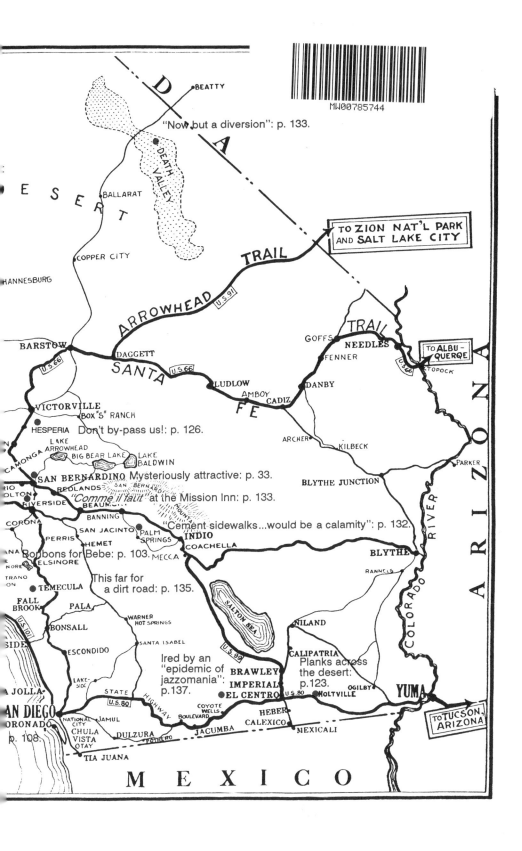

D A

BEATTY

"Now but a diversion": p. 133.

DEATH VALLEY

E S E R T

BALLARAT

COPPER CITY

HANNESBURG

TO ZION NAT'L PARK AND SALT LAKE CITY

TRAIL

ARROWHEAD

U.S.91

TRAIL

GOFFS

NEEDLES

BARSTOW

DAGGETT

FENNER

TO ALBU-QUERQUE

U.S.66

U.S.66

SANTA

U.S.66

LUDLOW

DANBY

TOPOCK

AMBOY CADIZ

VICTORVILLE

"BOX 'S'" RANCH

FE

HESPERIA   Don't by-pass us!: p. 126.

LAKE ARROWHEAD

ARCHER

KILBECK

CAMONGA   BIG BEAR LAKE   LAKE BALDWIN

SAN BERNARDINO Mysteriously attractive: p. 33.

BLYTHE JUNCTION

PARKER

REDLANDS   SAN BERN'D'O

RIO

OLTON

"Comme il faut" at the Mission Inn: p. 133.

RIVERSIDE   BEAUM...

MOUNTAINS

CORONA

BANNING

"Cement sidewalks...would be a calamity": p. 132.

SAN JACINTO   PALM SPRINGS   INDIO

PERRIS

HEMET

COACHELLA

ANA

Bonbons for Bebe: p. 103. MECCA

BLYTHE

NORE   ELSINORE

RANNELS

TRANO

ON

This far for

TEMECULA   a dirt road: p. 135.

FALL BROOK

PALA

SALTON SEA

WARNER HOT SPRINGS

BONSALL

NILAND

SIDE

ESCONDIDO

SANTA ISABEL

U.S.101

CALIPATRIA   Planks across

LAKE-SIDE

Ired by an
"epidemic of   BRAWLEY   the desert:
jazzomania": IMPERIAL   p.123.
p.137.   EL CENTRO U.S.80 HOLTVILLE OGILBY

JOLLA

STATE

U.S.99

COYOTE WELLS

YUMA

AN DIEGO

U.S.80

HIGHWAY

HEBER

ORONADO

BOULEVARD

CALEXICO

TO TUCSON, ARIZONA

p. 108.

NATIONAL CITY JAMUL

CHULA VISTA

DULZURA

JACUMBA

MEXICALI

OTAY

TECATE

TIA JUANA

A R I Z O N A

COLORADO RIVER

M E X I C O

The Great

CAR CRAZE

*How Southern California Collided
with the Automobile in the 1920's*

By
ASHLEIGH BRILLIANT

Published by

Woodbridge Press / *Santa Barbara*

First Edition

Published and distributed by

Woodbridge Press Publishing Company
Post Office Box 6189
Santa Barbara, California 93160

Copyright 1989, 1964 by Ashleigh Brilliant

All rights reserved.

Printed in the United States of America
Distributed simultaneously in Canada

Library of Congress Cataloging in Publication Data

Brilliant, Ashleigh, 1933–
   The great car craze : how Southern California collided with the
automobile in the 1920's / by Ashleigh Brilliant.
     p. cm.
   Bibliography: p.
   Includes index.
   ISBN 0-88007-172-9 : $19.95
   1. Automobiles—Social aspects—California, Southern—History.
I. Title.
HE5633.C2B75   1989
303.4'832—dc19

89-5453
CIP

To my Mother and Father

With Appreciation...

The author wishes to acknowledge and thank all those persons, organizations, and publications whose work during or concerning the 1920's provided the sources that made this present work possible. Especially to be acknowledged is the courtesy of the following with respect to the items indicated.

Clymer Publications, Overland Park, KS: photographs, pp. 168, 169; Floyd Clymer, *Cars of the Stars and Movie Memories,* ©1954.

Los Angeles Times: cartoons, pp. 160, 161; newspaper page, p. 166.

McGraw-Hill Book Co., New York, NY: photograph, p. 172; Bellamy Partridge, *Fill 'Er Up: The Story of Fifty Years of Motoring,* ©1952.

Simon and Schuster, New York, NY: citations, Caryl Chessman, *Cell 2455 Death Row* (Prentice-Hall), ©1954, 1960.

Sunset Magazine, Lane Publishing Company, Menlo Park, CA: photograph, p. 167; poem, "Motor Honeymoon," p. 131. Copyright © in the years indicated by *Sunset Magazine,* Lane Publishing Company.

Unocal, Los Angeles, CA: drawing of automobile, cover.

Westways (formerly *Touring Topics*), Automobile Club of Southern California, Los Angeles, CA: poem, "Tourists' Motor Camp," p. 130; acrostic, p. 93; photograph, p. 171; cartoon, p. 157. Copyright © in the years indicated by *Westways,* Automobile Club of Southern California.

Additional acknowledgement is given to:

Appleton & Lang, East Norwalk, CT: citations, Frederick F. Van de Water, *The Family Flivvers to San Francisco* (Appleton), ©1926.

Battelle Publishing Company, Los Angeles, CA: photographs, p. 174; *Building a Profitable Super-Service Station Business,* ©1927.

California Sports, Los Angeles, CA: photographs, pp. 158, 159.

Covici, Friede, New York, NY: photograph, p. 169; Benjamin B. Hampton, *A History of the Movies,* ©1931.

Duell, Sloan, and Pearce, New York, NY: photograph, p. 170; Frederic Thrasher, *Okay for Sound: How the Screen Found Its Voice,* ©1946.

Harcourt Brace Jovanovich, San Diego, CA: citation, p. 30 ; Lincoln Steffens, *The Autobiography of Lincoln Steffens,* ©1931.

Harper and Row, New York, NY: citations, p. 152; John Keats, *The Insolent Chariots* (Lippincott), ©1958.

George G. Harrap, London: citations; cartoon, p. 164; Jan and Cora Gordon, *Star-Dust in Hollywood,* ©1931.

E. F. Hill: the end papers, roadmaps of the 1920's, ©1928.

Kenmore Publishing Co., Los Angeles, CA: poem, p. 145; "Twilight in Los Angeles," by Daisy C. Breeden, in Marshall Breeden, *The Romantic Southland of California,* ©1928.

National Council for the Protection of Roadside Beauty, photographs, p. 172.

Nation's Traffic, photographs, pp. 162, 163.

The author invites additions or corrections to these acknowledgements for future editions of this book.

FOREWORD

Television viewers in the Los Angeles area were recently treated to a ghastly glimpse of their region's future. *Stuck In Traffic* was the title of a special program in which they were told that, if present dismal trends continue, by the year 2010, 50 percent of all their daily travel time would be spent *not moving at all*—a condition already dignified by standard dictionaries with the word *GRIDLOCK*.

Thirty-six traffic experts and community leaders were in the studio for this program, and when asked how they themselves got to work, only one person admitted to using public transportation. It was a vivid demonstration of the grip still held by the private automobile upon the lives and minds of Southern Californians, a grip which first took hold in the early decades of this century, particularly the third decade. This book is about what happened in those years, and it may help to explain how the current chaotic situation arose.

Some explanation may be in order as to how the book itself came about. It was originally written as a doctoral dissertation in American history at the University of California at Berkeley in 1963. It was something of a pioneering work in its field, and I soon discovered (somewhat to my surprise, since I had found the whole topic quite fascinating) that at that time there was little interest among publishers in the subject matter. The best I could do was to get an article based on it published in the scholarly journal, *Southern California Quarterly*, in June 1965, under the title, "Some Aspects of Mass Motorization in Southern California, 1919–1929."

From that point on, my own activities took me in other directions, but, as I expected, public interest in the social effects of the automobile has mounted over the years. My work has been used and quoted by a number of subsequent scholars, and I have even found myself being sought out and interviewed on National Public Radio as "an expert on the history of the car in early Los Angeles." When James J. Flink, now widely regarded as America's leading automotive historian, began to praise my dissertation in print, and urged me to get it published, I felt that its time must indeed have come at last—and the present volume is the result.

More recent research has of course done much to illuminate further the area of my own investigation. In addition to the works of Professor Flink—especially *The Car Culture* (1975) and *The Automobile Age* (1988)—the reader is referred, in particular, to Robert M. Fogelson's *The Fragmented Metropolis: Los Angeles, 1850–1930* (1967), John B. Rae's *The Road and the Car in American Life (1971)*, Warren J. Belasco's *Americans On The Road: From Auto-Camp to Motel* (1979), and Scott L. Bottles' *Los Angeles and the Automobile* (1987).

But none of these works covers quite the same territory as my study, and none appears to invalidate anything in it. It has therefore been felt justifiable for it to be presented here substantially in its original form.

Unfortunately, both Walton Bean and George R. Stewart, under whose guidance this work was accomplished, and whose own works have contributed so much to the study of California history and culture, are no longer alive to share with me the pleasure of seeing it finally published. Let it stand, then, in tribute to their memory.

Ashleigh Brilliant
Santa Barbara, 1989

CONTENTS

9

PART I

INTRODUCTION

Preface

> Considering the fixation of the American people upon auto-
> mobiles and their use, there has been surprisingly little of what
> might be called personal or imaginative writing on the sub-
> ject. . . . The social historians . . . seldom get much under the skin
> of the individual.[1]

This study had its origins in a desire to understand the significance of
the automobile as an outstanding example of the impact of technological change upon human life in general and American life in
particular. In the process of narrowing the topic to practical proportions, three important questions were asked and answered.

First, what aspects of the automobile should be covered? Answer:
Let no aspect be entirely ruled out, but let the focus be on the effects of
the private passenger car upon the lives and thoughts of ordinary
people.

Second, to what span of time should the study be limited? Answer:
Concentrate on the period during which the lives of the most people
were being the most drastically changed by the innovation. It took
very little research to establish that the decade following the First
World War most clearly filled that part of the bill.

Third, where should the geographical focus be fixed? Answer: Give
major attention to whatever area was most profoundly affected by the
coming of the automobile during the period under consideration. And
here it was soon apparent that California, and in particular the region
known as Southern California, best met the requirement.

11

As the study proceeded along these lines, however, it came to assume dimensions which seemed to be greater than the sum of its parts. The automobile, it began to appear, was more than simply the most notable of a great series of technological developments. It was different *in kind* from any other invention which had ever influenced the American public. The Nineteen-Twenties were not merely a period of accelerated change. The ethos of that decade set it quite distinctly apart from any other period in America's past or in her foreseeable future. And Southern California was not simply an extreme instance of the national experience, but was in many ways wholly unique.

This book must therefore be presented to the reader with some frank acknowledgement of doubt in the author's mind as to whether any of the material presented in the following pages may be generalized into any broader significance, or whether, after having started out in search of a topic of universal importance, he has found one whose importance begins and ends entirely with itself. An attempt has been made to preserve at least the illusion of momentous import by dividing the book into three sections with the impressive titles of MAN, MACHINE, and LAND. The first section concentrates on people; the second, on cars; the third deals in a broad sense with the landscape upon which people and cars came together (sometimes rather painfully). But the overall aim in all three sections is to get "under the skin" of the individual as Stewart urged, and to show in human terms what the coming of the Mass Automobile meant, at least in one remarkable region during one of the most colorful periods of its history.

Historical Background and Geographical Setting

A. Transportation

Before we plunge into the Nineteen-Twenties, there are a few things which ought to be made clear about the historical role of the automobile. The first point, which is often overlooked, is that what was really new about the steam-, electric-, and gasoline-powered "horseless carriages" which began to appear about the end of the Nineteenth Century was not that they were horseless, *i.e.*, self propelled, but that they were *carriages*, capable of being used by ordinary people in much the same way as horse-drawn carriages had previously been used. There was nothing new about self-propelled vehicles *per se*. Such devices had already been in existence, in a practical working form, for at least seventy years, mostly in the form of "locomotives," which for various reasons, not all of them technical, had been confined to special private roadways, usually consisting of parallel strips of durable material specially adapted to the wheels of the vehicle and known as tracks.

Thus the real significance in the history of transportation of the emergence of the automobile was that the long-familiar railroad locomotive was now for the first time released from its tracks, scaled down, and put into the hands of a multitude of individuals. But the heritage both of the railroad and of animal propulsion are interestingly manifest in the subsequent history of the automobile. For the new device really only required the substitution of one form of "track" for another, and the absence of an animate "motor" created a very understandable tendency to impart animate qualities to the new machine.

As an illustration of the latter point (and as a reminder that the people into whose social history we are going to be inquiring, urbanized as we shall mostly find them, had strong and usually very recent rural roots), consider the complaint of a California wife of 1927 that her husband's previous familiarity with horses and wagons, while making him quite adept at the tricky art of parallel parking, caused him also to be:

> . . . very hard on machinery. . . . He cannot quite believe that the car is inanimate. When it fails to respond, he yanks at levers and grinds gears with blood in his eye. . . . It is only the anatomy of the thing which keeps him from twisting its tail or blowing in its ear when it balks. I think if he were lost he would 'give it its head' in the expectation that the car would find its own way back to the garage.

Having thus condemned her husband's unrealistic attitude, the lady still could not refrain from adding, 'I am secretly aware that the car likes me best. I never swear at it."[2]

In this connection, it might also be pointed out that, contrary to much popular folklore, until the advent of the Mass Automobile in the Twenties it was in the rural rather than in the urban areas of the United States that the motor car was most widely accepted and applied as a machine of practical utility.[3] Indeed, one modern authority has gone so far as to assert that one of the principal reasons for the "unique concentration of urban automobiles" in Southern California was the fact that "migrants to the area were used to the ways of farms and small towns, where they had been dependent on the automobile for every movement."[4]

Getting back to the question of "tracks" for the new form of "locomotives," it is important to note that, whereas in building up a railroad system, the matter of laying down the track was primary and paramount, in establishing the American "automobile system," the building of cars was for a long time given much more attention than the building of roads to drive them on. Ever since the coming of the railroads, ordinary roads had tended to be neglected.[5] This was, in fact, probably one of the reasons why, also contrary to popular myth, the United States was comparatively slow in getting into the automotive act.

Vehicles and roads, it can be argued, are not so much separate entities as they are functions of each other. The type and quality of the road determines the kind of vehicle which may be used upon it, and the kind of vehicles in existence more or less determine what sort of roads there are going to be. (Just what factor comes first, in this chicken-and-egg situation, is hard to say.) Thus, in the early days of American motoring we find cars being designed to meet the very rugged driving conditions which then existed almost everywhere (hence, for example, the high road clearance of the famous Model-T Ford), while at the same time motorists were agitating for improved roads (which would ultimately render possible the road-hugging bellies of today's models). Automobiles, then, cannot be separated historically from their roads, and we will accordingly have a good deal to say about roads in discussing the social effects of the automobile.

B. CALIFORNIA

Both the track-tied and horse-drawn antecedents of the automobile had reached a remarkable stage of development in the state of California before the automobile itself came upon the scene. According to John W. Caughey, for example, as early as the mid-1850's California's stage-coach service was already "unsurpassed, except perhaps by England's Royal Mail."[6] In addition, the bicycle, another device which opened great vistas in the field of transportation (some predicted that the next war would be fought by armies on bicycles) had, by the end of the nineteenth century, attained tremendous popularity.

Indeed, the concern with good roads which, as will be seen, was largely responsible for California's early reputation as a motorist's paradise actually antedated the advent of the automobile. The first significant legislative act towards the establishment of a statewide system of good roads was passed as early as 1895, which also happened to be the year in which the people of Los Angeles saw their very first automobile.[7] The act set up a Bureau of Highways consisting of three men, two of whom, J. L. Maude and R. C. Irvine, along with Irvine's dog Maje, performed the rather remarkable feat of making a 7,000 mile tour of the state on a buckboard wagon to study the existing roads. Little was done about their recommendations at the time, but a bulletin written by Irvine in the following year paid rhapsodic respects to the bicycle as a powerful argument for better roads:

> The influence of the bicycle upon this agitation for improved high-
> ways cannot be overestimated. Millions of dollars have been in-
> vested in the manufacture of these easy and graceful machines of
> locomotion and this agitation for better roads is due more directly
> to the efforts of the wheelmen than to any other one cause. Any
> machine which enables a man to travel with pleasure, without
> discomfort, and practically without expense, forty miles a day, is
> evidently one which has come to stay, and the number of wheelmen
> will surely reach extraordinary proportions in the years to come.[8]

Irvine lived to see machines considerably less "easy and graceful" come to dominate the roads which the wheelmen had fostered. His own 7,000 mile horse-drawn tour was indeed probably a pleasure jaunt compared with that made for a similar purpose by automobile some sixteen years later, described by Highway Commissioner Charles D. Blaney:

> We covered six thousand eight hundred fifty miles on our tours. We
> were kicked off mountain roads by mules, we were stuck in river
> fords, we slid around dangerous mountain grades, we broke our
> windshield and punched holes in the bottom of our gasoline tank on
> the rocks of the desert, and after we had covered the trunk lines
> and laterals of California from Oregon to Mexico we went back to
> Sacramento and drew the State Highway routes on a big map of
> the state.[9]

But it was not only the bicycle but also the venerable horse-and-wagon which was prominent in the minds of California good-roads pioneers. In fact, as late as 1907, when automobiles had already furnished dramatic proof of their practical utility in the great San Francisco disaster of 1906,[10] Governor George C. Pardee's message to the legislature, in discussing the benefit of good roads, made no reference to the auto-mobile, but spoke of "the saving of money in horse flesh, harness, wagons, time, and draught power."[11]

Thus, the automobile did not immediately remake the world, not even California, in its own image. That part of the process did not really begin until the period with which this investigation is par-ticularly concerned. Rather, the motor car began, around the turn of the century, to infiltrate a world in which horse traffic, horseless rail traffic, and even rail-less bicycle traffic had all come to be taken for granted and had managed to achieve a relatively stable and harmonious relationship with each other. It was a world well-depicted in its urban aspects by Frank Norris in his description of a Central Valley town of about 25,000 in the 1890's:

> The business portion of the town was always crowded. . . . Saddle
> horses, farm wagons—the inevitable Studebakers—buggies grey
> with the dust of country roads, buckboards with squashes and
> grocery packages stowed under the seat, two-wheeled sulkies and
> training carts, were hitched to the gnawed railings and zinc-
> sheathed telegraph poles along the curb. Here and there, on the
> edge of the sidewalk, were bicycles wedged into bicycle racks
> painted with cigar advertisements. . . . The Yosemite 'bus and
> City 'bus [horse-drawn, of course] passed up the street on the way
> from the morning train, each with its two or three passengers. . . .
> The electric car line . . . did a brisk business, its cars whirring
> from end to end of the street, with a jangling of bells and moaning
> plaint of gearing.[12]

It is interesting to note, in connection with "the inevitable Stu-
debakers" mentioned here, that the John Studebaker who eventually
achieved fame as an Indiana manufacturer of wagons and, subsequently, of automobiles, began his career as a wagon maker in Placer-
ville, California, not long after the gold rush.[13]

This vehicular concord was, however, to be sharply upset by the
intrusion of an entirely new form of traffic. By 1906, the California
world described by Norris in the above passage had been penetrated
by about 6,500 motor cars. By 1912 there were about 77,000 registered
in the state, and by 1918 about 365,000. During the period 1919–1929,
however, the figures took a big jump, and the average annual increase
for those ten years was about 141,000; so that by 1929 the state had
about 1,900,000 automobiles (see Appendix A). But the really important change was not in the numbers of cars but in the lives and
thoughts of people, and in order to come to grips with that aspect of the
subject, it is necessary to narrow our geographical focus to that part of
the state where these changes were most concentrated and most intense.

C. SOUTHERN CALIFORNIA

> People! Automobiles! Buildings! Orchards! Farms! Oil! Ships! Fac-
> tories! Climate! Vast stretches of undeveloped land! Mountains!
> Resorts! The Ocean! Ah! Los Angeles![14]

Carey McWilliams has devoted two very fine books to showing that
California is radically different from any other part of the world and
that Southern California is just about as different from the rest of
California.[15] Without attempting to be too precise about its exact
boundaries, this book will accept the argument that there is something
quite distinct about the geographical region which has the city of Los
Angeles as its major metropolitan center, and will further maintain

that much of this distinctiveness is inseparable from the unique role of the automobile in the region—a role long recognized by the inhabitants. For example, the preface to a children's textbook on the geography of the region published in 1929 pointed out that:

> The children of Southern California enjoy exceptional advantages. Good roads and the almost universal use of the automobile have contributed to their first-hand knowledge of those areas which are outside the immediate home environment . . . Besides this, many of them have come [usually by automobile] from other parts of the country where life conditions are different.[16]

The growth of Southern California since 1870 has been characterized as "one continuous boom punctuated at intervals by major explosions."[17] Two of the greatest of those explosions, the booms of the Eighteen-Eighties and of the Nineteen-Twenties, were closely associated with developments in the field of transportation. In the Eighties it was the completion of the Santa Fe Railroad and its competition with the Southern Pacific which brought thousands of fortune seekers to the already fabled land of sunshine. In the Twenties it was, of course, the automobile. But the big difference was that, unlike the railroad, the motor car did not cease to have an intimate connection with the lives of the immigrants, and thus with the course of the boom, once it had deposited them upon the streets of Los Angeles. For this was a case, not of the locomotive bringing the man, but of every man bringing his own locomotive.

During this period, automobile registration in the Los Angeles area came to surpass that in any other urban center in the country,[18] and the city began to acquire a worldwide reputation for being, among other things, the most motor conscious on earth. The same three factors had helped to bring this about as had in general contributed so much to the development of the region: climate, scenery, and that ardent form of self-promotion known as "boosterism." Climate was particularly important because in the early years of motoring the vast majority of cars were open rather than closed models, so that driving was much less comfortable, as well as much more hazardous, under adverse weather conditions. In most areas of the country, it was common practice to put one's car into storage during the winter. But here was a region where one could drive in comfort all year round. And it was a beautiful region with varied and entrancing scenery, where many people lived who had wealth and leisure enough to be able to enjoy their surroundings in the most up-to-date fashion.

In December of 1900 a few such people gathered together to found the Automobile Club of Southern California, one of the earliest and eventually the largest and most influential of such organizations in the country.[19] Boosters of Southern California also realized the need for good roads to attract more tourists and contribute to the general growth and prosperity of the region. With roads, climate, and scenery to offer the motorist, Southern California soon took permanent lead in the world automotive sweepstakes. For this was a region constantly and almost pathologically bent upon advertising itself, one whose entire way of life came in time to be based upon the idea of growth for its own sake.

The number of automobiles soon came to rank next to the size of the actual population as an indicator of desirable growth, and indeed both sets of figures went soaring during the great boom of the Twenties. Between 1920 and 1930, Los Angeles County gained 1,272,037 people and 644,418 cars (see Appendices A and B). Such astonishing increase was, as usual for Southern California, far in excess of the state or national average.[20] But it is characteristic of a decade of phenomenally accelerated change.

D. *The Nineteen-Twenties*

Dear Children of Southern California: You live in the happiest land in all the world. Your homes are the most comfortable. The country about you is the most beautiful. The air you breathe is the softest. The food you eat is the best. The roads you travel are the smoothest.[21]

"In the Nineteen-Twenties," writes William E. Leuchtenburg, "the events of half a century finally caught up with America. . . . All the institutions of American society buckled under the strain."[22] The experience of Southern California illustrates this generalization with peculiar aptness, especially with regard to the automobile. Among the "events" which began to catch up with the region during this period were the local phenomenon of rampant boosterism and the national phenomenon of rampant industrialism, each being closely tied up with something called prosperity. The automobile manufacturing industry had actually in the space of a single generation risen from nothing to become a prime but somewhat shaky cornerstone of national economic well-being. And it seemed to some, even at the time, that the sudden influx of population into Southern California was "a culmination, at the psychological moment, of years of advertising both organized and individual . . . of the many advantages which this region offered as a place in which to live and prosper."[23]

But the great Southern California boom of the Twenties, a period which will be considered here as having lasted from about the beginning of 1919 to the 1929 crash, involved more than people and cars. It had to do also with one of the waves of real estate speculation which periodically engulf the region, with a mighty bonanza of oil discovery and production coinciding fortuitously with the unprecedented rise in demand for fuel oils and lubricants, and with the heady heyday of the young movie industry. "I've never seen anything comparable to Los Angeles in 1922," wrote Oliver Carlson, describing how he, as a new arrival at the railway station, was "literally seized and fought over by a dozen different real-estate agents." The town was "population mad, annexation mad, and speculation mad."[24] Inevitably such an atmosphere fostered social and individual disruption and corruption. In the view of Carey McWilliams who was there at the time, the whole decade for Southern California was "one long drunken orgy, one protracted debauch."[29] Nevertheless it is quite possible, and indeed the evidence seems to indicate, that many, perhaps a majority, of the people who lived in this highly abnormal society had no idea just how mad it was but managed on the whole to adjust to its bizarre patterns. The record of the problems they faced and the adjustment they made, in respect to the automobile revolution—of which their region was the first in the world to experience the full effects—constitutes the real substance of this book.

PART II

MAN

Numbers, Boosters, and Boom

The post-war decade in Los Angeles was the time during which the automobile took a firm grip upon the consciousness of the community. Cars had been around in growing numbers for a generation, and the ubiquitous Model T, which had been in production since 1908, was certainly no luxury vehicle; but in the popular mind a tendency had persisted to associate motoring with sport, recreation, and wealth. Now, however, cars had become much cheaper and more reliable, and suddenly it seemed that everybody was buying one, or more than one. Nothing like this this had ever happened before, and the resulting confusion took everyone off guard. It was years before the mess began to be sorted out, and in many ways of course it has not yet been cleared up. Much that is going to be said here about the situation in Southern California in the Nineteen-Twenties could apply to the same area today, and indeed to many other areas then and since. But it is quite evident from articles in national magazines of the Twenties, and from the comments of both visitors and local residents, that something extraordinary was seen to be going on just then in Southern California, and that it had very much to do with cars—the variety of uses to which they were being put, the extent to which they were already a part of everyday life, and the sheer numbers of them.

As a typical example, take a book written about California for children and published in 1925. As Junior and Beth, farm-children visitors from Illinois, drive with their uncle into Los Angeles, they experience the typical reaction: "It really seemed as though all Los

21

Angeles must be on the road. Where *did* all the automobiles come from?"

California, explains Uncle John:

> is a great automobile State. That is partly because it has so many
> good roads. Californians use cars for business as well as for plea-
> sure. I know a man who has an office in Los Angeles. During the
> summer he lives at the beach. He has a ranch near Riverside. He
> has mining interests in Randsburg. Occasionally his business takes
> him to San Francisco. He could not very well look after all his
> interests without a car. His wife has a machine for her own use.
> His son, another. Then they have a large touring car for pleasure
> trips. The family often spends the week-end at San Diego or Santa
> Barbara. At least once a year they go on a longer trip—to
> Yosemite, or perhaps out of the state.[1]

The children are appropriately impressed, as were many more sophisticated visitors by the same phenomenon. Alice Williamson, for
example, a New Yorker visiting Hollywood in 1928, lightheartedly
commented on the matter-of-fact acceptance of the car as a way of life:

> Why not go to Los Angeles for pins? It's only a motor spin of eleven
> miles, and quite a good excuse for a charming excursion. . . . All
> your friends have motor cars, fleets of them, last year's and this
> year's models. The husbands use last year's models to run out to
> the studios and direct films or write scenarios or whatever they do.
> The wives use this year's ones to take you into Los Angeles in
> order to buy pins, or lunch, or go to a matinee of a play just out
> from New York. . . . The idea seems to be, why should anybody
> walk, except for the purpose of getting thin, and even so, isn't it
> nicer to dance?[2]

Hollywood, of course, has long been taken to represent in even more
exaggerated fashion the extremes of behavior and outlook customarily
associated with California in general, and Southern California in particular. Interesting also, in the above passage, are the indications that
by the late Nineteen-Twenties women had become quite accepted as
drivers, and that it was of a certain social importance to be seen in an
automobile of the latest fashion. More on these topics later.

"Everybody who is anybody at all has his own car—and a goodly
number of others who are not anybody," Rider's California guidebook
informed the nation in 1925:

> They not only have them, but they use them, to an extent that the
> easterner does not dream of. Your Californian thinks nothing of
> running out from Los Angeles in the morning to take luncheon at
> Pomona, cutting back to dine in Hollywood, and spending the
> evening at Long Beach.[3]

And the *Saturday Evening Post* gave a pretty good indication of the national interest in Southern California's motor boom, when in 1923 it published an article called "California Takes to the Road," which began with a passage strongly suggestive of the spirit of triumphant boosterism:

> When, just the other day, its highway commission up at Sacramento issued its one-millionth automobile license, California was pleased as punch over the entire business. . . . Every time Don Daig of Los Angeles drives his new roadster, with 1000 000-CAL-1923 affixed to its bow and to its stern, down the streets of that incomparable metropolis, the Angelenos get their own peculiar thrill of pride. . . .[4]

A few years later, in February 1930, Jackson A. Graves, pioneer lawyer and banker of Los Angeles and by then an old man of seventy-seven, went up over the city for his first air ride, in a blimp belonging to the Goodyear Tire and Rubber Company of California. Whether he too felt a "peculiar thrill of pride" at the astonishing changes which the automotive revolution had brought to the area is not clear from his account. But he was deeply impressed by such visible effects as the sight from the air of huge densely packed parking lots occupying land which he could clearly remember as having been covered with vineyards and orchards.[5] To a man of his age, riding over the most thoroughly motorized city in the world in a machine built to advertise automobile tires, the change in the social role of the automobile must have seemed little short of fantastic. Mr. Graves, for example, had already been in his fifties at the time when Dr. H. Nelson Jackson of Burlington, Vermont, making what was claimed to be the first transcontinental motor trip, had been misdirected fifty-four miles by a California woman in order that her family mighty have an opportunity to see their first automobile (1903):[6] He was fifty-one when the city of Long Beach passed a law restricting the parking of automobiles to fifteen minutes, not because there was any lack of room, but because it was claimed that oil dripping from the vehicles was eating holes in the asphalt pavement (1904);[7] and it must have seemed only yesterday to him that the President of Princeton University, Woodrow Wilson, had declared "Nothing has spread socialistic feeling in this country more than the automobile. . . . They are a picture of the arrogance of wealth, with all its independence and carelessness." (1906)[8]

By any ordinary historical reckoning the automobile revolution had been accomplished with incredible swiftness. Yet the most intense changes were in fact crammed into a far briefer span than the generation or so which Mr. Graves had seen elapse since the turn of the century. It was actually the first few years after the World War which saw the real automotive deluge hit Southern California, paralleling one of the region's steepest rises in population.

In 1919 the *Los Angeles Times* still combined automobile news and sports news in one section of its Sunday edition; and *Pacific Golf and Motor* magazine, which at one time (July 1916 to July 1917) had been the official organ of *both* the California Golf Association *and* the California State Automobile Association, was still carrying items on motoring. (By May of 1920 it had dropped them entirely, though it retained the "*and Motor*" part of its title right through the Nineteen-Twenties as an interesting relic of the days when fashionable sport and motoring were so closely associated.) Such things as motels, trailers, and freeways had in 1919 not yet been heard of; the term "freeway" was actually not coined until 1930, and California did not see its first one—the Arroyo Seco Freeway in Los Angeles—until 1940.[9] Traffic lights, one-way streets, and boulevard stop signs were nonexistent. "Drive-in" and "hitchhiker" were terms yet unborn, and the very word "car" when used in a headline could still be generally understood to refer, not to an automobile, but to a railroad car.

Yet at the same time public interest in automobiles was very high and growing every day, fostered by advertising, by a reaction against the restrictions and shortages of wartime, by pride in the achievements of Detroit, by vicarious identification with the industrialists like Henry Ford who were at the forefront of those achievements, but especially, by the sheer and undeniable pleasures and advantages, of owning and driving an automobile, especially in Southern California.

Some wealthier families had already become remarkably dependent upon their cars which, for example, made possible a hilltop life of the kind enjoyed by Julia M. Sloane and her family somewhere between Los Angeles and San Diego during the war years. "Trains," she wrote in 1919:

> are becoming as obsolete in our family as the horse. We wish to take a trip: out purrs the motor; in goes the family lunch-box, a thermos bottle, and a motor-case of indispensables, and we are off. No fuss about missing the train, no baggage, no tickets, no cinders—just the open road.

But such dependence had its drawbacks too, for "Every now and then I am marooned on my hill, if the motor is 'hors de combat.'" And the leading local grocery store, Mrs. Sloane complained, which still made its deliveries by horse-drawn conveyance, "did not expect to deliver to people who had their own motors."[10]

Just four years later, however, car ownership had become so common in Southern California that it was almost a mark of distinction *not* to do one's shopping in one's own car. Such, at least, appears to be indicated in Mark Lee Luther's novel *The Boosters* in which George Hammond and his wife, post-war immigrants from Boston, having bought a home in the Hollywood Hills, decide that they must at last buy a car. "Of course we must have a car," says Mrs. Hammond. "I'm not the kind of housekeeper who depends on the telephone and the honesty of tradespeople." Her architect husband, a more sensitive soul, who earlier in the novel sold a new car he had won in a raffle shortly after arriving in Los Angeles because he preferred to have the money, accepts the inevitable—not without regret. "So endeth our exclusiveness," he sighs, "Gone our sole claim to distinction. We join the populace in their simple joys."[11]

As early as 1922 a report issued jointly by the U.S. Bureau of Public Roads and the California Highway Commission, based on a survey conducted at 103 counting stations throughout the state, had made a statement as laconically dramatic as the famous announcement by the Director of the U.S. Census of 1890 that a frontier line of settlement could no longer be determined. "In California," declared the report, "all traffic except motor vehicle traffic is negligible."[12] But there was no local Frederick Jackson Turner ready to spring forth with a thesis on the Significance of the Horse in California History. In fact one might argue that the true significance of the change thus officially recognized was not so much the end of a frontier as the beginning of one—the automotive frontier—whose end is not yet in sight, but whose wildest and most unrestrained period was certainly the decade of the Twenties.

By 1929 Rockwell Hunt could write that "the significance of the automobile in California to all the inhabitants thereof really needs no discussion,—It is too obvious." But what was really significant about this chapter of social history was not that "the privately owned car has come to be one of the ordinary requirements of everyday life,"[13] which was as far as Rockwell Hunt would go in attempting to assess a transformation of which he was, after all, still in the very middle. It was rather that, in attaining this position so quickly, the automobile required profound human readjustments. This new machine was the most blatant and formidable encroachment ever made by technology upon the daily life of the average man. And Homo Angeleno, through no real fault of his own, was the first to feel its full force.

Like most Californians, and indeed like most Americans of that era, Rockwell Hunt was imbued with a sense of material progress, as well as with his share of local patriotism. One can almost hear a throb of emotion as he describes the flocking of cars to California: "For weeks at a stretch the automobiles roll into the borders of the state where anticipations are exceeded only by realization. This is the innumerable motorcade!" The booster spirit so clearly exemplified in this celebration of the "innumerable motorcade" was the dominant response of Southern California to the auto era.

In fact, the state and many lesser governmental and private bodies took great care to enumerate the "innumerable," requiring all motor tourists to register upon entering the state and publishing the figures with frequency and pride, along with equally glowing statistics on automobile ownership and sales of new and used cars.[14] All such information was taken as proof of prosperity. It was a source of never-ending satisfaction to Americans in general that they owned the vast majority of the world's automobiles. Hunt himself, in the following passage from his history of transportation in California, shows how busy the enumerators were in demonstrating statistically the automotive superiority of California over any other state, and of Southern California over everywhere else. The reader will note the tone of jealous exultation:

> California is the automobile state par excellence among all the states of the Union. Registration within this highly-favored state has mounted with astonishing rapidity, passing the million mark in 1923 and leaving far behind the million-and-a-half mark three years later. In 1927 the thirteen counties of Southern California alone exceeded a million registrations. The only state that is able to show a greater total registration is New York with its teeming millions of population—but while New York has a slightly higher numerical total, she falls far behind when considered on a ratio basis.[15]

This is typical of the kind of treatment generally accorded the question of the significance of the automobile in California during the years when that significance was first really making itself felt. And this, of course, is only to be expected. In the midst of so astonishing a transformation, most observers could only take note of the raw figures and gasp with wonder at their possible implications. A columnist in a Los Angeles newspaper of 1924 well conveys this sense of groping for meaning amid a welter of statistics. "There is," he wrote:

> one automobile to every seven persons in this country, while in Germany there is only one to every four hundred. If this great difference keeps up, the kind of social and economic civilization which will result means a vast difference in the evolution of the two peoples.[16]

Just what kind of difference that might be, the journalist, like most of his colleagues who discussed similar topics, did not attempt to ascertain. It was enough to assume that God was on the side of the most motors.

In the forefront of those proclaiming the automotive millenium were two powerful organizations whose purposes were different, but whose fundamental interests were really very similar: The Los Angeles Chamber of Commerce and the Automobile Club of Southern California. The latter had by 1929 a membership of about 136,400. Its monthly magazine, called *Touring Topics* (later changed in 1933, belatedly but significantly, to the present title of *Westways*), was probably one of the best magazines published during the Twenties in Southern California—though this does not say much for the journalistic standards of the place and period. Both in *Touring Topics* and in the *Southern California Business* magazine of the Chamber of Commerce, magniloquent paeans in praise of the benefits being bestowed upon the region by the automobile were repeatedly to be found. Some notion of the fervor this concept evoked in its exponents may be derived from an article by Ernest McGaffey, a regular contributor to both magazines:

> Without the automobile, Southern California would be only comparatively advanced over the days of 1849. . . . Not even by one thousandth part would she be what she is now if motor cars . . . had not absolutely revolutionized the entire Southern half of the state as regards its commercial expansion, and its steady increase in population. . . . From whatever angle you may view Southern California's striking progress, you will be compelled to acknowledge that the automobile is responsible more than any other half dozen factors, for its phenomenal advancement. . . . If California ever adopts a new State flower, the motor car is the logical blossom for the honor[!]. . . . Whether commercially or socially, whether from the standpoint of business or sport, it is 'the same, the whole same, and nothing but the same.' All Hail Rubber! All Hail the Automobile![17]

California has not yet adopted the automobile as its state flower, but McGaffey was undoubtedly correct in his assessment of its importance in the development of the region. It is in fact arguable that the coming of cars, along with movies and the oil industry, to Southern California produced as profound a break in historical continuity as had the Gold Rush half a century before. As a guide for understanding present social conditions, the "returns" of California history seem to diminish as sharply for Southern California when one goes back before the Automobile Era as they do for the state as a whole beyond the great divide of 1848.

There were, of course, dissenting voices—there always are. Every now and then, for example, a letter like the following might appear in a Los Angeles newspaper:

> I think the automobile should be abolished altogether except for trucking purposes. It has done more harm than good in my opinion. It has brought sorrow into thousands of families who have been bereaved of their loved ones by it. It has aided holdup men in their nefarious schemes. It has led to wildness of modern youth. The little pleasure it has provided has been too highly paid for.[18]

But it is remarkable how few such protests were, and how close to unanimous was the conviction that the ever-increasing number of automobiles was an unmixed blessing. The vast majority readily agreed with Frederick Lewis Allen that the 23,131,000 passenger cars in the America of 1929 were "possibly the most potent statistic of Coolidge prosperity."[19]

Appeal of the Automobile

Whatever its economic implications, the automotive surge was based upon the tremendous appeal which the new machine had for vast numbers of individual human beings. It seems appropriate at this point, therefore, to inquire as to the nature of this appeal.

Most human material contrivances, as Hendrik Van Loon has pointed out in *Man the Miracle Maker*, can be seen simply as extensions of the ordinary functions of the human body.[20] A bridge extends the power of a man's legs; a hammer gives him a stronger, harder hand; a telescope multiples his visual range, and so on. Looking at the automobile this way, one may say that its basic appeal lay in the fact that it enormously extended the powers both of human legs and of human arms; in other words it was a vast magnification of the ability to move and to carry. It was not, as we have seen, the first practical device to perform that function on land; that distinction must be accorded to the railroad. But it *was* the first capable of being used and controlled by a multitude of individuals for their own private purposes. Hitherto the individual human being had had only his or her own strength, the immemorial horse, mule, etc., or the very recent bicycle. In each case some creature's or group of creatures' muscles had to do all the work, and this was a severe limitation upon the amount and nature of moving and carrying that was feasible. Now for the first time, an entirely different and infinitely more powerful form of force was applied to make the wheels go around—the virtually irresistible powers of expanding steam, of electrical energy, and of exploding petroleum vapor.

No single contrivance ever offered, before or since, to the public has been capable of satisfying so many individual human desires. Of course, when a multitude of individuals all set about attempting to satisfy their desires with a new contrivance within a limited area, serious problems are bound to arise; and that is just the kind of situation we find in an aggravated form in the Southern California of the Nineteen-Twenties. What results is a paradox of co-operation and conflict. People co-operate willingly to prepare the playing field, i.e., to get good roads built and maintained; they cooperate grudgingly to lay down a minimum of ground rules; but they refuse to cooperate at all when it comes to establishing just what the purpose of the game is to be—in fact everybody insists on his right to his own purpose. To complicate matters, new players keep joining the game who haven't even learned the ground rules. The spectators join in, the umpires join in, and the whole thing becomes a grand free-for-all. This, of course, is an exaggerated and perhaps a distorted picture; but there are many aspects of the subject which, even when seen in the perspective of today's unwholesome conditions, savor of anarchy.

Yet Angelenos drove through the decade with their eyes wide open. Their typical attitude was well summed up by Bailey Millard writing in the *Los Angeles Times* in 1926: "Our forefathers in their immortal independence screed set forth 'the pursuit of happiness' as an inalienable right of mankind. . . . and how can one pursue happiness by any swifter or surer means available to the mass of mankind than by the use of the automobile?"[21] There you have the only agreed upon purpose of the game.

Happiness for some people meant a sense of power, though this was not generally considered a socially acceptable desire, and tended to be attributed to the villains in the automotive fiction of the time. Thus Martin Plith, villain of a story called "Talion" which the *Los Angeles Times* published in 1927, was described as always enjoying

> a grandiose feeling . . . when driving his richly upholstered spark-ling car; the feeling of an emperor possessed of unlimited power. Nothing made him so happy as to hear the smooth hum of the motor, to swing sharply in and out of traffic lines and go flashing around and past all other cars. Ah, speed, richness, power, his, Plith's.[22]

For others, happiness meant escape, and this was a much more highly esteemed purpose, as long as one was not trying to escape from some form of social control. Paul H. Blades in 1921 commented with delight upon the new phenomenon of family motor-camping:

> . . . the grand fact about it is that it is absolutely wholesome. Not a thing is to be said against it. If there is a hyper-reformer, who would deprive us of various other joys of life, not a whisper of protest has he raised against the family wanderlust for the mountains of God.[23]

But, like the telephone, the automobile did provide the user with a certain irresponsible kind of freedom. It was now possible, for example, to get away with being much less mannerly towards the other driver or the pedestrian than had been the case when most human contacts were on a more completely personal level.

For the majority, however, at least on the level of their own conscious thoughts, the great appeal of the automobile lay simply in being able to get about from place to place with an ease, a speed, a convenience, and range of activity totally foreign to all previous experience.

The New Mobility

> I had a world before me. I felt lifted up to another plane, with a wider range. I could explore regions I had not been able to reach. . . . The whole world was open to me. I need not imagine it any more, I could go and see.

Lincoln Steffens, in the above passage, was describing his sensations, not at first becoming a motorist, but at being given a pony when he was eight years old in 1874.[24] The words seem peculiarly appropriate, however, as an indication of the wonder of automobility which the ever-amassing humanity of Southern California began to discover in the Nineteen-Twenties. Above all else, the motorcar was a machine for going places and doing things on an unheard of scale. An environment of beaches, mountains, and desert areas, which formerly had seemed hostile and foreboding, now beckoned even the most timid traveller. But, much more importantly, the internal life of the city underwent an astonishing metamorphosis. The automobile, Ernest McGaffey reminded his readers in 1928,

> has enabled the working man, and the man of moderate means, to live a considerable distance from his work, thereby enabling him to own his own home, and to have lawns, flowers, and shrubbery, and sufficient room so that he is not crowded into tenement houses or cheap apartments where living conditions tend to the certain deterioration of the races. It also gives the dweller in cities the opportunity to attend lectures, art exhibitions, outdoor exhibitions of athletic sports, and visit friends in distant parts of the metropo-

lis where in the old and tedious days of street car travel such recreation and enjoyment would have been next to impossible.[25]

That there was something in this argument can hardly be denied, and we cannot blame Mr. McGaffey for failing to foresee that there might come a time when the "old and tedious days" would be looked back to by many with a rather fond regret, and when the automobile itself would come under serious scrutiny as a possible factor in the "deterioration of the races." Clearly there was a close connection between the popularity of individual urban and suburban housing units, each with its own little patch of surrounding land, and the advent of the mass automobile, though the railroad in its various forms had already begun the process of vastly extending the area in which a city worker could live.

The New Dislocation

But there were (at least) two sides to this picture. It was all very well for the boosters to boast about how cars were bringing distant friends closer together and everyone closer to the finer things in life. From another point of view, however, the new automobility tended to separate people from each other and from the natural environment. Old values of "home," "family," and "neighborhood," were being sharply challenged, while the automobile itself, especially as the "closed car" began to predominate was, after all, a sort of portable room, which as long as you remained inside it did not necessarily take you *to* anything even if it had taken you *away* from something. Very few Southern Californians were consciously concerned about this problem; but foreign visitors like Jan and Cora Gordon, an English couple who lived in Los Angeles for an extended period during the late Twenties, were constantly struck by it. Judging from the daily life, as they observed it, of their neighbors in a typical bungalow court, the image of the convivial outdoor-loving Southern Californian appeared to be a complete myth:

> The truth is, the people seemed to venture rarely into the open air. If they wished to go out they slipped from the back door to the garage, shut themselves primly into a closed car, and drove away. If they wished to do the family shopping they drove into large open-air grocery shops specially arranged so that they could select their provisions without getting out of the car. If they wished for distraction they drove to the sea or up into the hills and stared at the view through the windshield. They seemed to be almost as destitute of friends as they were of personal furniture. . . .[26]

Also concerned were a few sociologists, to whose works the following pages will frequently refer. On the local level such scholarly concern as was in evidence centered at the University of Southern California in the work of Drs. Emory S. Bogardus and Bessie Averne McClenahan, who made what might be regarded as pioneer studies of youth problems and changing social patterns in Los Angeles.[27] On the national scene, historians now and in the future will always be indebted to Robert and Helen Lynd, who chose Muncie, Indiana, as a representative American community, disguised it under the name of *Middletown*, and published in 1929 a remarkably illuminating study of social changes and trends which they and their investigators had observed there.[28]

Taken as a whole, the works of these sociologists revealed a decided agreement on the importance of the automobile as an agent of social change, and a decidedly more critical approach than that of the boosters to the question of just what these changes implied. The Lynds, for example, were not nearly as sure as our friend McGaffey that the motorized family took great pride in the "lawns, flowers, and shrubbery" which the new automobility enabled it to own, cultivate, and enjoy. They stressed rather that the car itself had come to rival the yard as a center of family attention, and that ease of getting away from the home had made "a decorative yard less urgent."[29]

Dr. McClenahan's study focussed upon the social implications of the new mobility in terms of what it appeared to have done to the concepts of "neighborhood" and "neighborliness" among the residents of a twenty-block, middle-class section of Los Angeles in an area not far from the USC campus. It was very true, she found, as Ernest McGaffey had pointed out, that people could now much more easily "visit friends in distant parts of the metropolis." But, as a result of this, it seemed that friendships based upon local proximity were on the decline. The whole idea and ideal of a neighborhood as a physical area within which one developed and maintained the closest of one's everyday social ties was in fact dying out: "A new definition of a 'friendly neighborhood' is apparent; it is one in which the 'neighbors tend to their own business.'"[30] Here, for example, is how one householder replied to the questions of the interviewer:

> I don't know anything about the neighborhood. I don't like it and take no interest in it. We have been here a year, and bought only for investment. We have nothing whatsoever to do with my neighbors. I don't even know their names or know them to speak to. My best friends live in the city but by no means in this neighborhood. We belong to no clubs and we do not attend any local church. We go auto riding, visiting, and uptown to the theaters.

Another man stated "We have had sickness in our family since we moved here [two years ago], and we, therefore, know nothing about the neighbors. . . . Our friends live in various parts of the city and in the small cities around Los Angeles." The whole story of the waning of neighborliness in Southern California seems to be summed up in that poignant "therefore."[31]

The change, however, need not necessarily be regarded as an unfortunate one, though its immediate effects were bound to involve dislocation and insecurity. Dr. Bogardus maintained an optimistic outlook, postulating the evolution of a new pattern of human relationships involving greater freedom on a possibly higher plane of development:

> The role particularly of the automobile . . . had cut down spatial distance and tended to increase social nearness to such an extent that every person may live in wide-flung communalities of his own, in place of the old closely-circumscribed neighborhood. [It is] increasing the psycho-social range of human beings.[32]

Nevertheless, the dominant picture of Los Angeles society which emerges from the chaotic first decade of mass motorization is one, not of new "communalitization," but of a phenomenal, frantic restlessness, well–characterized by Dr. McClenahan in her comment upon the high proportion of families found in her study to be unsettled and thinking of moving again:

> This straining against the bonds that hold them in the area makes residence for many families an uneasy, unsettled, uncertain state. . . . They are like branches or tree-trunks caught in a swirling river current which find lodgement here and there against the river bank, only to be caught up again and hurried to another resting place.[33]

Mobility, then, had many faces. A car made it easier for people to come to you; but it also made it easier for them to leave you. Hence the perplexity, for example, of the Riverside booster-editor who complained in 1927 that, while many people from nearby San Bernardino were coming to do their shopping in Riverside, which was fine, many from Riverside were " always running over to San Bernardino" to shop there, which was, to say the least, "a mystery."[34]

It was universally recognized, however, that the most socially significant aspect of this problem was its effect upon family relationships, and in particular the behavior and attitudes of the younger generation.

A. *Youth*

It is hardly surprising that during an era remarkable for conflict between the generations, when the very term "Youth" had connotations which it has almost entirely lost today, a significant part of that conflict should have found expression in connection with that era's most notable agent of social change. Cars plus kids tended to spell trouble of one kind or another, and it is not difficult to see why. The Mass Automobile had burst so suddenly upon the scene that there had been no time to evolve laws, methods, traditions, and attitudes for dealing with the many problems to which it gave rise. If mature adults were thrown off balance by an innovation which so amazingly augmented the powers of an individual human being, it was even more likely that those still growing up would be affected.

In many ways, therefore, the social problems associated with motorized young people were only intensifications of difficulties of adjustment faced by the population as a whole. For example, the questions of mobility and dislocation already touched upon here were manifested in their most alarming aspects in connection with the changing structure of family life. In many quarters the automobile was seen as a tremendous threat to parental control, enabling children to escape entirely and with great ease from all the restrictions of their home environment. Dr. Bogardus, for one, made no bones about it. "The automobile," he declared flatly, "is the undoing of many a boy. . . . With the automobile at his command, the boy easily speeds up beyond home control."[35]

The Lynds, however, found that "Many families feel that an automobile is justified as an agent holding the family together." They quoted one business-class mother as declaring that "I never feel as close to my family as when we are all together in the car," and pointed out that about 60 percent of Middletown's high school students claimed "that they motor more often with their parents than without them."[36] Nor did California car salesmen hesitate to assert that "automobiles are known to bring greater domestic happiness, particularly when there are children. . . ."[37]

Nevertheless, Dr. Bogardus, whose study of the problems of boys in Los Angeles devoted an entire chapter to problems centering around the automobile, was able to marshall impressive testimony to corroborate his concern for the future of family ties in the motor age. Statements like these from persons interviewed fill his pages:

A teacher: 'Too many fellows have a machine too early. . . . whenever we get a fellow we can't do much with, who is always playing hookey and getting into trouble, we ask his parents to take his car away from him.'

A social worker: 'Nearly every Jewish home has a car, even among the poorer people where they have second-hand Fords, but these tend to separate the children from their parents.'

A principal: 'One father bought his two children, still in this elementary school, an automobile. They burnt out a bearing which cost $75. Father had auto repaired. The mother is worried every minute they are out in the car. Still she says "They are beyond our control; what can we do?" '

Parents were often blamed for making cars too easily available to their children; but this was only part of the story. For the juvenile society of Southern California had become at least equally as car crazy as the adult segment of the population, and possibly more so. The boy denied a car by his parents "may work for one, or steal one, or several."[38]

Desire stimulated from so many different sources was too great to be suppressed by mere parental disapproval. Such disapproval, in fact, only tended to heighten the desire, making the automobile a potent symbol of rebellion against authority. And indeed in the entire history of man, no discovery, no movement, no leader, no cause, had ever been able to offer to the adolescent mind and spirit such a wide range of stimuli, challenges, opportunities, and satisfactions as this incredible box on wheels which moved by itself. Speed, danger, adventure, independence, glamor—the automobile seemed to embody the very essence of youth. It was the most exciting toy which had ever yet been offered to a generation to play with.

With so many factors to recommend it to the young, possession of an automobile or access to one became, for many of those whom we would now call teenagers, a social essential. In particular, that element of the mating process known as "dating" came more and more to require a car. By 1926 this had gone so far that one Los Angeles teacher said that he could not blame a boy for stealing a car for this purpose, since "he has to do it if he wants any kind of a girl at all." According to Dr. Bogardus, the social pressure upon boys to take girls to parties in cars was "almost beyond comprehension."[39] Thus the acquisition of a car came to mark a stage in the process of growing up. When Jimmy's father bought him a car, in Peter Viertel's fine novel, *The Canyon* (about the life of a group of young Angelenos during the Nineteen-Twenties and Thirties), a remarkable change came over the boy; childish things were suddenly put away: "I'll be able to take girls out, you know, and this damn fooling around the canyon will be over. I guess I'll get rid of my bike."[40]

But to have young people of both sexes moving together unsupervised over the landscape and sitting close together in portable cubicles entirely beyond the reach of all external restraint was, in the eyes of many social commentators, a most deplorable state of affairs. As old Jackson Graves put it, "I fear that the automobile, encouraging all sorts of night excursions on the part of the young, . . . [is] not for the best interests of society or the social state."[41]

At the Southern California Conference on Modern Parenthood, held in Los Angeles in December 1926, a speaker on "Social Conditions Influencing Youth" described with evident alarm the behavior he had recently observed of some young people returning in automobile parties from a football game:

> . . . boys and girls together, stimulated by the feeling that they were by themselves, given that reckless expression which is the result often of a stimulus of being under that detached environment, laughing and attracting attention and doing things that would have hurt their character, right in the public eye as they passed by.

The coming of the automobile, according to this speaker, had thus created a situation in which "even vice is different" from what it used to be.[42] A close association generally existed in the minds of many critics between automobiles, movies, alcohol, and sexual misbehavior. Towards the end of the decade, the radio also began to come in for its share of the blame. Those very critical English observers, the Gordons, for example, lumped radio, cars, and movies together as "insidious drugs, moral morphias that can render habitues insensible to any vacant spaces of mental life unfilled with thought," and went on to link them, in a rather vague way, with "bootleg liquor and the growth of flagrant and cynical concupiscence among youth."[43] Censure of this kind was, incidentally, as Professor G. H. Knoles has pointed out, particularly common in the accounts of America written by English visitors during the Nineteen-Twenties. In his opinion it stemmed largely from a jealous resentment of American prosperity.[44]

Another speaker at the Parenthood Conference, Dr. William Kirk, Professor of Sociology at Pomona College, took a more tolerant view:

> As I left my home this morning . . . in a 1927 automobile . . . I could not help but feel that my youth was an entirely different affair from the youth of these youngsters . . . We didn't have the radio . . . we didn't even have electric lights . . . the movie was unknown; the automobile unthought of. . . . We are living in a changing world. . . . We are not yet emotionally educated up to the many demands which modern life is making upon us. . . . Our control over physical forces has gone far beyond our control over the moral forces of life. . . . Our boys and girls who have been caught up in this great onrushing tide are neither good nor bad on general principles; they are either weak or strong. . . .

Dr. Kirk was confident that the boys and girls who were then growing up were "being trained emotionally," and that "when they reach our age they will not be so bewildered or so perplexed as we find ourselves today."[45]

Nevertheless, the public at large continued to see a close connection between cars and the corruption of youth. It was not until 1929 that the Lynds cited statistical evidence that a majority of juvenile "sex crimes" were now occurring in automobiles.[46] But according to a novel of Upton Sinclair's, as early as the war years the practice was quite common in Southern California whereby

> the rich high-school kids would go out hunting in pairs in their fancy sport-cars, and would pick up girls and drive them, and if the girls did not play the game according to their taste, they would turn them out on the road, anywhere, a score of miles from a town. There was a formula, short and snappy, 'Pet or walk!'[47]

In 1921 the *Los Angeles Times* quoted an unhappy report delivered by Captain Cannon of the County Motorcycle Squad to the Board of Supervisors:

> The practice of making love on the highways is becoming alarmingly prevalent. In many cases it is flagrantly open. . . . Numerous complaints have been received of night riders who park their automobiles along country boulevards, douse the lights and indulge in orgies.[48]

Four years later, the problem appeared to have changed somewhat. The new popularity of the closed car had enabled automotive lovemaking to be somewhat more private (the age of the motel, which would much alter this entire situation, was yet to come); and the chief concern of the police, judging from the following item, was now not that it was "flagrantly open" but that it was becoming harder to ferret out:

CLOSED CAR BLAMED FOR CONDITIONS

[According to an address by Pasadena Police chief Charles Kelley], 'the greatest menace now facing the morals of Pasadena youth is the coupe and sedan which . . . have replaced the old-time red-light districts.' The house of ill fame on wheels, as the new menace is referred to, has become one of the Pasadena Police Department's greatest problems, it was disclosed. The astounding number of 'coupe lovers' who park on dark streets in the Crown City necessitates the use of nearly all the police machines on patrol duty.[49]

Just what role the automobile really played in the process of changing attitudes towards sex remained a point of dispute. Some people thought that the sheer sense of speed had something to do with it. "When young people get out in autos, theorized one youth worker, they always want to go as fast as the car will go, and that gives an exhilarating effect upon the occupants and tends to break down the barriers that before existed." Some thought that some types of cars were more dangerous in this regard than others, that "other things being equal, a couple in a sport car are more liable to step over the bounds . . . simply because the car they are in is different or a little off color, so to speak." It is interesting, though, that there appears to have been a general tendency, when the question of blame was discussed, to fix it upon the car rather than upon its occupants. Thus a boys' worker declared:

> I think [the automobile] is the most important factor in what might be called downright immorality; a couple get off into the country in some secluded spot, and there are very few people who would not be tempted. I do not think we can blame the young folks too much.[50]

Just how the young folks came to be there in that secluded spot was, of course, another story.

In any case, the institution of automotive lovemaking was by the end of the decade quite well-established in Southern California, though it had its hazards and inconveniences. Caryl Chessman, who grew up in Los Angeles and eventually died in the San Quentin gas chamber for a crime involving the sexual molestation of women in parked cars, handed down to the world in his autobiography a boyhood memory suggesting some of the less attractive features of motorized romance:

> One sunny summer day he [Chessman] came down from the cabin high in his hills, B.B. gun in hand, and stood at the edge of a bank looking down at a car—and the three people in it—parked where the street ended at the foot of the hills. In the back seat of the car a nearly naked couple were engaged in a sex act. A tiny, crying girl stood on the front seat and called pitifully for mama. The woman kept shushing her child and all the while responding to the huge hairy man. Then the tiny girl set up a more insistent wail for her mama and climbed up on the back of the front seat. With a curse, the man reached out and struck the girl down. While the child cowered and whimpered in the front seat, the mother and her lover proceeded to concentrate on the gratification of their lust. They didn't proceed very far.
> In a flash [the boy] raised, aimed and then squeezed the trigger of his B.B. gun. A moment later a bellow of pain issued from the throat of the hairy individual and a surprising amount of activity, none of it co-ordinated, took place in the back seat of the car. [The boy] ran off down a trail; he didn't want to see any more.[51]

For all its power and mobility, an automobile could not always protect an amorous couple from the importunities of other members of the family or from the sensitivities of wandering youngsters with B.B. guns!

One term, of many, to which the auto mania of the Twenties gave wide currency was "joy ride,"[52] a term most expressive of the spirit of abandon so commonly associated with the young people of that era then and since. But when, after all, had it ever been possible for so many people to derive so much joy out of riding? There had usually been more trouble than pleasure associated with travel—the very word "travel" stemmed from "travail," or labor. But "joy riding" connoted far more than joy and riding. It meant recklessness, immorality, and youthful decadence. It was less descriptive than pejorative. As an illustration of such usage, consider the following account by an outraged Californian published in 1927:

> One night I helped dispose of two boys and two girls who were out joy-riding in a small car. We noticed this auto racing madly around town . . . with these four high school kids in it. They were yelling at the top of their voices. . . . About midnight or later we found the car on its side in the center of a very dark vacant lot with the curtains drawn. There were the two couples locked in each other's arms, two in the front seat and two in the back seat; all four bodies were nude. . . . All four were paralyzed drunk. We put their clothes on as best we could. We took the girls to one hotel and the boys to another . . . and then went . . . to find the parents.[53]

It turned out in this case that the parents had also been misbehaving. They had "been out to a country club," presumably in their own automobiles, "indulging in a little liquid refreshment themselves." Such incidents were no doubt hardly typical. But they tended to receive wide publicity because, as the *Los Angeles Times* editorialized, "the super-heated fires of flaming youth" were "one of the burning questions of the hour," so that when "the rompish rubber-tired flivver heads youth into a peck and sometimes a barrel of trouble, [it] makes better headlines."[54] (*Flaming Youth*, incidentally, was the title of a popular novel by Werner Fabian, which Mark Sullivan branded "an improbable tale almost exclusively concerned with sex and alcohol."[55])

Yet there was no real agreement on what part the automobile was playing in all the different social changes which seemed to be going on at an accelerated rate during the Twenties. There were too many variable factors to be considered. For every observer who worried about the number of babies being produced by illicit lovemaking in automobiles, you would find another concerned that the automobile might be a threat to the birthrate because people would rather spend money on mobility than on having children.[56] And closely tied in with matters of youth and sex was the intriguing question of the new status of women.

B. WOMEN

There could be no doubt that the coming of the mass motorcar was playing havoc with longstanding social conventions, particularly where women were concerned. Even so eminent an authority on "correct" behavior as Emily Post could only complain, without offering any solution, about the inconsistency with which polite society continued to insist that "absolutely no lady . . . can go to dinner or supper in a restaurant alone with a gentleman," while seeing nothing wrong in allowing even "a very young girl [to] motor around the country alone with a man," so long as she had her father's consent.[57]

That the social position of women, and consequently to a considerable extent also of men, was changing, few could deny.[58] And the driving of automobiles was one of the ways in which women could assert their new claim to equality. On the defensive, resentful men created two great and enduring stereotypes to bolster their damaged egos: the incompetent "woman driver" and the "backseat driver," who, in the classic situation, was generally a wife harassing her driver-husband. The *Los Angeles Times* reflected the typical masculine reaction when in 1925 it described as "a genuine jolt" an announcement by the American Automobile Association that tests had proved conclusively that women drivers were just as competent as men and even less variable.[59] The jolt, however, had little permanent effect, and the following year the same paper was assailing Woman for being "so temperamental in driving! She fills the heart with love in the home, but with the jim-jams on the highway."[60] Newspapers in general delighted in such stories as that of a woman driver who held up traffic at a busy Hollywood intersection while she stopped to powder her nose.[61]

Nevertheless, the phenomenon of women at the controls of automobiles soon became a very common one in California, a subject for remark only by visitors from abroad such as the Englishman William A. Robson, who wrote in 1925 that:

> . . . it is a perpetual surprise to see the remarkable competence with which the American woman manages her own car. . . . When we visited a women's college in California my companions and I were taken out for a drive one afternoon by a group of the senior students in three enormous throbbing monsters driven by three small college girls whose little feet could hardly reach the pedals. It was magnificent![62]

The growing number of women drivers was reflected in changing editorial policies of The Automobile Club of Southern California magazine, *Touring Topics*. In February, 1924 the magazine carried its first cover picture of a woman at the wheel of a car, and about the same time began publishing regular articles on fashions in dress, and frequent, usually rather mawkish, love stories with some kind of motoring theme. For example, "Cupid in the Fog," by H. B. Ross, tells of a woman driving late at night from San Francisco towards Los Angeles to marry a man she does not want to marry, and of a man driving in the opposite direction to marry a girl *he* is not in love with. They just happen to collide, but escape injury, and realize upon first meeting that they are each other's ideals. The fact that the man, (who had caused the accident), had been driving drunk at high speed through a fog at the time of the crash appears to have had no moral implications for anyone concerned, including author and editor.[63]

Women were still painfully self-conscious about their new freedom. There was more than humor in Mrs. Nancy Barr Mavity's advice:

> Never let your husband teach you to drive;—be the first to learn! In fact, if it is at all possible, be the one to teach him. That will just about even things up psychologically. But if you reinforce his ingrained sense of masculine superiority with the authority of a teacher, if you let him be the expert while you are still the novice, you will never catch up—never!

The same writer confessed that her backseat driving had been "responsible for the only bitter quarrels of our married life," but protested that this vice had nothing to do with her being a woman:

> The impulse of a driver to drive when he is not driving is not a sex character. It is so deeply rooted in human nature that it is more like original sin, dormant until something—the invention of automobiles in this case—brings it out.

She also admitted that, while perfectly capable of changing a tire herself, she preferred to have a man do it for her because "I merely hate it." Her excuse for this apparent inconsistency in her feminism was charming: since "the automobile is accused of wrecking the morals of the nation, leading our young people astray . . . and stimulating the crime wave, it may well bear the onus of my own peccadillo, my bit of petty graft from the masculine tradition."[64] Apparently unwilling to challenge such graft, the Automobile Club of Southern California, when it began its own emergency service program in 1924, offered to change tires "when car is operated by a woman unaccompanied by a male companion. This service will not be rendered to a man physically able to change a tire himself."[65] Since then, however, men have been able to achieve equal status with women in this regard and are no longer presumed by Automobile Club rules to be any less helpless in motor matters than members of the opposite sex.

C. *Crime*

In his annual report for the year 1920–1921, Los Angeles Police Chief Lyle Pendergast, commenting on the recent rapid development of the motorcar, expressed the opinion that "this new means of transportation has had the effect of greatly increasing the number of offenses" committed in the city. He explained that he was referring, not only to traffic offences, but also to car-, and car-part theft and to such crimes as holdups in which it was now possible for "a party of hoodlums [to] hold up several pedestrians and be outside the city before the first dazed victim has been able to make a report of his misfortune."[66]

Whether or not there was any actual increase in the *amount* of crime committed during the Nineteen-Twenties, there was certainly a change in its types and methods, as well as in methods of dealing with it. It was only to be expected that an object as desirable and useful as an automobile would figure largely in the record of conflict between individual man and society as a whole, and that where there were the most cars, there would be the most automotive crimes and criminals. As early as January 1919, David R. Faries, General Counsel for the Automobile Club of Southern California, was warning its members that "Automobiles may be involved in almost any crime human beings may commit."[67] And as the age of mass motorization got under way, it became more and more the case in Los Angeles not that a car gave a criminal an advantage, but that he was disadvantaged without one.

Of all the crimes associated with the automobile, by far the most common was that of stealing the cars themselves. This was not only because of their great desirability and high intrinsic value, but also because of their usefulness in the commission of other crimes. Los Angeles Police Department records showed an average of about 8,000 cars stolen per year during the period 1921–29 with a peak of 11,541 being reached in 1926.[68] Frank G. Snook, Chief of the State Motor Vehicle Division, reported in 1929 that stolen automobiles were associated with "at least 70%" of major crimes.[69] As the Gordons remarked concerning a newspaper item of 1928 to the effect that eighteen highwaymen were known to be at large in the city area, none of whom was a pedestrian, in a town where car thefts were so common, "he would have been a fool bandit that went afoot."[70]

The trouble was that, as with many other problems arising from the motor age, society had not anticipated the problem of mass motor theft, and was at first quite unprepared to deal with it. Cars were remarkably easy to steal and very difficult to trace if taken to another city or state. A 1921 article on car theft in California described it as "the least risky and the most profitable of all the major criminal operations." Thieves were helped by the inadequacy of locking devices, especially in the days when open cars predominated, by a surprising carelessness on the part of motorists, by the increasing number of cars on the roads, and by a great lack of co-ordination and communication between the police departments of different communities, combined, of course, with the mobility which the stolen car itself gave to the thief.

What recourse did the motorists have against this menace? The police, of course, were not entirely to be discounted, although, according to the article cited above, they had been "forced to confess themselves helpless against the rising tide of auto theft."[71] That they had lost the confidence of the public, however, was indicated by the fact that private advertisements occasionally appeared in newspaper "lost and found" columns requesting aid in the recovery of stolen cars. One could attempt to have one's car guarded in various ways, as the following want ad of 1919 suggests: "Dogs for sale . . . Male Boston terrier, handsome and gentle, for watchdog for auto or home."[72] Or one could purchase one or more of a variety of mechanical protections, such as the "Stop Thief Auto Lock," which prevented the steering wheel from being turned,[73] or the popular "Security Auto Theft Signal," a metal protuberance made to lock around the front wheel, which did not actually immobilize the car at all but bumped and made a noise if the car was driven with it on.[74] Some of the manufacturers of these devices tried to increase their value by public offers of not-too-generous rewards ($100 to $250) for the apprehension of persons attempting to circumvent them.

Most drivers, however, appeared to find security methods of this kind too much trouble to bother with. A survey conducted by the Gilmore Oil Company in Los Angeles in 1926, based on 3,000 cars checked in both business and residential areas, found that 85 percent of parked cars were left unlocked. (Incidentally, the same survey also found that the most careful motorists in this respect were the owners of cars in the *medium* price range, *i.e.*, the $900–$1600 class. Those with cars both less and more expensive took fewer precautions.)[75] It is easy, therefore, to understand the note of urgency in such pronouncements as that of Victor Killick, statistician of the Los Angeles County Sheriff's Department, in 1927, that "every citizen who does not take ordinary precautions to prevent the theft of his car is indirectly guilty of conditions that help the hold-up, the burglar, the murderer and all other types of lawlessness against society."[76]

The most effective recourse against the auto thief which his victims seem to have had, at least until police techniques began to improve, was the private Theft Bureau set up by the insurance companies. Detectives employed by this Bureau soon became so proficient that it was claimed, for example, that over 90 percent of the cars stolen in 1920 were recovered and returned to their owners.[77] But this high recovery rate was also due in part to the fact that a large proportion of the cars stolen in Southern California were taken by youngsters for some specific purpose and then simply abandoned afterwards. According to a police worker interviewed by Bogardus, "Almost all of the cases of auto theft are with kids, fellows about eighteen, but many go down to thirteen."[78] The *Times* sermonized:

> Cars are stolen by reckless youth every week in this city merely for joy rides, the thieves afterward leaving them in byways. . . . This shows what great risks young fellows will take for the transient satisfaction of a brisk run out to the beach or into the country—risks which more sober and discerning people would consider far from commensurate with the pleasure thus enjoyed.[79]

And the superintendent of a state reform school, when asked in 1929 to state his opinions on the causes and prevention of crime, pointed out that 35 percent of his inmates had been committed on a charge of auto theft, largely the result of the boys finding "most of the cars unlocked or with defective locking devices." In his eyes, one of the most effective ways of fighting crime would be "a simple campaign of education through the press and over the radio urging automobile owners to lock their machines when parking."[80]

With regard to the more violent and sensational aspects of auto-mobilized crime, virtually any edition of a Los Angeles newspaper during the Nineteen-Twenties will serve to demonstrate the already thorough motorization of society. For example, an edition of the *Times* chosen entirely at random (June 1, 1925) yields local car crime news in the form of one definite murder (of a Los Angeles car salesman in his own car), one suspected murder (two men were seen by a passing motorist bundling a man's body into the rear of a touring car near the foot of the new Hollywood Dam), one armed robbery (two men robbed a Los Angeles taxi driver and drove off with his taxi), and the confiscation of $25,000 worth of cars for transporting intoxicating liquor in violation of the Prohibition law.[81] ("Don't try to use your car as a brewery wagon," the District Attorney had warned motorists.[82] But the county treasury, for whose benefit confiscated cars were sold, reaped a handsome harvest from those who disobeyed.)

The California Crime Commission gave some indication in 1929 of the frightening range of auto-crime problems yet to be dealt with when it complained that the state had no adequate border patrol "so that automobiles entering and leaving the state could be checked for stolen automobiles, concealed weapons, narcotics, intoxicating liquor, and criminals."[83] Perhaps the most vivid portrayal of such aspects of Los Angeles life during the decade is to be found in Don Ryan's novel, *Angel's Flight*, with its descriptions of the activities of bootleggers (their car armed with a machine gun mounted on the hood),and bank robbers (who used a "series of waiting automobiles into which they change in making a getaway—the first or lead car being a stolen one.") But even in Ryan's book, as in so much else of the literature of the time, what is most remarkable to the student of automotive social history is not the prominence accorded to the automobile in the narrative but the extent to which so recent an innovation is taken for granted. Only in a passage such as that in which a police car goes to investigate a murder in the Mexican Quarter is the reader reminded that there was then still a section of Los Angeles "where automobiles seldom stray" and where they were sufficiently unfamiliar to the "darting eyes" of the Quarter's inhabitants for those eyes to "devour every shining nickel device on the big car [and] feast on the rolling wheels."[84]

Automobiles figured prominently in many of the most sensational Los Angeles murder cases of the era. One of the first and most famous of such cases was that of Clara Phillips who in 1922 was found guilty of murdering her husband's paramour, Alberta Meadows. Alberta worked in a downtown bank to which she commuted in her own car. One day Clara, who knew Alberta, met her after work and asked for a ride to somebody's house on the east side of town. Their route took them to a road in a hilly section of Highland Park called Montecito Drive, where Clara contrived to get Alberta to step out of the car with her and then proceeded to smash in her skull with a hammer which she had bought specially for the occasion, attempting subsequently to hide the body under a large rock. Clara then drove home to her husband, Armour, in Alberta's car, a Model T Ford, and announced (according to his later testimony), "She's dead and I killed her!" Armour at first decided to help his wife. The major problem was to get rid of the Ford which they drove thirty miles to Pomona and abandoned there. Author George Worthing Yates, from whose entertaining account of the case these details are taken, comments, possibly with some exaggeration, on the difficulties such a recourse might present to the police in those days:

> The [Ford] abandoned in Pomona had yet to be reported. . . . It might molder there unnoticed for months without causing comment, for it was the habit of the Southern California motorist, when his easy payments grew onerous or the machinery went

haywire, to cast a car away as casually as an empty match book. In
whole or in part, they abounded along every gutter and highway.[85]

In this case, however, finding the car did not prove essential, for
Armour Phillips soon changed his mind and turned his wife in. After an
amazing subsequent escape to Central America and recapture by Eugene Biscailuz (later to become in 1929 first head of the California
State Highway Patrol), she was eventually given a life sentence. It is
interesting, but of course fruitless, to speculate whether such a crime
might not have taken place at all had it not been so easy for the
murderess to have herself and her intended victim transported together in a few minutes from the heart of the city to a relatively
isolated spot where no screams might be heard.

Perhaps an even more striking example of crime in the motor age,
and surely the most publicized and horrible Los Angeles murder of the
decade, was the kidnap-slaying of young Marion Parker by William
Hickman.

Hickman was a youth of about nineteen who on December 15, 1927,
appeared at a Los Angeles elementary school with word that twelve-
year-old Marion Parker's father, a bank official, had been seriously
injured in an automobile accident and that he had been sent to get her.
Such calamities were by then so common that no question was apparently raised by the school authorities, and Hickman was allowed to
drive off with the child in his own car. Soon Marion's distraught father,
who had not been in any accident, was receiving anonymous letters and
telephone calls threatening death to the girl and demanding $1,500 in
ransom to be handed over at a rendezvous which both men were to
reach in their own cars with no police in attendance. The best that
could be said of the Los Angeles Police Department during that period,
as J. Francis McComas has written in his account of this case, "is that
it was by no means the finely equipped, splendidly staffed organization
of honorable, able men it is today."[86] The police persuaded the child's
father to allow them to follow him to the appointed place, which they
did quite openly in two large cars. The tactic was wholly ineffective, for
Hickman, with Marion then still alive beside him in the car, had kept
watch on the Parker house and saw the police cars following Parker's
car when he left. He then apparently followed *them* far enough to see
just what the plan was, but he naturally failed to show up at the
rendezvous. In a note which he subsequently sent to the father, the
kidnapper took care to show how well he had observed the trap and the
vehicles of the trappers:

> When those two closed cars followed your car north on Wilton to
> Tenth and stopped shortly off Wilton on Tenth and then proceeded

to circle the block on Gramercy, San Marino, Wilton, and Tenth I knew and you knew what for. One was a late model and the other had disc wheels. . . .

The next time Parker arranged to meet Hickman, he went alone, and when Hickman appeared, the father could see Marion sitting in the car. Hickman got out of the car, took the money from Parker, and instructed him to remain there while he drove further up the block where he said he would release the girl. When Parker reached the spot where Hickman had deposited his daughter before driving rapidly off, he found only her legless, armless corpse. Its hair had been combed; its face powdered; and the eyelids sewn open with black thread to make it appear that the child passenger in the car was alive. Only the convenience of the private automobile had enabled Hickman so smoothly to carry out this ghastly act.

The automobile also played a large part in Hickman's subsequent identification and capture. (He was executed at San Quentin in 1928.)[87] But even more pertinent to the present purpose were the words of an anonymous contemporary ballad, circulated in California and other states, which commemorated the case:

Right here in California bright and gay, and gay,
A family wrapped up little gifts for Xmas day.
One of them was Marion, such a pretty child,
All the folks on that block loved her pretty smile.

She went out next morning, here in bright L.A.
Going to her grade school just a couple blocks away.
She got to her school all right, but a dirty fiend
Got her in his jalopy and drove her from the scene.

He wrote her daddy a ransom letter for a thousand five,
But also thought poor Marion might talk if left alive.
So this dastard took a shiv and cut her joints away,
It was the cruelest thing e'er done, here in old L.A.

Her daddy he was honest, he brought the cash along;
If only Hickman also was, nothing would be wrong.
He sat there in his fine car, tossed out ears and eyes;
The father he was weeping, distressed by Hickman's lies. . . .

The father, he was honest. Why wasn't Hickman too?
He had no call to kill her, poor Marion so true.
She was probably as brave as any girl could be;
If he had asked, she'd keep shut, on who did that deed.

If he had only been more fair and had not cut her dead,
He might have got a better car and never be afraid.
But some men are so cruel, nothing does them touch:
He was a hard-hearted skunk, so he is in Dutch. . . .[88]

What is most notable here is that the anonymous balladeer apparently assumed that the entire motive behind the kidnapping had been to enable Hickman to buy a better car, and furthermore, that such a motive was in itself quite sufficient to justify kidnapping, if conducted honorably. In fact, Hickman's motives were never very clear, but buying a car was certainly not one of them, since he was already an accomplished car thief and had performed this and previous crimes entirely with the aid of stolen cars. He himself actually claimed, upon capture, that he had wanted the money in order to go to Bible college! If only the kidnapper had been "honest," "nothing would be wrong," and "he might have got a better car and never be afraid." Just how Hickman's "jalopy" of the second verse became a "fine car" at the very time of the handing over of the ransom money is not easy to explain, except perhaps by a sort of figurative anticipation in the mind of the poet. So there passed into the folklore of Southern California, during a period in which the creative literary talent of the region was in general conspicuous by its absence, at least one splendid tribute to the spirit and values of the era.

Not only in killing other people was the new machine found to be of use. By 1929, "jumping in front of vehicle" had become sufficiently common as a means of suicide to be given a separate listing in the annual City Police statistics.[89] At least as early as 1923 it had been discovered that automobile exhaust gas, when directed into gopher holes, was an effective means of destroying their inhabitants.[90] Car owners who tired of the struggle were soon employing the same method upon themselves, though it was still sufficiently unfamiliar in 1931 to require special explanation in John O'Hara's novel *Appointment in Samarra*. Later the great structures built for conveying the new vehicles smoothly over deep obstacles, especially the graceful Colorado Street Bridge, would act like magnets for would-be suicides. It is interesting to note that in 1928 Southern California showed the greatest increase in number of suicides of any place in the country, and that most of the people who committed suicide were relatively recent arrivals.[91]

Class and Status

It must be remembered that the popular picture of the automobile had altered drastically in the course of a relatively few years. The vehicle which had once been a symbol of "the arrogance of wealth" had now, at least in Southern California, become virtually a symbol of democracy. The following, from a highly colored contemporary account of the San Francisco earthquake-fire of 1906, gives a good idea of then prevailing attitudes:

> Down the street came a great automobile. It was occupied by two society women. . . . They were out to see the sights—the awful heartrending sights. . . . It was heartless, cruel, inhuman, unnatural, fiendish—for they laughed as they came through the lines of suffering mortals and between the rows of wounded and dying.[92]

By the Twenties, however, it was a very different story. "Everybody owns an automobile . . . and they got fine paved roads all over Southern California," says a character in one novel of the period. "I don't see's the workin' man's got any kick coming' "[93] The transition from the one image to the other, however, was neither abrupt nor complete. People who had grown up in the days when it was a mark of wealth and status merely to possess an automobile naturally liked to cling to that image when they themselves acquired cars, even though everybody else was doing the same. As late as 1920, we still find an author, wishing to emphasize the wealth of the movie colony, boasting, "Millions, probably, are represented in the property owned by men and women of the movies. . . . Their automobiles are numbered by the thousands!"[94] Before much longer, however, mere ownership of an automobile said very little, in itself, about the social position of the owner. The type, the condition, the newness, the accessories, and in general the monetary value were factors which now became very important in that regard. In consequence, there resulted what might be called a remarkable confusion of automotive images and associations.

To a certain extent, the automobile was, like the six-shooter, a "great equalizer." In terms of actual use, there was not a great deal of difference between one type of car and another, provided both were in equally good running order. The power, the mobility, the escape potential, were relatively the same, as compared with any other form of transportation. But the more widespread automobile ownership became, the more the finer distinctions came to count. The motorized portion of society was thus lifted in its entirety to a different plane, but there it developed a hierarchy all its own.

As an indication of the double imagery characteristic of this "motor-domocracy," consider the following from Alice Williamson:

> . . . There are none so humble here as not to own a car. While you wait your turn for a strawberry sundae . . . you hear the sleek-headed white-clad attendant offering to take a friend home that night in his automobile. All stenographers own their cars, though some may be year before last's Lisettes.[95]

"Lisette" here is presumably a pseudo-polite of "Lizzie," a term applied since about 1917 to an old, cheap, or dilapidated car, usually a Ford, and similar in meaning to "flivver." But the really significant word is "though," indicating the existence of an important scale of preference. Even more revealing is the statement, in an article of 1923, that the Automobile Club of Southern California seeks "to provide a service organization rather than a social club. They do not make the almost fatal error of trying to mix in a clubhouse the owner of the flivver with him of the twin-six."[96]

On the open road, however, and especially in the motorcamps which sprang up everywhere during the Twenties, class distinctions tended to disappear in response to the fact of common immediate circumstance, as did regional differences. The *camaraderie* of the road was a subject remarked upon by almost every motor traveller, so much so that one often detects in their comments a heavy note of class consciousness, particularly with regard to auto status, as in the following last stanza from a poem called "Tourists' Motor Camp," published in *Touring Topics* in 1927:

> T.M.C. is no respecter
> Has no choice in cars or states
> Lordly limousines nudge flivvers
> 'Bugs' creep close to shining eights.
> Sleep, impartial, democratic
> Blends in nightly strong refrain
> Snorts of sleeping Colorado
> Snores of travel-weary Maine.[97]

"Bug," as indicated by the context, was a term for a small automobile.

The "lordliness" of some cars as opposed to others, then, came to be as much taken for granted as the predominance of cars in general. Hence, for example, the phraseology of the lead paragraph of a 1926 *Times* report on a "Closed-Car Salon," an exhibition of expensive models, being held out at the Biltmore Hotel: "Imperialism still lives, even in our democratic America, in our ultra class-levelled Los Angeles! The nobility of motor-cardom holding court at the Biltmore proves this."[98] "Ultra-class-levelled Los Angeles" indeed cherished and nourished its auotomotive class distinctions, perhaps because in so fluid and unstable a society such distinctions afforded one of the most ready means of passing those necessary judgments upon one's fellow men which everyone has frequently to make in order to keep a sense of social perspective. To that extent the idea was no doubt a useful and healthy one. But it led to all kinds of perversions and extremes.

Because the automobile became accepted as a ready indicator of social status, people began seeking to advance their status by means of their cars. Thus in Upton Sinclair's novel *Oil!* the newly oil-rich Mr. Bankside:

> moved himself out to an ocean-front palace . . . and bought himself . . . a big new limousine, also a 'sport-car,' in which to drive himself to the country club to play golf every afternoon. . . . Efficiency was the watchword out here in the West, and when you decided to change your social status you put the job right through.[99]

And we find items in "fashionable" magazines with such titles as WHAT THE SMART SET SELECTS IN MOTORS: HERE ARE THE THOROUGHBREDS OF THE CALIFORNIA HIGHWAYS,[100] (See Figures 2A–2B). Approaches embodying suggestions of this kind were of course the bread and butter of those engaged in advertising and selling the more expensive makes of cars. A point was soon reached when it became apparent, as the Biltmore Salon reporter pointed out, that a whole class of automobiles existed which could hardly be regarded as "merely a means of transportation."[101] Eventually, though the present writer has found no such usage of the term in the Nineteen-Twenties the very word "transportation," when applied in the marketing of automobiles, would come to connote an inferior specimen having no other virtue than that of providing a means of getting about, a term used only in connection with the cheapest of used cars.

As with a good many other kinds of attitudes towards the automobile, it was particularly in connection with the movie industry that ideas of status evolved. Then, as now, Hollywood not only helped to form public attitudes, it also tended to reflect them—though usually in an exaggerated or distorted form. And the lives of film folk, whether on or off the screen, constituted a sort of perpetual show for which the people of Southern California had grandstand seats. Perhaps because of the constant inpouring of newcomers, Southern Californians never became blasé about the presence of the film colony. A *Touring Topics* article of 1921, for example, told how the Hollywood fashion for very ornate cars, trimmed in gold leaf or bedecked with elk antlers or large monograms, was beginning to spread to the general public which had taken to "using the bejewelled motor bus and getting itself taken for Pauline Frederick or Tony Moreno as it tours down Broadway." Meanwhile the stars themselves had begun to react against this trend, leaning instead towards the "sedate sedan" and leaving the "mere public a lap behind." Among the stars themselves, however, rivalry for prestige was keen, and "practically every motion picture star . . . [was] planning to outdo friend neighbor in the matter of something nobby but not gaudy in automobile designs."[102]

The automobile was one of the symbols most readily employed by satirists of the ostentatious unreality of Hollywood. In Carl Van Vechten's novel, *Spider Boy*, Imperia Starling, the big star who has lured Broadway writer Ambrose Deacon to Hollywood to write the scenario for her next film, has the following conversation with him shortly after his arrival:

> 'Now I just can't bother with you today. I'm much too busy . . . Tomorrow I'll try to get together a dinner party for you. Today, work on my story if you feel like it . . . Or take out one of the cars. I have twelve: Pierce-Arrow, Marmon, Chrysler 80, Packard, Lincoln . . . whichever you prefer. I use the Hispano. Can you drive?'
> 'No.'
> 'It doesn't matter. There are two chauffeurs.'[103]

And it is interesting that an automobile figures significantly in the episode of Harry Leon Wilson's *Merton of the Movies*, perhaps the best novel of the decade about Hollywood, in which the hero, Merton Gill, a movie-struck boy from the Midwest, first begins to become disillusioned about the craft which he has hitherto idealized. In this episode, Merton witnesses the shooting of a scene in which a horse is supposed to panic at the approach of a motorcar. By this time, the surviving Southern California horses have become quite accustomed to the presence of cars, and this particular horse, not being a very good actor, has to be assisted in his "panic" by "a couple of charges of perhaps rock-salt" fired at him with a shotgun by someone hidden in a clump of shrubbery. This height of unreality—and what could be more unreal than trying to pretend that a car could still frighten a horse in the Nineteen-Twenties?—shocks even Merton: "For the first time in his screen career he became cynical about his art. A thing of shame, of machinery, of subterfuge. Nothing would be real, perhaps not even the art."[104]

Hitchhiking

It was not, of course, only those who owned or drove cars whose lives and values were affected by them. Nor was it necessary to own or know the owner of a car, or to engage in auto theft, in order to take advantage of the new mobility provided by the private automobile. The advent of a new means of mass transportation called into existence a new and quite unique method of individual travel, which eventually came to be known as hitchhiking.

This institution, which has since spread with the automobile to most corners of the world, appeared very early in Southern California. The same conditions which favored the early development of motoring in the region also tended to favor those who sought to obtain free rides from passing motorists. The practice appears to have begun in the days when motoring was still primarily a pleasure activity and to have been originally associated with Los Angeles boys who sought to join motorists on their excursions out of town. As early as 1916, the A.C.S.C. was urging its members to "be stony-hearted" towards such solicitations because the boy would often be a truant and "you are helping him to rob himself of the education he is going to need so much in later years. . . . But if it is Saturday, or you are sure he isn't playing hookey, that's a different thing again."[105] The camaraderie of the road could also come into play between the motorist and those less gifted with mobility in a way well expressed by Julia Sloane:

> One late afternoon a friend of ours was driving alone and offered a lift to two young men who were swinging along on foot. 'Your price?' they asked. 'A smile and a song,' was the reply. So in they got, and those last fifty miles were gay. That is the sort of thing which fits so perfectly into the atmosphere of this land. Perhaps it is the orange blossoms, perhaps it is that we have extra-sized moons, perhaps it is the old Spanish charm still lingering. All I know is that it is a land of glamour and romance.[106]

Besides the adventurous young, the ranks of this new class of travellers tended to be filled by hoboes who had formerly relied on a more traditional but less comfortable means of increasing their mobility—the railroad. A writer of 1922 described the change which was taking place:

> . . . Many of the bindle stiffs [tramps] . . . are abandoning their characteristic bindle [bundle] and the sidedoor pullman for a suit case and an easy riding motor car. The writer has watched casuals discriminatingly waiting along the highway for a large touring car, explaining that 'flivvers' were too hard riding; besides the large touring car went faster, farther, with less chance of breaking down. This form of travel is frequently called 'Hitting the Highway.'[107]

The modern name did not, apparently, come into use until some time later. Mathews' *Dictionary of Americanisms* finds its earliest usage in a *Nation* article of 1923. But three years later the term still seems to have been something of a novelty, at least to Californians, as indicated by a *Times* editorial of 1926: "What is a hitch-hiker? He is what many

California motorists call a ride-moocher—a person who asks for a lift in almost any car that happens to come along."[108]

By the time it acquired a permanent name, however, the practice was already firmly established and had already acquired a set of rather unpleasant associations. In a society and an economy becoming more and more based upon an ever-increasing number of private automobiles and motorized public transportation, it was, perhaps, only to be expected that social pressure would be exerted against any practice which tended to limit the need for an individual to contribute to this process in some way. Much publicity was given to instances of crime and violence committed by hitchhikers, and little or nothing was ever said about possible means of making the practice safer and more respectable. The problem of tremendous waste incurred when so many cars had unused room for extra passengers tended to be ignored. Even the right of a group of workers to form what is now known as a car pool was challenged in a Los Angeles court before it became firmly established.[109]

In 1923 the Automobile Club of Southern California came out very strongly against picking up any hitchhikers, prompting an indignant letter of protest from an old Wobblie who signed himself "Sacramento Goldie, Card no. 47437":

> We are starting a campaign telling how it is a gippo game between the stage [motor bus] lines and yourself . . . I'm just hoping one of you birds gets in the desert without water and gets a touch of it.[110]

The two arguments most frequently advanced against giving rides to hitchhikers were those of possible danger and of increased liability in case of an accident. As one Angeleno put it:

> From the motorist's point of view we think it bad policy to give . . . lifts, for if any accident occurs the driver is responsible if it was caused in any way by his negligence and it is hard for him to prove his innocence in such a case. Also, a short time back a man gave some boys a lift out on the edge of the desert but the boys were not satisfied and rapped him over the head and buried him out on the desert, and went merrily on their way, to be apprehended at T--- and sent through life in a hurry, electrocuted I believe.[111]

Nevertheless, the practice continued and the young people of Los Angeles continued to make use of it. A boys' worker complained in 1926 that "positively 25% of our truants are such because of being able to get rides in automobiles."[112] Thus the automobile conferred, even upon the children of carless families, a chance for adventure and escape beyond the wildest dreams of any previous generation of youngsters. "Boys are begging rides to everywhere now," said another youth worker in 1926,

". . . Boys twelve years of age and older are getting rides to San Francisco, going as far as each driver goes, arriving there with no money except what they can beg or earn in stray ways or steal."[112] Dr. Bogardus saw the whole matter as one element of what has since come to be called juvenile delinquency:

> Begging a ride to the beach, 'hooking [stealing] a bit to eat,' falling in with other boys and bumming around for the day, and then, in order to get home with as little trouble as possible, a Ford is stolen, [sic.]. Starting out on an innocent jaunt, and ending in jail, is not uncommon for a boy who is 'begging a ride.' Motorists with 'hearts bigger than their brains' are partly responsible. . . .[113]

But it was not, apparently, only males who formed this new group of travellers. A *Touring Topics* article of 1923 reported the comment of a Los Angeles driver that it was "surprising how many women are bumming rides nowadays":

> Neat looking dames nail me all the time around L.A. . . On the road to the beach, most of them. They go back and forth just for the fun of riding in nifty cars. I picked up one gal who wasn't more'n eighteen and a good looker too. I asked her if she didn't get in a jam, sometimes, grabbing rides with strangers. 'Oh no' she answers, chipper as can be, 'you'd be surprised to know how many nice fellows there are. The young guys is nearly always O.K. too. It's the old papas with a flock of kids at home who get to showing signs of an affectionate disposition. . . . When I meet a man who starts telling me that he's misunderstood by his wife, it's time to get out and walk.'[114]

Just when the extended thumb achieved currency as the universal hitchhiker's signal of solicitation, the present research has not revealed, but California hitchhikers of the Nineteen-Twenties appear often to have preferred much less direct methods. One such traveller, whose comments were published in 1923, described his technique thus:

> I just sit and wait for the right car to come along. When a nice easy-going bus pulls up, I hops to my feet, hold up one hand and look just as pleasant as possible. Nine times out of ten the car stops. The driver thinks you are a flagman put there by the highway gang for some reason.[115]

Another authority, two years later, advised prospective hitchhikers never to ask or signal for a ride at all: "You get more rides by not asking, as the average driver prefers to pick out his own objects of charity. You can take it for granted the autoist suspects you want a ride."[116] Both the above experts showed in other remarks how dangerous the practice of giving rides had already become in the public mind. "I never try to flag a car at night," said the "flagman," ". . .

There's too many stick-ups done that way. Drivers are leary and won't stop.[117]" The other, who described himself as "a modern tramp—one who prefers the automobile to the railway train," advised motorists never to pick up more than one man at a time "unless your party is the stronger," but offered assurances that a carload of hitchhiker passengers was quite harmless so long as each was picked up separately: "Murder, arson, robbery or mayhem plots are not concocted on the spur of the moment between strangers. Your second guest is a protection against the first."[118]

Unfortunately, with hitchhiking as with many other aspects of the newly motorized society, it was the more lurid features and incidents which were more likely to be recorded for posterity. Less noted were such factors as the happiness afforded to countless persons for whom the joys of motoring would otherwise have continued to be as far out of reach as they had ever been, and the widening of social horizons through contacts between drivers and hitchhikers of backgrounds so diverse that they would ordinarily never have met. The author is not without personal bias in this particular matter, since most of his own youthful travelling was accomplished by this means.

Morality and Religion

Despite the tendency to sensationalize the various social problems consequent upon the automobilization of society, there appears, on the whole, to have been very little discussion in Southern California of the deeper moral implications of this new phenomenon. The region was too caught up in the process to be able to adopt an other than pragmatic approach to it. To a lesser extent, this also applied to the country as a whole. But there did appear from time to time during the decade items in the national press of a more than usually analytical nature whose relevance makes them worth considering here.

Those who gave any serious thought to the question of whether the automobile was good or bad frequently came to the conclusion that it was neither, and that this was in some ways the most frightening thing about it. Like the nuclear energy with which the next generation would have to deal, it was a powerful new force capable of being used by good men in good ways and by bad men in bad ways, but, because of the frailties of the human condition, not entirely under the control of either. In this respect, it seemed to symbolize, in a way that brought the matter closer to home than any previous invention had done, the utter amorality of the universe as seen by a civilization which had, in its pursuit of technological progress, departed so far from the theocentric outlook of medieval man. Joseph K. Hart expressed this viewpoint very well in an article which he wrote for *Survey* in 1925:

> There is, of course, no place in [a "moral" universe] for an automobile. An automobile will not hold together and give one more gasp because a doctor is hurrying to the bedside of a dying bishop; neither will it fall down and smash merely because some villain is running away with 'the daughter of an honest woman.' A load of booze is no heavier to an auto than is an equal weight of deacons. A faithful horse, or a chivalrous universe will protect a lady in distress; and maybe, in the long run, even the poor working girl. But what interest has the 'family auto' in the fate of either? The horse used to bring the worn out reveler and the tired doctor home. . . . Now the auto, its steering wheel slipping from exhausted hands, flings them both into the telegraph pole and leaves their broken bodies as warnings that a mechanism does not supply its own intelligence. The universe of the auto along with the auto itself, is no longer to be counted as either the Enemy or the Friend of men.[119]

The question, as Hart indicated, was far from a purely academic one. The lives and outlook of millions who had scarcely been shaken from their moral complacency, even by the greatest war of all times, were touched profoundly by the indifferent power of the new machine to which they had so readily become attached. And, as usual, it was only to be expected that the effects would be most marked where the cars were most numerous. One victim of this amoral juggernaut was Caryl Whittier Chessman, whose mother, while he was still a child, was severely injured in an automobile accident at a busy Los Angeles intersection and left permanently paralyzed from the waist down. Chessman has left his own account of his feelings:

> Whit cried 'But why, Mom? Why?'
> Hallie told him simply, giving the only answer she knew. 'It's God's will, Whit'. . . . Yet, if God were truly responsible, why had He caused or allowed this to happen to his mother? And if God were not responsible, who or what was? These were questions the boy was not prepared to answer . . . for a suspicion lurked behind the questions, a frightened suspicion of what the answer might mean, and he desperately wanted to believe in God and good, and an ordered, controlled reality.[120]

Whatever its cosmic indifference as a machine, however, it could hardly be denied that the automobile was placing a great strain upon existing social mores and institutions, so much so that there were some, like Leo L. Ward, who openly longed for the pre-auto era, which was coming to be known as the "horse-and-buggy days," a term soon indiscriminately applied to anything old-fashioned and out-of-date:

> We now have a thousand roads reeking with the national neurosis
> of hurry, and burnt gasoline. The swoop of a million wheels past
> every road gate has gotten into our blood. The horse and buggy
> have vanished from our roads, and all happy days seem to have
> gone also. For who can be constantly in a hurry and ever really
> enjoy himself?[121]

But, of course, the more realistic approach was to accept the new
phenomenon and seek means of incorporating it more agreeably in the
culture. This, in the opinion of some, was merely a matter of time, and
the chief remedy was patience. As Allen D. Albert wrote in *Scribner's*
in 1922, "It is absurd to expect a great new social agency to come into
use without abuse . . . Automobile outlawry and lawlessness are now
more serious, I believe, than they are to be hereafter."[122] Addressing
itself to the same problem, the *Christian Century* expressed serious
alarm at the existing state of affairs as it viewed them:

> Undoubtedly our motorized society is less regardful than it was of
> time-honored institutions and programs of culture. Many a deserv-
> ing book is not being read. Due consideration is not being given
> . . . to the crucial issues of the day. Rather, the population is
> whirling along country highways, drowzily shifting the gaze from
> half-open eyes now to this side of the road, and again to that. . . .
> The automobile . . . is just now making the American volatile and
> reckless—reckless of the passengers behind his own wheel and
> those whizzing by on the other side of the road—reckless of costs,
> of mortgaged homes, of unpaid grocery bills, of many of the social
> values which we have accounted the most substantial and inviola-
> ble of our civilization.

This was placing a heavy burden of censure upon the automobile.
But there followed the admission that "We must allow a place for the
automobile. It is here to stay. . . . All of our social institutions . . .
must adjust themselves to the motorized age and its new ideals."[123]
Just what this meant and how it was to be accomplished, particularly
in the religious context which was the magazine's chief concern, was
not explained. Joseph K. Hart had an explanation, though it would
probably not have satisfied the *Christian Century*. In his view, the
automobile was helping people, especially young people, to evolve a
new and more realistic morality based upon power and scientific actu-
ality. The freedom of activity which it provided was encouraging a
freedom of thought which in the long run could have only a beneficial
effect.[124]

Abraham Cronbach, however, was not so sure. Replying to Hart, he
voiced doubts shared by many:

> Mr. Hart very properly . . . insists upon the importance of inde-
> pendent thinking. . . . But what if some of those moral adventures
> for which Mr. Hart plays the apologist were to impair young
> people's ability to think? What if intoxicants, joy rides, jazz, road
> houses and sexual risks were to render young men and women not
> more capable but less capable of mental independence? Will the
> fact that these diversions constitute voyages of moral discovery
> save the day?[125]

Mr. Hart made no published reply. And the present author thinks it
best to take refuge in the reply reputedly offered recently by an old
Chinese scholar when asked his opinion on the effects of the French
Revolution: "It is perhaps too early to tell."

"One feature of the debate over the moral effects of the automobile
was the controversy concerning its influence on conventional religious
observance in the form of churchgoing. Were the temptations of plea-
sure-driving taking people away from the churches? A report issued by
the Committee on Social and Religious Surveys of the Interchurch
World Movement in 1922 expressed fears with regard to the people of
Southern California, that the "comparative freedom" provided by their
prosperity, in combination with the climate "which makes possible
outdoor recreation at almost any time of the year" was serving to
create "a love of pleasure . . . so extravagant as to be unhealthy."[126] On
balance, however, it appeared, as an observer writing in 1924 put it,
that "the automobile has created a give and take in this matter of
church attendance that just about cancel each other."[127] For every
family who now preferred Sunday driving or weekend camping to
church-going (and, as the Lynds pointed out, to the old leisurely
Sunday noon dinner),[128] there was another for whom possession of an
automobile now rendered church attendance more pleasant and conve-
nient, and therefore, more frequent. Nor, of course, was mere absence
from home a necessary obstacle to religious observance. A popular
handbook on motor-camping published in 1926 made a point of this:

> The week-end camper need not neglect his religious duties [for he]
> is not likely to camp in a place so remote as to be more than a
> fifteen-minute, or thereabouts, motor ride from a church of some
> denomination where he will be likely to get as much good as he will
> be able to assimilate.[129]

And it was noted that, although many churches far from the highways
were in decline, those on the highways were flourishing.[130]

But as far as those Southern Californians of the Nineteen-Twenties
whose opinions are on record were directly concerned, this whole issue
does not appear to have worried them very much. The region was in

fact noted throughout the decade, despite its high degree of motorization, for equally high extremes of religious enthusiasm; and the churches, even the poorer ones, were both as ready and as obligated as most other social groups to make whatever use they could of the new mobility in order to further their work. An item in a Los Angeles Negro newspaper of 1921 tells a typical story:

NEW PASTOR WELL RECEIVED

. . . Because the members [of the First A.M.E. Zion Church] believe that Rev. Grantt can bring harmony out of chaos, and that he would be handicapped by the great distances in Los Angeles in doing that that would make for greater harmony, the church gave our pastor an automobile costing $1350, and after three weeks someone stole the car and thirty days later we bought another car at a cost of $1685, a Cleveland Six. Now he goes after and takes back the old and infirm members of the church, who otherwise would be deprived of the blessing of attending church, and he considers this one of the most pleasant tasks of his ministry.[131]

In general it might be said that, because of its head start in matters of mass automotion, and because of the extraordinary extent to which its inhabitants soon became dependent upon the automobile, Southern California had no choice but to play down the fundamental questions of motor morality. The new system of mechanical slaves, becoming as much a part of the way of life as that of human slaves had been in the Old South, was soon even more jealously if less consciously guarded from criticism. What might be called a form of technological totalitarianism had gained control of the region, and it became virtual anathema to attempt to challenge the idea of automotive primacy. Only within the context of that idea might criticisms be offered, and even these were usually phrased in a semi-facetious form. Thus an article which the *Times* headed "Garage Man Convinced Motoring Has Dispelled Honesty" concerned nothing more basic than a mechanic's complaint that many motorists who borrowed gasoline cans failed to return them.[132] This profundity, which was, of course, merely a switch on the already traditional notion that those who made their living from servicing or repairing automobiles were habitually dishonest, was about as far as Angelenos appeared ready to go in assessing the moral implications of the motor age.

The Motor Mentality

Modern sociologists have some difficulty in defining "crazes" and distinguishing them from mere "fads." The difference seems to hinge on the degree of emotional involvement and commitment. A fad can be some relatively superficial and external piece of behavior, hardly affecting a person's ordinary routine. But a craze siezes the whole psyche, to the point of extinguishing critical ability, and diminishing awareness of future consequences.[133]

In the light of the above definitions, the automobile boom which hit Southern California, and to a lesser extent the whole country during the post-war decade, though it embraced many fads, may itself be characterized as a craze, a craze of unprecedented proportions. A resident of Middletown expressed the characteristic mood: "Why on earth do you need to study what's changing this country? . . . I can tell you what's happening in just four letters: A-U-T-O!"[134] To a few observers, elements of frenzy were evident in the situation even at the time. Ward described how socially contagious the infection seemed to be, how within a few short years the horse stable became an abandoned relic, while

> the new garage was built in a week, or perhaps two days, made of galvanized tin, the roof put on while you were learning to run the car. Then the neighbors bought cars and threw up their garages. . . . (Who cannot remember the anguish of waiting till he could afford his first automobile?). . . . Everybody was infected by automania. By one leap rather than by any development the country arrived at the full age of the motor car.[135]

The President's Research Committee on Social Trends could hardly be accused of overstatement when in 1930, attempting to assess the results of this phenomenon, it declared that "It is probable that no invention of such far-reaching importance was ever diffused with such rapidity, or so quickly exerted influences that ramified through the national culture . . ."[136]

Los Angeles appeared to be in the forefront of the trend towards a new way of looking at life based upon the automobile, a frame of reference which may be characterized as the motor mentality. This was evident in a great popular concern with matters automotive and a tendency to see even non-automotive matters in automotive terms. *The Los Angeles Times*, then, as now, the leading newspaper of the region, not only devoted much space to news, features, and advertisements of interest to drivers, but revealed a sort of subconscious preoccupation with the motor image. By 1925 its regular Sunday section on motoring was fourteen pages long, including, among other things, items on road conditions and improvements, suggested tours, car improvements and new models, maintenance tips, auto club news, business news, safety exhortations, and historical notes on the early days of motoring. With

regard to the latter, it is remarkable how comparatively early in its
career the automobile became a subject of nostalgic reminiscence. By
the early Nineteen-Twenties the public was already showing an interest in "ancient models," though it was not until the latter half of the
following decade that American devotees and collectors of "antique
automobiles" began formally to organize, their base of operations, as
one might expect, being Southern California.[137]

Even while the war was still on, Julia Sloane discovered, somewhat
to her surprise, the high interest and wish for personal participation in
motoring on the part of Southern Californian newspaper readers:

> If I feel at all lonely or bored, I generally advertise for something.
> Once I wanted a high-school boy to drive the motor three after-
> noons a week. The paper was still moist from the press when my
> applicants began to telephone. I took their names and gave them
> appointments at ten-minute intervals, all the following morning,
> only plugging the telephone when J— and I felt we must have
> some sleep. . . . When they arrived they ranged in age from six-
> teen to sixty. The latter was a retired clergyman who said he drove
> for his wife, and . . . he thought he could fit us both in![138]

With such a reservoir of eager and informed readers, it is scarcely
surprising that, once the war was over, newspapers should have sought
to appeal to the actual and potential motoring public. As early as 1920
the *Times* was carrying "Gasoline Alley," a syndicated cartoon feature
whose career in a sense epitomizes the story of the incorporation of the
automobile into American life. Beginning as a single picture cartoon
which revolved entirely around the subject of cars, "Gasoline Alley"
changed during the Nineteen-Twenties into a regular comic strip in
which the interpersonal relationships of the characters became at first
at least equally as important as their car problems and eventually
replaced them altogether as the story content. When this change
occurred, the *Times* had to introduce a new comic strip of its own with
a definitely and permanently automotive flavor, called "Along Figueroa
Street." The name was taken from that of the thoroughfare which had
already become firmly established as the commercial center of the car
trade in Los Angeles, though the family whose car activities the strip
portrayed did not presumably live on that street. Meanwhile "Gasoline
Alley" went on to become one of the oldest American comic strips still
running, being one of the few in which the characters change and age
with the passage of time. Very few of its current followers have any
more idea of the real significance its title once had than they have of
what the automobile once meant to a generation starving for mobility.

Other newspapers also had their auto comics. Cornelius Vanderbilt

Jr.'s tabloid, the Los Angeles *Illustrated Daily News*, for example, had a strip called "Carrie and Her Car." It was also remarkable how many different types of journals and periodicals published in Southern California apparently felt obliged to cater to their readers' new interest in cars. Thus, for example, the *California Jewish Review* and the *Citizen's Advocate*, a Negro weekly, had regular automobile sections. Even *California Southland*, a very fashionable, glossy, lavishly illustrated monthly magazine published in Pasadena, experimented in 1922 with a section called "The Garage . . . For People Who Drive Their Own Cars," but dropped the idea after three months, perhaps because by then motoring had become too popular to be considered in good taste.

A preoccupation with the motorcar was particularly evident in the use of motor imagery by editorial writers and political cartoonists. Sometimes a journalist would take some aspect of motoring as a kind of scriptural text for a sermon, attempting to derive from it some profound generalization about the state of the world, though often the connection seems extremely forced. Take the following extract from a *Times* editorial of 1925 for example:

> According to the expert, brakes are responsible for 75% of highway trouble. Probably the proper proportion is ⅓ engine and ⅔ brakes. One-third liberal and two-thirds conservatism seems to be about the proper adjustment for state as well as for motors. There have been too many smash-ups in the world. And it has been largely due to lack of sufficient brake. We have been holding the radicals responsible. The motor expert locates the responsibility upon the brakes.[139]

Only to a population obsessed with motoring could so tenuous an association, of a car's engine with political radicals and its brakes with conservatives, have made much sense. Again, consider an even more shaky employment of the motor metaphor, from a *Times* editorial of 1926 entitled "Back-seat Drivers":

> Most men in this region are at home at the wheel, though such motorists do not make the best back-seat drivers. To shine resplendently in this role one needs to know nothing whatever about shifting or steering, but should be a good manager.
> In a general way the back-seat driver is running about everything in the world that is worth running. In Europe, where the wobbly monarchical flivvers defy the efforts of the throne occupants to keep them in the rough post-bellum roads, the big dictator in the back seat reaches over from behind, grabs the wheel and steers the machine, running it more or less effectively. What

would Victor Emmanuel III do without that excellent back-seat
driver Mussolini? . . . . No wonder the back-seat driver is so
popular in Italy and other European countries in these perilous
times.[140]

What did the metaphor add to the somewhat nebulous points being
made in these quotations? One is tempted to hypothesize that in each
case the point was being made for the sake of the metaphor, rather
than vice versa. And why not, after all? Were not the readers of the
Los Angeles Times of the mid-Twenties far more interested in engines
and brakes and backseat drivers than they were in radicalism or
Mussolini?

Similarly, though usually with more metaphorical logic, political
cartoonists saw local and world issues in terms which conveyed most
meaning to their motor-minded readers. The picture of Great Britain,
for example, seated at the wheel of a car containing Canada, South
Africa, and other dominions—all of whom are thinking, "Wish I had a
bus of my own,"[141] (see Figure 3) says at least as much about the great
and ever-increasing popularity of the private automobile in Los Angeles and the desirable status attached to motor ownership as it does
about the problems of the British Empire (a good deal more, in fact,
since the analogy, as far as political realities were concerned, was
essentially unsound). And a cartoon as technical and complicated as the
one showing the "clutch" of Mexico's Carranza "slipping" because he is
unable any longer to keep his "foot down" (a very clever cartoon,
incidentally, which contains at least five automotive puns—see Figure
4) could only have been appreciated by readers familiar with the
transmission system of an automobile.[142] Nor did it seem at all strange
to liken the city's need for water to that of an automobile radiator,[143]
though this was surely reversing the "normal" stream of association
(see Figure 5). Such reverse associations had, however, by this time
become almost habitual with Southern Californians. How else could
the manufacturers of "Cactus Corn Cure" have had the temerity to
advertise their product by showing a big bare foot, with an automobile
in the background and the engaging caption, "GET MORE MILEAGE
OUT OF YOUR FEET"?[144]

Here indeed was one region of the world—probably the first—where
the very act of walking was coming to be seen as an exception to the
predominant act of riding. Such a situation is clearly indicated by the
following extract from an article on the "Charm of Hiking":

In these flivver-cluttered days when folks drive . . . more miles in
an hour than you will walk in a day, it is quite common to hear
lamentations from flivver-less people that they can have no enjoya-

ble vacation. The economical, healthful, body-invigorating vacation is made on foot, carrying blanket and supplies, as you see the boy scouts do it.[145]

In a society where values appeared to have undergone so sudden a reversal, it was hardly surprising to find a corpse in a novel comparing itself with a car:

Heigho! Nobody knows I'm here! The living thing that was in me has gone and I am left to clutter up the driveway . . . They'll never be able to start me running again—like the Ford coop there. They'll have to tow me away like a car that is dead—when the engine plays out.[146]

And a sociology student of Professor William Kirk's at Pomona College, writing a paper on common faults of parents, found it apparently quite natural to compare children with cars:

A man will treat his young off-spring as a sort of possession of which he is inordinately proud . . . He is also proud of his car. The difference is that if anything happens to his car he has it fixed at once, and he detects the slightest knock. The young son's nervous organism . . . may start knocking, and his father never knows anything is wrong, unless a more or less complete smash-up occurs.[147]

To compare a broken car with a sick or dead human being—that is one thing; but when men in all seriousness start comparing dead men with cars that won't start, one senses a significant threat to humanistic values. How long before the parts of the body begin to be named after the parts of cars or other machines? How long before all human activities are seen in purely mechanical terms? Perhaps no such threat, with all that it implies, actually exists; or perhaps, if it does exist, it ought not to be regarded as a threat. The author only knows that he was slightly alarmed to find that in one of the world's newer states (Israel) any human delay, however caused, is now universally known as a "puncture"!

With the motor beginning to supercede the body, both in fact and in metaphor, some very interesting assertions were made by supposedly responsible authorities concerning the effects of this change upon human health. The following remarkable example of the motor mentality emanated in 1922 from U.S. Senator Royal S. Copeland, who had formerly been Health Commissioner of New York City:

Of course motoring bestows its greatest benefits on the person who drives the car. Not only does the driver get the full benefit of open road and fresh air, but he gets actual physical exercise in a form best calculated to repair the damages wrought by our modern

existence. The slight physical effort needed in moving the steering
wheel reacts on the muscles of the arms and abdomen. . . . The
slight but purposeful effort demanded in swinging the steering
wheel reacts exactly where we need it most. Frankly I believe that
steering a motor car is actually better exercise than walking,
because it does react on the parts of the body least used in the
ordinary man's routine existence.[148]

Even allowing for the facts that open cars were then more prevalent
(producing as much exposure to dust as to fresh air) and that there was
somewhat more work involved in driving in 1922 than there is today,
such a statement savors very strongly of rationalization. This and
similar pronouncements, however, enabled automobile salesmen to
make such claims for their product as that "it is a proven fact that it will
increase the length of your life."[149] Advocates of motor-camping were,
of course, on much firmer ground when they argued that, despite the
acknowledged decline in walking and cycling, the automobile was
bringing countless people, for whom such experience would otherwise
be rare or impossible, into a physically and psychologically regenerat-
ing contact with the out-of-doors.[150]

There were also, however, certain alleged motoring health hazards
which were perhaps as far-fetched as some of the supposed motoring
benefits, though they appear to have had an equal fascination for the
motor-mentality. In 1923, for example, Dr. Herbert R. Stoltz, California State Director of Physical Education, announced the discovery of a
new malady, afflicting only motorists and of particular concern to
young women, since it resulted in unshapely legs. He named the new
condition "bulging shin" and described it as an "over-development of
the elongated muscles covering the shin bone." Presumably it was
caused by the need for frequent foot pressure upon the pedals of an
automobile. Apparently the right leg, which controlled the principal
brake, was in particular peril, for the doctor went on to warn that "the
girl who drives much discovers that her right calf is much larger and
more unshapely than her left."[151] Whether or not this was intended as
an attempt to discourage girls from driving does not appear. If it was,
it certainly had no detectable success. Instead, it doubtless served only
to heighten the clamor from women for automotive improvements
which would render cars and driving more congenial to them.

The motor mentality, however, thrived on such stories. To those
bitten by the motor bug it appeared to be almost as much of a delight to
contemplate the social havoc caused by and/or attributed to the automobile as to proclaim its virtues. What mattered to the average Angeleno, as has already been pointed out in our discussion of morality,

was not whether the mass automobile was good or bad but that it was something big, a power which could not be denied. Some hint of this perverse exultation is to be derived, for example, from an article written in 1926 by Chester Hanson in which, through the voice of "J. Augustus Wetblanket, prominent local dealer in dire prognostications," he satirized alarmist sentiment directed against the automobile by speculating as to the probable social consequences of the introduction of a "flivver airplane":

> You know what a wave of crime and violence the automobile has brought. What do you suppose is going to happen when airplanes get to be as popular as Fords? The automobile . . . has brought about an increase of 102% in murders, 110% in divorces, 127% in burglaries, and the bobbed hair craze—all within the past decade. . . . [It] has broken up more homes than all the ornery mothers-in-law put together. . . . Think what the family air flivver is going to do! We'll have the neighborhood jealousies and family quarrels over the automobile doubled by the air flivver. . . . And who knows what new kind of necking parties the air flivver will bring?[152]

The reference here to the bobbed hair craze is worth commenting on, since both hair-bobbing and skirt-shortening have then and since been said to have come as a response to automotive necessities—long hair being too easily tousled by the wind in an open car and long skirts becoming tangled in the pedals.[153] Unfortunately for the social historian, changes of fashion in dress are by no means so easily explained in terms of practicality, nor indeed, as far as the author can see, has any other principle yet been advanced which satisfactorily accounts for them. The idea, for example, that long hair and prominent bosoms and hips disappeared in the Twenties as a reflection of women's desire to be the equals of men seems strikingly inconsistent with the rising hemline and the unprecedented sale of comestics. Nor does it in any acceptable way explain how the same anatomical features have continued to reappear and re-disappear. In any case, it seems that the bobbed hair style spread to America from Europe where the exigencies of driving were far less likely to have any bearing upon women's fashions.

One other characteristic feature of the motor mentality which ought to be emphasized was the phenomenon of sacrifice to which its new standards gave rise. Owning and operating an automobile was a large expense, even when new car prices were at their lowest in history. Bringing a car into one's life meant, for most families, new economies somewhere along the line. Yet such sacrifices were in most cases willingly, even eagerly, made. The Lynds found twenty-one working class families in Middletown who had cars but no bathtubs, and they quoted one woman as saying, "I'll go without food before I'll see us give up the car."[154] Ray U. Brouillet, a Californian who in 1925 published a book called *Objections and Answers*, giving automobile salesmen advice on how most effectively to persuade their prospects, explained the technique of inducing the car-hungry client to forego old satisfactions for his new mobility. Should a potential customer protest that he could not afford the monthly payments, Brouillet advised this approach:

> By a careful analysis of what your prospective customer does during the week—that is—how much money he spends for shows, poker games, enjoyments of all kinds, recreations on Saturday and Sundays, you will find that the sum he spends . . . is a great deal more sometimes than the monthly payment, and he still has nothing to show for it, whereas the money he is putting monthly into an automobile is like a savings account, and he has something to show for it, and is also getting a great deal more pleasure.[155]

Thus was a whole population prevailed upon to abandon its customary amusements. For who could resist the appeal of having something material "to show" for one's expenditures and the promise of "getting a great deal more pleasure" to boot? Put in these terms, it hardly seemed like a sacrifice at all. Consider also the striking fact, pointed out by John Chynoweth Burnham, that the gasoline tax, which was adopted in state after state beginning in Oregon in 1919 and reaching California in 1923, was one of the few taxes in history which people seemed almost glad to pay.[156] One authority has in fact described the tax as "extremely popular."[157] This was largely because it was known that the money would be used only for road improvements. There could be few more vivid demonstrations of the extent to which the inhabitants of the new motor era were willing to endure deprivation for the sake of their new dream of power and escape.

PART II

MACHINE

Part I was primarily concerned with aspects of human thought and behavior seen as a response to a great technological innovation. In this second section we will be more particularly concerned with that innovation itself, both as a mechanism and as the focal point of a tremendous problem of social reorganization and readjustment. Just what connection existed between the emergence of the mass motorcar and the emancipation of women may always remain a subject for dispute, but there can be no question about its relationship with the problems of traffic congestion and road safety which bedevilled the Nineteen-Twenties. The discussion ought, therefore, from here on, to be on a somewhat firmer footing.

Automotive historians appear to agree that the year 1919 marked a turning point in the development of the motorcar in America, separating the "experimental period" from a period of vigorous expansion. The experimental period was characterized, relatively speaking, by high costs, low standards of service, limited demand, and small-scale manufacture.[1] By about 1919, these birth pangs of the auto age had passed. Cars were much less likely to break down, and when they did it was now much easier to get help. A steady progression of technical improvements made cars more comfortable, more reliable, and easier to control. Among these were the self-starter, balloon tires, and four-wheel hydraulic brakes. The development of the all-steel enclosed body eliminated the price differential between open and closed models, and between 1919 and 1929 there was a change in the U.S. from 90 percent open models (touring cars and roadsters) to 90 percent closed models (sedans and coupes).[2] Interestingly enough, the latter change seems to have been nearly as much in evidence in Southern California as every-where else, despite the climatic advantage. Jan and Cora Gordon commented that:

> The climate of Los Angeles-cum-Hollywood is a little like the benefits of Christianity—very much boasted about, but of little practical effect. . . . About 80% of the cars in which Los Angeles spends the greater part of its leisure are closed. The people may boast of their climate, but they drive about in glass boxes.[3]

For all its improvements, however, the automobile still displayed some revealing vestiges of its equine ancestry. There still had to be a "driver," though he no longer had any animals to "drive." He still had to sit in front and control the progress of the vehicle, but now, instead of leather reins, he grasped a steering device directly connected to the front wheels, and a much higher degree of alertness was required of him than of any previous kind of driver. For not only were there neither animal intelligences nor steel tracks to assist him in piloting the vehi-cle, but he had also at his not always perfectly adequate command more speed and power than had ever before been loose upon the public highways. The motor, or motion-giving force of the vehicle, was situ-ated in front of the driver, largely because that had been the position earlier occupied by the horse.[4] This was hardly the mechanically log-ical place for it, however, since it was only the *rear* wheels which were turned by the motor, and the separation, requiring a long shaft to transmit the power from front to rear, inevitably meant a loss of efficiency. Such considerations were hardly of prime importance in an economy which was coming to be built upon abundance and waste.

The driver and passengers sat in rows facing the direction of move-ment, since to designers brought up in an age of horse speed, there seemed no particular danger in such an arrangement. But this meant that any sudden arrest of motion, such as that caused by most colli-sions, would tend to throw all occupants of the vehicle violently for-ward (the degree of violence depending, of course, upon such factors as the speed at time of impact) with great hazard to life and limb, since the forward motion of the occupants alone would in turn be arrested by part of the vehicle or its contents against which they were flung. It was in such occurrences that many denizens of the new motor age were killed or injured, under circumstances which gave a new dimension to the meaning of the word "accident."

But despite its horse-and-buggy heritage, the automobile as a ma-chine owned by private persons was in other respects quite unprece-dented. It was physically large, dwarfing its owner and largely concealing him. It made noises and emitted odors unlike any to which he had previously been accustomed. It demanded care and maintenance of a thoroughly unfamiliar kind. Not only could it be easily stolen, but since, unlike a horse, it consisted of various detachable and largely interchangeable parts, it could, once stolen, be dismantled and lose its identity without losing its usefulness. It could even have parts stolen from it separately, especially such easily removed items as spare tires (mounted on the outside) or ornamental radiator caps. But above all, it represented a variety of hazards totally new to the experience of the average man: it burned a highly combustible fuel; it produced a highly poisonous gas; and it attained dangerous speeds while creating a highly false sense of security.

Traffic and Congestion

Besides being exposed to death by suffocation, combustion, and concussion, the motorist was beset by numerous new minor perils and harassments, many of them resulting from the sheer number of the new machines which had so suddenly appeared, and from the attempts of society to create order and safety out of the consequent chaos. For, in addition to worrying about the maintenance and control of his own machine, every driver had more and more, especially from about 1919 onwards, to reckon with the fact that there were thousands of other drivers and machines about, endangering his life, competing for the space he wished to occupy and the mobility he wished to enjoy, and crowding the roads and other facilities which had never been intended for so incredible an invasion by an army of machines.

It was in fact in connection with this new and alarming congestion that an event occurred in Los Angeles which may be said to have marked symbolically the true beginning of the motor age in that city, and thus perhaps in the entire world.

Before we go into that, however, let it not be thought that traffic congestion as a social problem was in any way a special product of the motor age. Lewis Mumford reminds us that the problem had been a subject for legislative concern at least as long ago as the days of Imperial Rome. One of Julius Caesar's first acts on seizing power had been to ban wheeled traffic from the center of Rome during the day, and Marcus Aurelius subsequently extended this prohibition to all the towns in the Empire.[5] Another modern writer on urban problems, Jane Jacobs, offers vivid evidence of the extent to which excessive traffic had become a major social ill in the modern city even before the advent of the automobile. In some ways, congested horse traffic was even worse than that of cars, since it was even noisier and in addition created serious problems of hygiene.[6]

Be that as it may, the burgeoning boom town of Los Angeles does not appear to have taken official cognizance of the fact that it had a traffic problem of mammoth proportions until April of 1920. In that month, the City Council took the unprecedented step of virtually banning daytime parking of automobiles in a large section of the downtown area. It adopted this drastic measure largely at the behest of the streetcar company, which had complained that the downtown streets along which its cars operated, had become so congested with automobile traffic that they were no longer able to adhere to their schedules. The theory was that a ban on parking would discourage automobiles from using those streets, or at least maintain a freer flow of traffic in them. There was little opposition to the no-parking ordinance before it went into effect, for downtown traffic congestion had already become notorious, and there was general agreement that something had to be done.

What resulted, however, was hardly anticipated. As soon as the ordinance was put into operation on Saturday, April 10 (with 1,000 arrests being made the first day), downtown merchants on the affected streets began to notice and complain about a falling-off in business transacted by their establishments. Here was a first vivid demonstration of the fact that, at least in this one corner of the world, the automobile had become something much more than a mere pleasure vehicle.

Actually the process had already been going on for some time. In the 'help wanted' columns of the *Times* for January 5, 1919, for instance, three out of fifty-three, or about six percent, of the advertisements for salesmen or solicitors already specified that the applicant must have his own car. A similar check for October 20, 1929 finds 16 out of 133 or about 12 percent with the same specification, but by that time many advertisers probably assumed that applicants would have cars.

The public controversy which now developed over the no-parking law was the first prominent acknowledgment of the fact that the status of the automobile in Southern Californian life was undergoing a highly significant change. For a great outcry now arose against the new ordinance. It seemed that both motorists and businessmen had suddenly awakened to the fact that they had become dependent upon the automobile. The *Times*, which gave strong support to their cause, viewed the situation this way in an article headed "Motor Cars Are

Essential. Two Weeks of No Parking Proves That Business Can't Do Without Them":

> The only good thing that can be said for the no-parking law is that it has served once and for all to demonstrate the extent to which the automobile has become a part of our everyday life. The vast majority of people have in a general sort of way, felt that the business pulse of Southern California throbbed in unison with the purring motors of its automobiles, but not until the automobiles were practically driven from the downtown streets of Los Angeles by the no-parking ordinance had the fact ever been brought home with such force.[7]

The same newspaper also took up the question from the point of view of the rights of the motorist. In a scathing editorial, it charged sarcastically that the Council had not made the ordinance severe enough: "So far the Council has merely deprived motorists of the rights of citizens and taxpayers, and has failed to make it clear, except by inference, that they are also outcasts, not entitled to the reasonable privileges accorded human beings."[8]

As the evidence mounted every day that people who normally shopped downtown were now taking their business elsewhere, to places like Pasadena where there was no limitation on parking, opposition to the ban began to organize. It culminated on April 24 in a demonstration typical of the ballyhoo of the era. The glamour and influence of Hollywood were recruited in support of the aggrieved merchants in the attractive form of film actress Clara Kimball Young, who claimed to have received "no less than two hundred protests . . . from admirers who assert they have been unable to attend matinees at film houses owing to the parking law and that they live too far to come downtown at night." On April 24 Miss Young led a protest parade of automobiles through the downtown streets. Five days later the parking ban was amended to allow up to forty-five minutes of parking between 10:00 a.m. and 4:30 p.m. Only between 4:00 and 6:00 p.m., at the height of the evening rush, was parking still completely forbidden.

The implications of this episode were quite fully understood at the time, at least as far as the new importance of the automobile was concerned. Gilbert Woodill, who had served as chairman of the protest committee of the Motor Car Dealers' Association was quoted as exulting that:

> The day when the automobile was a 'pleasure car' as the gentlemen of Congress called it during the war, is long since past. The motor car is just as much a necessity to business as the street car. And for the reason that the no-parking ordinance has emphasized this

fact, the motorist owes the city council a vote of thanks. These
gentlemen will think twice before they pass measures hampering
the use of the automobile again.[9]

Touring Topics similarly rejoiced: "It has taken a mighty long time to
make people understand that the automobile is no longer a luxury or a
plaything."[10] In effect, the car had now been recognized as King of the
Southern California road, or at least as heir apparent. During the
decade, the street-railway system which had once been recognized as
one of the finest in the world would yield precedence almost without a
struggle.

Yet the problem of traffic congestion remained virtually un-
answered. And the struggle for space, in which the 1920 outcome had
been after all only a symbolic victory, continued. Similar attempts to
increase mobility by decreasing utility occurred repeatedly, despite
Mr. Woodill's optimistic prognostication. During the Christmas holiday
shopping rushes of 1922 and 1923, conditions became or threatened to
become so impossible that parking bans had temporarily to be re-
imposed; but each time as soon as the festive season had passed,
opposition from commercial interests defeated re-enactment of the
measures.[11]

Actually, of course, the parking of automobiles was not in itself at the
root of this problem at all. It was understandable that when cars first
began seriously to interfere with a well-established and hitherto highly
efficient streetcar service, the initial reaction should be to try somehow
to get rid of the cars. But as it became apparent that the cars were not
to be got rid of, and were in fact going to continue to multiply at an
astonishing rate, the problem began to be investigated more deeply
and to be seen in terms not of too many vehicles but of too little space.
Since cars would continue to increase, space must be found or made for
them. Once this mental step had been taken, a process was begun
which has not abated even yet, with two-thirds of central Los Angeles
currently occupied by streets, freeways, parking facilities, and
garages.[12]

It would be a mistake, however, with the benefit of hindsight, to
condemn out of hand the lines along which Southern Californians of the
Nineteen-Twenties sought to solve their traffic problems. For one
thing, the magnitude of those problems was enormous. For another,
those who sought to deal with the situation had no precedents to guide
them. In fact they were setting precedents for the rest of the country
and the world, and the space given to Los Angeles in national magazines like *Nation's Traffic* made it plain that her experience was something from which other cities hoped to learn.

The chaos of congestion produced by the advent of masses of automobiles in a city completely unprepared to deal with them is attested by many sources. One has only to glance at Figure 6, a photograph showing a downtown Los Angeles intersection about 1919, to understand how great the confusion must have been when streetcars, motorcars, horse-drawn vehicles, and people afoot all endeavoured to negotiate their own quite independent courses at a time when there was virtually no traffic regulation other than that provided by an inadequate and overwhelmed police force. One of the great and horribly frustrating paradoxes of the motor age was beginning to emerge: that a machine which was supposed to provide speed and mobility could only too frequently become a source of stifled motion, wasted time, and tormented patience.

Early in 1919, the *Los Angeles Times* printed an article by Irma Armand highlighting this new problem. In it the story is told of two men who have an appointment to meet downtown, for which both are late. One of them walks to the meeting place, and he blames the vehicular traffic for making him late. The other comes in his own car, and *he* blames the pedestrians who, he says, "simply monopolize the crossings and make a big fuss if we run over them."[13] It would be some time before any but the most visionary thinkers began to question why pedestrians and cars should be on the same street at all.

It was not only the congestion itself which produced frayed nerves, but the fact that many of the inhabitants of Los Angeles were newcomers from rural areas. Eugene Crandall, a visiting Canadian motor journalist writing in 1920, observed that these newcomers "were not brought up to city alertness and city ways." Crandall commented that he had never been in a city "where I saw so many drivers who appeared tense, frightened, or even partially dazed in heavy vehicular traffic," and was surprised at the number of crushed fenders and bent bumpers he saw. The pedestrians, too, seemed just as unfamiliar with heavy metropolitan traffic.[14]

This type of phenomenon seldom failed to impress visitors to the city. James Montgomery Flagg, the famous artist, compared the traffic chaos to "a piece of ripe cheese seen under a microscope," and added: "I thought New York was the original Bedlam, but in 'Los' the traffic is like a sack of a city in its confusion."[15] A tourist from Boston in 1929 described the city as "simply one big jam; people tore and rushed along as fast as gas and electricity could make their motors go. All the pedestrians had a strained look on their faces, as they too rushed along."[16]

Besides the pedestrians, the city motorist, as has already been indicated, had also to contend with streetcars, large electrically-operated vehicles of public transportation which ran along tracks set in the middle of the thoroughfare. Not only were the streetcars themselves a great obstruction to freedom of movement from the motorist's point of view, especially with their frequent stops, but passengers, in order to reach or leave a streetcar, had to cross part of the roadway—clogging things up even more. From the point of view of streetcar drivers (called "motormen") and their passengers, however, it was the automobiles which were the nuisance, cutting in front of the streetcars, encroaching on the "safety zones" (areas of the open street beside places where the streetcars made their stops in which passengers waiting before boarding or after alighting were supposed to be able to stand in safety), occasionally stalling on the tracks, or simply refusing to move off them.[17] An indignant letter from a streetcar passenger to the *Los Angeles Times* in 1926 complained that a woman motorist had caused the streetcar on which he was riding to miss a traffic signal, thus delaying it about five minutes. Since the streetcar was carrying about a hundred people, there had been a loss of "500 minutes of valuable time . . . because that silly willy woman, whose time was not worth ten cents a day, wanted to impress the world that she owned an auto and as much of the street as she wished to use."[18]

Complaints about the extent to which automobiles were hindering the performance of public services came from other quarters also. Clarence J. Sweeney, chief of the Los Angeles Police Bureau of Transportation, protested in 1929 that, despite sirens and gongs, motorists were refusing to give way to ambulances: "The automobile driving public seem unable to grasp the fact that a police ambulance . . . must have a clear street."[19] At about the same time City Fire Chief Scott was complaining that both the mobility of the automobile as a fire-reaching competitor and its immobility as a jammed obstacle were impeding the efficiency of his department's service:

> In the old days when the great bulk of the sightseers responded to fires on foot, conditions were bearable. No matter how dense a crowd, it was usually fluid enough to squeeze out a space for the Fire Department to get through. But you know . . . how helpless a four-wheeled vehicle is to give way when blocked front and rear by other vehicles. To all intents and purposes, the street is blocked as effectively as if a four-story brick building was moved into the middle of it. Besides, in the old days we could beat most of the spectators to a fire anyway, but conditions have changed. . . . What chance have we to beat the several hundred autoists who, by the law of average, must be in the vicinity, and, by the law of human nature, consider it their sacred duty to see the fire?[20]

But no matter how much trouble resulted from the conflicting purposes of motorcars, pedestrians, streetcars, ambulances, and firemen, drivers of private automobiles soon found that, as far as the problems of congestion were concerned, the greatest trouble they had was with each other. There were so many cars that they were continually getting in each other's way. Here again was a cruel paradox of the motor age. The wondrous vehicle which was supposed to enable a person to "get away from it all" gave the same capability to everyone else who had one. In consequence, the intending escaper in his four-wheeled metal box was only too likely to find himself surrounded by other escapers in their boxes, coming in many ways between him and whatever it was that he was seeking to enjoy. This was, of course, especially true on occasions such as public holidays when everybody was free to try to escape at once. Jan and Cora Gordon were particularly sensitive to the irony inherent in such a situation:

> We took a trip along . . . Palisades Road . . . a pleasure trip on Independence Day, down to the sea in cars. . . . The Americans have raised car-jaunting to a most dismal craze. To work up the conviviality proper to Independence Day we joined a procession of cars, bonnet [hood] to spare tire, like a line of processional caterpillars, that crawled along the seafront for some fifteen miles at an average speed of five miles an hour. All the way we breathed one another's exhaust gases mixed with ozone. Then having come to the end of the road, we turned back and crawled home. We estimated that about a tenth of the car-owning population of Los Angeles joined this melancholy and insanitary procession. (see Figures 8 and 9)[21]

This was the other side of the picture rosily painted by the boosters with their statistics. It will, however, be apparent to the reader that many of the difficulties associated with traffic congestion were not inevitable consequences of a sheer multiplicity of cars seeking to operate within a limited space, but were rather aspects of what we have called the motor mentality. The novelty of the new machine and the technological naivete of the society which encountered it, combined with a certain strong cultural tradition of individualism, tended to dull the sense of social responsibility which alone could have ensured a sane start for the age of the mass motorcar. Why did drivers in their bright new steel chariots so often seem to care so little about their obligations to organized society as a whole? Was it only another aspect of the general "lawlessness" of the decade, like the nullification of Prohibition, the revolt of Youth, the rise of organized crime, and the alarming spread of police brutality? Or was there something in the machine itself, the magic box which turned every man into a superman, that made all pre-motor codes of conduct seem obsolete? Whatever the final answer—and the author does not pretend to possess it—the world's first generation of mass motorists cannot have failed to be influenced in their behavior by the fact that they *were* the first. Nor can the attitudes and behavior of their society as a whole have failed to be reflected, to some extent, in their conduct as drivers. In this regard, it was perhaps unfortunate that the world's first experiment in mass automotion took place at a time of great social turmoil, in a country whose values were in an exceptional state of flux, and in a region of that country which was in many ways still close to a frontier stage of development. For, as will be seen, many of the precedents then set, particularly in attitudes towards authority, have not served to make it any easier for the world to adjust itself to the phenomenon of mass automobility.

The New Terror

Beyond all doubt, the most ugly concomitant of the motor age was the new form of peril which it introduced into the lives of every member of society. Never before in human history, except in time of war, had so many people been exposed in the course of their daily lives to the risk of violent death. The Mass Automobile brought a terror to the streets of Los Angeles far more real than any which had accompanied the wild days of the cattle boom in the previous century. Unlike any previously known violent large-scale danger, the automobile accident was especially prevalent in public places. It preyed especially upon the young and the elderly, yet it was completely impersonal, uniting in horror, people and groups of people wholly unknown to each other beforehand.

Not all accidents, of course, were fatal. During the years 1926–1929 inclusive (pre-1925 records are unreliable), an average of about three hundred thirty persons per year died as a result of automobile accidents on the streets of the city of Los Angeles. The annual average of injuries from the same cause for the same period was 11,946, meaning that for every person killed about thirty-six were injured.[22] Since nearly every death or injury meant suffering to additional others who were not involved in the accident at all, the toll in human distress may be seen to have had appalling ramifications.

The automobile seemed to have an affinity for accidents. In the year 1905 there were only two drivers in the whole of Kansas City, yet they somehow managed to meet one day in a head-on collision.[23] In that same year Los Angeles had its first automotive fatality. A son of one of the owners of the Los Angeles street railway system hit and killed a girl while driving into Azusa. He was subsequently charged with manslaughter, but acquitted.[24] It was soon found that most automotive injuries and fatalities tended to result from accidents of this kind— collisions between cars and people on foot.[25] As Bellamy Partridge points out, this was at least partly because the standards of judgement, particularly with regard to velocity and maneuverability, by which city dwellers had conditioned themselves to dodge horse-drawn traffic, served only to confuse them when it came to dealing with the new machines.[26]

As the true motor age dawned, it began to appear that a new class of persons had come into existence, a class known as pedestrians, a term which, in view of the excesses of the motor mentality, was peculiarly apt in both its connotations. For to most motorists there came indeed to be something very pedestrian about being a pedestrian. The modern pedestrian was as much a product of the mass automobile as the modern motorist. "Driver" and "pedestrian" were not, of course, fixed characteristics, but roles which people played. Yet the roles were of a peculiarly absorbing nature. Even though the same man might within a few minutes be a driver, a pedestrian, and then a driver again, there was all the difference in the world between being the controlling agent behind the wheel of a powerful, deadly machine and being a defenseless human body standing in its path. No relationship quite like this had ever before existed in civilized society. Thousands of anonymous human beings were constantly at the mercy of thousands of anonymous others. Only when, as all too frequently happened, an accident took place did names and addresses suddenly become important. And, as has already been discussed in a previous section, the fact that there had been no intention on anybody's part to do harm served only further to de-humanize the entire situation.

As two of the principal ingredients of traffic, automobiles and pedestrians were so very different and their purposes so often in conflict that accidents were almost inevitable. And it must be remembered that when the post-war decade began, although there were already about 150,000 cars registered in Los Angeles County, there was scarcely any regulation of traffic as we know it today. Such laws as existed to govern the situation were very poorly enforced. Moving about in the streets was largely a matter of competition between various types of traffic.

Under conditions so trying, it was hardly surprising that motorists and pedestrians should become resentful of one another, or that old attitudes of animosity towards the motorist should persist most strongly among that section of the public most exposed to danger and inconvenience. Leon Mirp was a columnist for the *Los Angeles Citizen*, a labor newspaper which had opposed the downtown parking ban of 1920 as an alleged instrument of the streetcar monopoly.[27] But by 1922 Mirp was so disgusted with the hazards and delays of downtown traffic that he was portraying the pedestrian as representative of the down-trodden masses:

> According to the law, pedestrians have the right of way in crossing the streets . . . but like all rights, natural and otherwise, unless the pedestrian fights for them, he gets nothing. With traffic officers on the job we have some slight chance, but when they are absent we have to take chances in dodging the machines whose drivers evidently have never heard of the above-mentioned law. . . . Why not eliminate most of these 'plutocratic' autos for the well-being of the mass of the people?[28]

A few years later, however, when Mr. Mirp had acquired an automobile of his own and was reporting on his tours of California and further afield, his readers heard no more about the iniquities of city drivers, nor about those he had once stigmatized as "the rich idlers who have their . . . automobiles that can get them out into the beautiful country in a few minutes."[29]

The dangers inherent in being a pedestrian nevertheless continued to mount. The mere act of crossing a street had become a perilous adventure. Drivers often seemed utterly oblivious of persons attempting to accomplish such a feat in their path. As a writer of 1923 put it:

> One thing I've learned is that it isn't automobile etiquette to ever see a person on foot after they have stepped off the curb. . . . Many is the time after reaching the middle of Wilshire Boulevard by super-human leaps and bounds . . . I have stood on that imaginary line that is supposed to separate the two lines of traffic [it was only later in the decade that such lines began to be actually painted on the road]. Bending now convex and now concave to avoid the camping outfits and dogs on the running boards, I have tried to catch the eye of some approaching motorist, but never yet have I been able to connect up.[30]

Yet it was not drivers alone who seemed to be lacking in awareness. As early as March of 1920, the *Los Angeles Times*, despite its tirades against "murderous" drivers, had pointed out that "the pedestrians . . . are by no means blameless;" and, foreshadowing its stand on the parking issue, had urged that "the automobile is now too common a possession for their owners to be considered a race apart, and with the belligerent antipathy once accorded them. They, too, are the public."[31] Pedestrian behavior, indeed, often appeared almost suicidal, as Tom Connor, a Los Angeles traffic officer, complained in 1922, citing that of young women as particularly bad:

The flappers that flip up and down Broadway with their rolled-down stockings, short skirts, red lips and blooming cheeks . . . make us more trouble than all the rest. . . . A stocking is not rolled just right, lips need a wee bit more lip-stick, cheeks are not blooming enough, and the toilet is commenced just as the young lady steps from the curbing into the traffic. . . . When this happens on my crossing I make a quick change from a traffic officer to a life saver; the pedestrian is trying to commit suicide. . . . Between the fenders of passing automobiles, I have to dodge and run to reach the young lady before she is killed. As a rule, I get there in time and conduct her to the curbing. By the time the passage is made, the toilet is complete and with a merry smile and the flash of a bare knee she steps to the curbing and skips away.

The behavior of elderly pedestrians was nearly as bad. They were "just like children. They never seem to do the right thing at the right time. They step from the curbing directly in front of motor traffic and then flutter around not knowing which way to turn."[32]

But it was children themselves who were the most tragic victims of the new terror. Ninety-five percent of the boys and girls appearing in 1926 before Presiding Judge Stephens of the Los Angeles Superior Court to exhibit their injuries in claim adjustment cases had been injured "from contact with automobiles, and mostly from playing in the street."[33] Mrs. Helen Lucille Holt wrote in 1928 of the deep personal impact such conditions made, especially upon parents:

With the increase of automobile traffic came the increasing horror of seeing the lifeless forms of friends and neighbors carried, crushed and mangled to their last resting place. . . . As the horror of these deaths became impregnated in the minds of California motherhood, the breakfast table, instead of being a cheery scene welcoming a new day, became a tense stage of fear and glinted glances between loved ones. Whom would the fates sacrifice this day?[34]

Accidents were especially frequent on weekends and public holidays. Monday morning newspapers were notoriously full of automobile accidents. A "Comic Dictionary for Motorists" published by *Touring Topics* in 1925, in fact, defined "Accident" as "the principal topic of Monday newspapers."[35] and, according to the *Times*, the undertakers made provision for a special rush of business following Sundays and holidays."[36] Of course, running into pedestrians was only one of numerous kinds of accidents which a motorist could have. A car could crash into or be crashed into by other vehicles; it could leave the roadway and collide with whatever natural or man-made obstacle stood in its way; it could run off a cliff, or catch fire, or simply turn over on top of its occupants. These things not only could happen but did, and they happened so frequently that the automobile accident itself soon became a kind of institution, something accepted and more or less incorporated into the culture, a favorite topic for jokes, for personal reminiscences, for sermons, and for fiction of all kinds. Thus the new terror, while its danger continued to exist, soon lost most of its capacity to inspire fear. People learned to live with it as they had learned or were learning to adjust to many of the other hazards of modern life. In fact they became hardened to such an extent that, in order to bring home to a public who seemed to have forgotten just what it meant in human terms to be involved in a serious automobile accident, it was necessary in the next decade for a writer concerned with preventing accidents, J. C. Furnas, in his *Sudden Death* (1935), to stress the horrifying physical details:

> . . . the flopping, pointless efforts of the injured to stand up; the queer, grunting noises; the steady, panting groaning of a human being with pain creeping up on him as the shock wears off. . . . the slack expression on the face of a man, drugged with shock, staring at the Z-twist in his broken leg, the insane crumpled effect of a child's body after its bones are crushed inward, . . . an hysterical woman with her screaming mouth opening a hole in the bloody drip that fills her eyes and runs off her chin. . . . the raw ends of bones protruding through flesh in compound fractures, and the dark red, oozing surfaces where clothes and skin were flayed off at once.[37]

Such passages are hard to find in the literature of the Nineteen-Twenties. Instead, as will be seen presently, we find, especially in Southern California, expressions of outrage soon being superceded by a superficial public attitude of indifference, colored only by a highly self-conscious attempt to laugh off the horror which it seemed was not otherwise to be avoided.

Public Reaction

How did Southern Californians deal with the problems of congestion and safety which were so clearly attributable to the coming of the mass motor car? The difficulty at first lay in identifying the exact nature of the problems. In the matter of congestion, as has already been pointed out, it took time for the emphasis of public thinking to change from "too many cars" to "too little space." In the matter of safety, the initial tendency was to regard the whole thing as a moral issue and look for some party upon whom blame could be fixed and public wrath wreaked. While the motorist was still in a minority, he and his machine made good scapegoats. But once it became apparent that the entire community was becoming motorized, it was better to forget the moral question, concentrate on bringing some sort of order out of the chaos, and learn to accept whatever unpleasant aspects of the motor age could not be brought completely under control.

The pages of the *Los Angeles Times* in the spring of 1920 demonstrated very strikingly the confusion of images concerning the automobile and the driver then prevalent. At the same time that it was proclaiming that the automobile had now become essential to business, the *Times* was still carrying its motor news in the sports section of the paper. At the same time that it was urging its readers to accept the idea that motorists, too, were members of the public, it was carrying other editorials alleging, in no uncertain terms, that a sizable proportion of that particular section of the public were "maniacs." At the same time that it was recommending desperate measures against "murderous speedsters," it was glorifying the speed and violence of organized motor races.

Compare, for example, the following two items. On March 18 1920, the *Times* published a virulent editorial headed "Murderous Speed Maniacs," advocating stronger measures against speeders, such as compulsory jail sentences and at least temporary confiscation of the car:

> It is a particularly mean and despicable form of depravity, this attitude of ME FIRST AND THE DEVIL TAKE THE HINDMOST . . . it is all a part of the spirit of greed and avarice that besets the land. . . . What is there about the possession of a four-wheeled chariot that transforms ordinary humans into vicious fiends?. . . . These people must be drunk with the sense of a little power . . . one can only suppose a previous condition of crawling on their bellies . . . people who are used to power and possession know how to use them.[38]

Yet only four days earlier, the same paper had carried an article about the races to take place on March 21 at the new Beverly Hills motor track which fairly reeked with enthusiasm for the spirit of "Me first and the devil take the hindmost," exalting in the sheer speed, the rivalry, and the possible violence to be anticipated.

BLOODTHIRSTY BUGS TO RACE. . . .

'Fiendish Five' to Get Under Way Next Sunday

Gentlemen harboring a bloodthirsty desire to knock all the paint from the other gentlemen's wheels will be accommodated as far as possible by the committee in drawing for heats in next Sunday's sprint program at the Beverly Hills Speedway. Every driver entered seems to have picked out some other pilot upon whom to

> empty the vials of his wrath. . . . Jimmy Murphy, the grinning
> demon . . . seems to be universally chosen as a prospective vic-
> tim. . . . The drivers are going to nail the throttle to the floor at
> the start and drive the whole fifty miles with their motors wide
> open. . . . They'll have to pour water on the track to keep it from
> catching fire.[39]

The fiendish villains of the editorial page are the fiendish heroes of the
sports page, the only essential difference being that the two forms of
fiendishness occur in places where they are respectively socially disap-
proved and socially approved. Even this distinction cannot have been
too clear, however, in the mind of the average reader who, after reading
the above speedway article, glanced down to the bottom of the page
and saw there an advertisement for a car which he himself might buy
and operate on the public highway, bearing the slogan: "Peerless . . .
The car that wrecks the records." Why the insistence upon breaking
records (which immediately carried the association of speed), and why
the use of so violently suggestive a word as "wrecks"? Under such
circumstances, we can hardly blame drivers for having a very hazy idea
of their new social role (see Figure 10).

Similarly baffling and even more alarming to drivers was another
contradictory set of attitudes evident in the same paper at the same
time concerning the treatment and behavior of drivers involved in
accidents, especially those accidents in which a pedestrian was hurt or
killed. During the same period that the *Times* was practically thundering lynch law against motorists who were caught in such situations, it
was thundering equally strongly against the baseness of motorists who
hit and ran, not having the courage to wait and be lynched. Thus we
find sentiments like these:

> Public indignation is reaching a point where a vigilance committee
> would not be condemned by many for taking the law in its own
> hands and meting out summary punishment to the offenders. . . .
> If a murderous automobile driver were to be shot down at his
> wheel by an indignant pedestrian, it must be apparent that it
> would not be easy to pick a jury that would vote for conviction.[40]

> Some day when the public temper is at boiling point a child will be
> killed and the slayer, innocent or guilty, fall into the hands of a mob
> that can see nothing but the poor mangled body in the gutter.[41]

followed closely by indictments like this:

> There is one fiend of the public highways of whom it is impossible
> to think calmly or to write within bounds. We refer to that com-
> pound of cowardice and brutality who, after knocking down his
> helpless quarry, speeds up his engine and leaves him to his fate,
> preferring to read in the next morning paper that the unfortunate

one died in the gutter, where he left him, than to stay and . . . face
the music.[42]

It was in this spirit of righteous public anger that the *Times* welcomed what was possibly the world's first organized community campaign for highway safety in the motor age. In March of 1920 the
Automobile Club of Southern California, in co-operation with the Los
Angeles Police Department, announced the formation of a corps of
"Traffic Vigilantes," a group consisting of several hundred substantial
citizens who, according to the *Times*, were to be selected from among
"civic officials, local bank directorates and motor car dealers who are
known to. . . . have keen judgment in traffic matters, and whose integrity is beyond reproach." This group, which the *Times* hailed as "the
first modern Vigilance Committee in the West," was to remain anonymous and to have no power of arrest. Its members were to be furnished
with cards on which they were to record instances of reckless driving
which they witnessed, together with the license number of the guilty
car. These cards were then to be turned in to the traffic office of the
police department where they would be kept on file and used as
evidence against any driver subsequently arrested by a policeman for
another traffic violation. Despite the relatively innocuous nature of
their powers, the *Times* chose to depict the members of this committee
as acting in the great tradition of frontier justice against public en-
emies even more threatening than those their predecessors had faced:

> Members of the Automobile Club of Southern California deserve
> commendation for organizing a vigilance committee to deal with
> the speed maniacs who take a fiendish delight in cutting corners,
> racing over crossings, and converting city thoroughfares into lanes
> of death. They are the lineal descendants of the bad gunmen of the
> early days who terrified communities with deadly weapons. But no
> Remington or Colt ever manufactured is as deadly as a heavy
> automobile driven by a reckless speedster. The vigilantes proved
> the only force capable of meting out summary punishment to the
> gunmen of the early fifties, and the community will rejoice to see
> their spirit revived to cope with the speed fiends whose harvest of
> death is greater than that reaped by all the other criminal ele-
> ments of the city. . . . Conscienceless brutes at the wheels of deadly
> cars are keeping a community in a state of terror. . . . Denouncing
> the offenders through the press is not sufficient. For a vulgar brute
> who holds murder of less consequence than losing some joy-ride
> wager takes a pride in the notoriety that his reckless driving gives.
> Some of them are as vain about their killings as were the bad men
> in the days of the Argonauts.[43]

The expression of such sentiments, however, became comparatively
rare during the decade as it became more and more possible that

oneself or some member of one's own family might become exposed to the charge of being a conscienceless brute at the wheel of a deadly car. Attitudes of condemnation tended to be replaced by attitudes of indifference, tempered by a positive sympathy for violators of certain traffic regulations, particularly those involving speed limits.

But flagrant abuses such as hit-and-run driving continued to be universally execrated. In 1927 a man named Pat Goidacan, who had killed a woman in a safety zone while drunk, became the first Californian hit-run driver to be convicted of murder (second degree);[44] and the offense was in general held to be so heinous that cases occurred such as that in which a Los Angeles dentist committed suicide rather than face a hit-run charge.[45]

It was, of course, the increasing familiarity of the public with automobile accidents, together with constantly improving methods of detection, which made it both safer and more in the interests of a driver involved in an accident to remain and face the consequences. But it was never possible to identify, catch, and punish all those who were considered to be guilty of causing accidents, and, in consequence, much of the public anger against the most irresponsible types of driver behavior had to take the form of large doses of moral censure not too specifically aimed. A *Times* editorial of May, 1926, on the problem of hit-run drivers contented itself merely with hurling imprecations at the "heartlessness and criminality," the "frightful . . . inhumanity," and the "cowardly . . . craven . . . diabolism" of such offenders, without offering any suggestions as to how the problem might be better understood or dealt with.[46]

The same exaggeratedly moralistic tone is to be found in much of the fiction of the period in which public reaction towards automobile accidents is reflected. Almost at the same time the above editorial appeared, for example, *Touring Topics* was carrying a story called "Festina Lente—or the Wisdom of Making Haste Slowly." In this story Cyrus G. Hunt, an evidently prosperous Southern Californian, hits someone while driving near his home one day, but does not stop. Hearing later that his little son has been involved in an accident, his guilty mind immediately comes to the conclusion that it was his son whom he hit. Terror-stricken, he rushes to the boy, only to find that it was not his son but his son's dog. The dog, in fact, is expected to recover, but Cyrus, it is plain, never will. Until now he has been selfish and negligent in his driving habits (which, the author implies, is somehow connected with the fact that he is wealthy and has a fine car). But from now on, of course, he will be a model of caution and courtesy.[47]

A similar image of arrogant wealth at the wheel was presented in the form of Martin Plith in William Gilmore Beymer's short story of 1927, "Talion," already referred to. Here Plith, a substantial Los Angeles business man, out driving with his wife and two children, attempts to overtake another car, and in the process collides with a car coming in the opposite direction. Plith and his family survive unhurt, but three occupants of the other car are killed. The accident is clearly due to Plith's carelessness, but this cannot be proven, and he denies any responsibility. The voice of public condemnation is heard through that of a Japanese gardener with whom, shortly afterwards, Plith nearly causes another accident:

> 'You are rich man. You can get away with it. Roadhog! No look—no signal. Other fellow always to blame. I see. I see. You—Mr. Plith. I read in newspapers about you . . . You still road hog. Mebbe some day you kill more. Then they hang you. I hope so.'

It is interesting also that in each case the culpable party receives a moral but not a legal punishment. Cyrus Hunt has the scare of thinking he has killed or injured his own son. Plith is punished in an even more terrifying and dramatic fashion. One person in the other car survives the crash, though lamed for life—Hugh Arnott, a man whom Plith's action has rendered a childless widower. Having no legal recourse, Arnott decides to take private vengeance by haunting Plith and his family with the blood-stained wreck of the car in which his own family died, arranging to have it parked at various times outside their home, school, and club. When even this fails to shake Plith's nerve, Arnott decides to re-stage the original accident by colliding head-on with Plith when Plith is driving alone to Ventura, thus ending both their lives. At the last instant he is unable to go through with it and just barely misses Plith's car. But Plith, "blood guilty," has finally been broken. He

> has not since taken and possibly never will take, his seat behind the wheel again. He gets into automobiles only when unavoidable, and is sick with apprehension from the moment he gets in until he gets out again.[48]

Such stories give one the impression of a society expressing some of its frustration at the presence of a new evil with which it is unable fully to cope. Many attempts were, however, made to cope with it. The traffic vigilante system was at first thought to be a great success. It was claimed that during its first month of operation there were sixty fewer traffic accidents;[49] and even as late as September 1922 Captain of Traffic, Cleveland Heath, was predicting that "if this system . . .

continues to increase as it has during the past six months, the vicious traffic law violator will almost disappear from our streets."[50] But after a three-year trial period the system was abandoned as ineffective, though the Automobile Club pointed out that it had at least served to reveal the most common types of driving offenses.[51] Another and more grimly direct approach to the problem was taken at about the same time by the Pasadena Chapter of the American Red Cross, which in 1920 decided to place marked boxes containing first aid supplies fixed on posts at thirty-five local highway danger-points.[52] Such a gesture did at least help to publicize the very real danger which existed.

Sporadic efforts of this kind were, however, not enough. Both pedestrians and drivers were coming to realize that, if the automobile was truly here to stay, large-scale changes in traffic regulation and street and highway planning were eventually going to be necessary.

The first major step towards a concerted campaign was taken in 1922 with the formation of the Los Angeles Traffic Commission. This began as an unofficial volunteer body organized by various groups and individuals concerned with traffic problems,[53] but it soon acquired official status and began making studies and issuing reports. In 1925 it recommended and secured the passage of a new traffic ordinance which for the first time officially put the pedestrian in his new place as a sort of two-legged vehicle, required to obey the same kind of restrictions upon freedom of movement as were now being imposed upon all other vehicles. Traffic signals had been in use in Los Angeles since 1921, but hitherto they had been regarded as regulating only the traffic on wheels. Now pedestrians, also, for the first time were required to obey them, to keep to marked crosswalks, and in all other places to request right of way across a street by raising one hand, palm out, against opposing traffic. Meanwhile, on both the state and local level, a mass of legislation was accumulating to tell the motorist for the first time where, when, how, and under what conditions he might, must or must not drive, turn, stop, or park. Among the most notable of these new regulations was that concerning the "boulevard stop" signs which required motorists to bring their machines to a complete halt before entering certain intersections. This remarkable innovation in traffic control was soon seen to be necessary to supplement the earlier simple rule that when two vehicles were approaching an intersection the one coming from the right always had the right of way. It went into effect in California in 1925.[54] Within a few short years much of the sense of freedom associated with motoring, which had flourished briefly between the time when cars became relatively dependable machines and the time when massive regulation began to come into effect, was gone forever.

On the surface, the change was almost universally welcomed. In an article of 1926, for example, Walter V. Woehlke praised Los Angeles as being the only Far Western city to recognize and come to grips with "the full size of the traffic and transportation problem of the future" and claimed that there had been a definite decline both in congestion and in accidents.[55] Whatever advances had been achieved, however, were soon more or less cancelled out by the constantly increasing number of motor vehicles. And on a personal level, acceptance of the new regulations was far from enthusiastic. It was remarked in November 1926, for example, that, despite the new law about pedestrian hand signals, "few pedestrians exercised this privilege, the majority apparently taking the position that it was useless."[56]

It took some time too for the new automatic traffic signals to gain public acceptance, especially from motorists. A Los Angeles Traffic Officer complained in 1922 that:

> Although the semaphore signals have been at my intersection for well over a year, scores of drivers who pass in their machines every day seem unable to remember that they can not drive on when the little arms say 'stop.' Others insist on bringing their automobiles to a full stop when the signal says 'go.' Others just drive on without attempting to see what the semaphore says.[57]

Pedestrians, however, seem on the whole to have readily grasped the social necessity of the new system once it applied to them; and it was easier for people on foot than for those in cars to bring pressure to bear upon each other to obey the new law. Walter Woehlke, after telling of the intensive educational campaign which had preceded the innovation, described typical pedestrian behavior when it went into operation:

> Almost at once the public learned to derive considerable amusement from the new rule. When the stream of traffic halted at the sound of the bell, the law-abiding citizens gleefully lined up along the curb looking for some absent-minded or stubborn individual to attempt to cross the street through the moving traffic. The progress of the venturesome individual was followed with breathless interest that reached its climax when the whistle of the cop blew shrilly and the blushing offender was forced hurriedly to retrace his or her steps to the curb while the spectators guffawed. It was the discomfiture of others that acted as a deterrent and the fear of ridicule proved to be a far stronger factor in the enforcement of the ordinance than the fines that were levied after the initial week.[58]

There is little evidence of any awareness at the time of the possible meaning of this innovation in terms of the process of mechanizing urban man. Yet the automatic traffic signal was surely even more remarkable than the automobile itself as an item in the strange story of man's relationship with machine. For the first time in history, human beings were by common consent obeying the quasi-arbitrary commands of a man-made mechanism. And, although the device had previously had small-scale and experimental use elsewhere, it was on the streets of Los Angeles in the Nineteen-Twenties that it made its formal entry upon the world stage, with 492 intersections being controlled by these new robots before the end of the decade.[59] To the average citizen, however, the new signals were more important as a saving in man-power (and expense) than as an increase in machine-power over his life, as was indicated in the following account of the extension of the system to Pasadena in 1928:

> An interesting experiment in human psychology is being tried out in Pasadena where a system of automatic signals is installed. At its busiest crossing, that of Colorado and Marengo Streets, the controlling officer has been removed for a month, and drivers and pedestrians are put on their honor. They are informed, through the local press, that if they obey without supervision, more signals will be placed at other needy intersections, more officers freed for other duties, and—blessed be!—city expenses lowered. So far the signal self-control is working well.[60]

This was indeed an important practical consideration at a time when, as one police chief complained to the California Crime Commission, ". . . no city . . . has a sufficient number of police officers since the automobile has come into common usage, for the reason that so many officers had to be taken from the ranks of the various police departments for the purpose of handling traffic [and] officers have not been added to replace them."[61]

Along with their new status as elements of traffic, pedestrians were also accorded the distinction of a special form of delinquency which only they could commit—the offense of "jaywalking." This term, which simply meant the act of crossing or walking in a street without due regard for traffic regulations, was not, as Mr. Phil Townsend Hanna of the Automobile Club of Southern California believed,[62] first applied to violators of the 1925 ordinance, since it was in use in Boston at least as early as 1917.[63] "Jay" was a colloquial term for a stupid, inexperienced person, usually with a rural or small-town background.

It is interesting that no equivalent term ever came into use to connote the "jay driver" who, especially with the ever-increasing flow of motor tourists, many of them from rural areas, was just as common in Southern California. It was in fact very difficult for visitors to cope with the multiplicity of unfamiliar traffic regulations which confronted them. As early as 1921, fears were raised that the profusion of new laws might actually frighten tourists away. As one writer in *Touring Topics* put it:

> You've no idea how much the effect of a sunset is heightened for
> the jaded tourist by the knowledge that in pausing at the edge of
> the coast road by the wide Pacific while the horizon is filled with
> the glorious tints of rose and purple, Traffic Officer Cyrus M. Jones
> is liable to appear at any moment with a summons for violating
> section 476, Sub-section D, of the Revised Ordinances of the City
> of Santa Monica, returnable before Police Justice Wilson on the
> following morning.[64]

It was, after all, the motorist upon whom the greater part of the new
legislation pressed. As one indication of the tremendous legal changes
undergone by California motoring in the Nineteen-Twenties, it might
be pointed out that until July 24, 1925, although drivers' licenses were
required by the existing Vehicle Act, practically anyone over the age of
fourteen could obtain such a license upon payment of a small fee,
without any kind of examination. There was nothing in the Act authorizing refusal of a license to a blind, crippled, or insane person.[65] Such
a state of affairs naturally aroused vigorous protest, especially from
such seasoned observers as traffic policemen, one of whom wrote in
1923 that:

> Police officers could tell of many instances of where they have
> found . . . armless women, old, feeble, nervous, and sick people,
> folks whose eyesight is impaired, and in many cases people who
> have to use the old-fashioned ear trumpet to hear what the officers
> tell them, driving automobiles around town, carrying the neces-
> sary legal permission to do so.

He asked why it should be so easy to obtain a license to operate a car
when "one has to pass a somewhat severe examination before being
granted a license to run an elevator."[66] Not until 1925, when the state
already had some 1,225,000 private automobiles registered, did its
legislators begin to tackle this problem, and even then the new driver's
license law which they passed merely required a sworn statement as to
the applicant's physical and mental health—and even this did not apply
to those already holding licenses.[67] It was not until the following
decade that actual tests of driving ability were made mandatory. This
tardiness in the introduction of legal controls, as compared with the
speed with which the automobile itself became an important feature of
daily life, perhaps helps to explain the persistent nature of many of the
difficulties of social adjustment associated with the mass automobile.
The motor age was born in a kind of chaos which it has had much
trouble in outgrowing.

Safety

One of the many words to whose meaning the Mass Automobile
brought a new dimension was the word "safety." More and more fre-

quently, in general usage, the word was understood to apply particularly to safety from the danger of motor vehicle accidents. Throughout the Nineteen-Twenties, beginning with the Vigilante experiment, safety campaigns of various kinds were almost constantly being conducted in Southern California. There was, of course, no rigid distinction to be drawn between attempts to relieve congestion and attempts to prevent accidents. But there was a difference of emphasis. As the *Times* editorialized in May 1920:

> Say what you will, the most important automobile question is not one of delay, discomfort, or congestion. . . . The main issue before the public is to end the maiming and the killing. . . . One cannot watch the . . . anxious faces of the crowds who daily feel that they are dodging death whenever they cross a downtown street or mark the lines of harassment and care on the drawn countenance of the average automobile driver without feeling that this great means for increasing human efficiency and happiness is through a common perversity being turned into an agent for spreading fear and panic.[68]

Nearly all students of the problem soon came to the conclusion that, important as were improved streets and roads, safer cars, and better laws better administered, the principal and underlying need created by the mass motor car was for improved public attitudes, which would be manifested in more careful driving and walking and in a greater willingness to support whatever practical public measures were necessary to prevent accidents. Just how this change was to be best accomplished, however, was a matter of much disagreement. There were inevitably some people, mainly non-motorists, who felt that the main solution lay in stricter enforcement of the laws and heavier punishments for violators. Leon Mirp complained in 1920 that:

> These alleged severe sentences for automobile speeders are a joke. An ambulance driver, not on a hurry call, runs by a standing street-car at great speed and kills a girl. What punishment does he get as a warning to the others? A suspended sentence, which is nothing. Another fellow up for driving while beastly intoxicated and liable to kill an innocent pedestrian also gets no punishment— suspended sentence. Don't these judges realize that these reckless drivers read of the lack of penalty attached to speeding accidents and act accordingly?[69]

There were inevitably others, principally motorists, who looked upon the problem as chiefly one of educating the pedestrian. *Touring Topics*, which was, of course, the voice of organized motorists in Southern California, came out in September 1923 with an editorial alleging that the most important cause of city accidents involving pedestrians was not so much carelessness as simple ignorance on the part of the pedestrian as to "the difficulty of controlling a machine." Too many pedestrians appeared to regard an automobile simply as a machine which would automatically stop for them, not realizing that it was entirely subject to the control of a fallible human being. It was therefore obvious, claimed the magazine, that people with a knowledge of driving made the best pedestrians; hence the best cure for traffic accidents was to give all pedestrians "a personal course in automobile driving. . . . Then, if there exists the rudiments of intelligence on which to graft an idea, those persons will realize that a car bearing down on them at a street crossing contains an element of danger that can't always be averted by frowning at the driver or looking beseechingly at the traffic officer."[70]

The dominant viewpoint, however, appeared to be that safety campaigns should be directed not at any one special group but at the public as a whole. The first major effort of this kind seems to have been a "No-Accident Week," a massive publicity campaign conducted in December 1921. There was no appreciable decrease in the number of accidents during the designated week. In fact, the overall number was higher than during the previous week, though there were slightly fewer fatalities. But its backers called the campaign a "moral success," stressing its long-term educational value.[71]

Education, indeed, was clearly a long-term matter, and it was wisest, therefore, to begin with the young. Soon the safety theme was being carried into the schools, and before the decade was over it had become recognized as a standard part of the curriculum. An article of 1926 explained the effort which Los Angeles schools were making to coordinate this new kind of learning with other subjects:

> In arithmetic problems, the students arrive at answers that contain a moral telling why they should be careful; posters showing the dangers of traffic are made in the drawing classes; stories, songs, and writing lessons carry the moral of caution; safety plays are presented by the dramatic classes. . . . Emergency first-aid instruction is given to all boys and girls in the 6th grade. . . .[72]

Some of the literary efforts produced by children subjected to such indoctrination displayed a striking awareness of the grim realities which had given rise to it. Here, for example, is a "safety jingle" which according to *Touring Topics* was written by an elementary schoolchild:

D is for Driver who lets his car run wild
E is for Excuses made when auto hits a child
A is for Ambulance that gathers up the scraps
T is for the speedy Turn where many meet mishaps

H is for the little Hearse, for those who meet the worst
It all spells DEATH for those who don't stick close to
SAFETY FIRST!![73]

There was as yet, however, no thought of a regular school course in "driver education." The comment in 1926 of a Juvenile Court judge, weary of dealing with traffic violations, that "Along with the well-known 3 R's it seems to me an hour should be taken now and then by school teachers in which to instruct their pupils in the art of driving an automobile" was unusual enough to merit a special item in the newspaper.[74]

In 1924 the Los Angeles Police Department organized a Bureau of Public Safety, consisting of a police sergeant and six patrolmen, with the specific aim of bringing about changes in the habits and attitudes of both drivers and pedestrians. The Bureau employed a variety of media to get its message across, including films, radio, and lectures to school children. Four of its members constituted the "Los Angeles Police Safety Quartet," which appeared at children's matinees and sang "safety songs." This was possibly the first time in history that policemen had assumed the role of entertainers in the course of their work, but Los Angeles was a very appropriate place for such phenomena to originate, and other cities were soon taking note of the general idea of selling "safety" in an appealing form.[75]

The idea of direct action against those who appeared to menace the public safety continued, however, to have a certain appeal of its own. In 1928, for example, Mrs. Helen Lucille Holt, who was a Director of what was known as the California Public Safety Conference, described the activities of the "California Caution Club" which she had been instrumental in establishing, and whose methods were very similar to those of the defunct Vigilantes. Members of the club jotted down the license numbers of cars they observed committing traffic violations. They then traced the addresses of the guilty motorists and sent each a copy of the following letter:

CALIFORNIA CAUTION CLUB

Working in the Interest of Street and Highway Safety

You are cordially invited to become a safe and cautious driver, and as such a member of this Club of thousands of California citizens who are putting forth every effort to lower the great toll of deaths and injuries due to lack of caution in driving.

You are sponsored by a member of the Club who chanced to

notice you _____ (note *offense*) _____ while driving _____ (note the place and highway) _____, on _____ (date).

Your duties as a member of this club will be to use the California Caution Signal—three horn blasts, one short, one long, one short—which means in the language of the California Highway Code, S.O.S., Safety or Sorrow, which is a cautious way of saying to your fellow motorists whom you notice violating the code of safe driving, 'Please be careful!'

Sixteen hundred California citizens were killed in automobile accidents last year.

(Signed)
  California Caution Club
(Auspices)
  California Public Safety Conference[76]

It seems likely that such a communication would be of more value in relieving the feelings of the sender than in altering the habits of the recipient. Caution was not, after all, one of the dominant characteristics of the Californians of the Nineteen-Twenties. And there must have been more than a small element of personal expiation or guilt transfer in much of the safety talk of the era. This is especially worth considering in view of the fact that, despite continued emphasis upon the theme of personal responsibility, when it came to taking positive public action to make accidents less likely—especially where expense was involved—the response was often notably lacking in enthusiasm. For example, one of the outstanding causes of accidents was the fact that large numbers of children played in the streets, having nowhere else to play. In 1926 the voters of Los Angeles were asked to approve a Municipal Proposition authorizing the issue of $1,500,000 in bonds to finance the building of city playgrounds. Judge Stephens of the Superior Court urged support of the measure, writing that:

> If every voter could sit beside me for a week and observe the little boys and girls who are exhibited to me in claim-adjustment cases, there would not be a dissenting vote. . . . Every day from one to ten of these little ones show me their cuts, or bruises, scars and effects of broken bones, each one of which is conclusive evidence of the thrilling escape from death . . . most of them from playing in the streets.[77]

The proposition, however, was defeated, as was another at the same time which asked $500,000 to help eliminate another notorious cause of accidents, the existence of large numbers of "grade crossings," places where ordinary roads and railroads intersected at the same level. Such neglect gave added point to the wisecrack that "grade crossings seem to be abolishing people faster than people can abolish grade crossings."[78] And it contrasted significantly with public willingness to spend large amounts of money on making roads smoother, wider, straighter, and more numerous. One is almost forced to the conclusion that there was at least as much symbolic truth as humor in the current joke about the man who, when asked by the Judge, "Why did you run down this man in broad daylight on a perfectly straight stretch of road?" replied, "Your Honor, my windshield was almost totally obscured with 'Safety-first' strickers."[79] It did indeed seem that all the various safety campaigns served more to appease than to arouse that public concern which in theory all agreed was so vitally necessary.

There was, however, one type of safety structure which the voters were willing to approve; and it was one which very vividly symbolized the new subordination of the pedestrian to motorized traffic. This was the tunnel, or "pedestrian subway," which permitted people to cross a street in safety by walking beneath it. These tunnels were mainly constructed near schools where children had to cross busy streets. The first one was built in 1925 at a cost of $10,000 under Sunset Boulevard opposite Micheltorena Street School where, according to an article by R. H. Bacon, several children had been hit by cars "although an efficient traffic officer was regularly on duty." The opening of the tunnel was celebrated by the schoolchildren as an important event, with an elaborate historical pageant.[80] Many more were built subsequently, of which most are still to be seen today—unpleasant, gloomy structures which require so many additional steps going down and up stairs that most pedestrians prefer to take their chances on the surface of the street. Ironically too, the tunnels, which were built to provide safety from one kind of danger, soon acquired a reputation for harboring dangers of their own; for they proved ideal places for conducting various kinds of assaults. But at least they helped to relieve the motorist of some of his sense of responsibility, and at least theoretically helped to put the pedestrian where, from the point of view of the motorist, he belonged—anywhere, so long as it was out of the way (see Figure 11).

The Humor of Violence

Despite the safety crusade, accidents continued to occur in large numbers. It is, therefore, surely a matter of more than slight significance that a strikingly large proportion of the humor based upon the automobile which circulated in and emanated from Southern California in the Nineteen-Twenties had violence, death, and destruction as its principal theme. Humor of this kind seems to have served as a release for feelings of fear, frustration, and guilt to which, for various reasons, it was impossible or undesirable to give direct expression.

In characteristic booster fashion, Angelenos found ways to brag about their traffic problems and laugh at them at the same time. The *Los Angeles Examiner*, for example, published in 1920 a book called *California, Its Opportunities and Delights*. Among the items included was an imaginary conversation between two New York Jews named "Abe and Mawruss" about Abe's recent trip to Southern California, which managed to convey a sort of humorous pride in the sheer danger of driving in a city which had so many cars:

> '. . . What I am trying to tell you is that this here Mannie Immerglick give me one of the most wonderful rides in his automobile around the outskirts of Los Angeles that I ever took in my life.'
>
> 'Do you mean to say that schnorrer has got an automobile yet?' Morris asked.
>
> 'A question!' Abe said. 'In the city of Los Angeles alone, there is an automobile for every ⅔ of a human being. If all the automobiles in Los Angeles were to form a procession and pass a given point at a rate of 20 miles an hour, I don't know how many years it would take, except that from what I seen of automobiles in Los Angeles, it wouldn't be possible for Los Angeles automobiles to pass a given point at less than 40 miles an hour unless something was the matter with the engine [the statewide speed limit at this time was 30 m.p.h.]. Honestly Mawruss, the way them Southron Californian people take their lives in their hands every time they go automobile riding, Mawruss it makes you wonder is it because they are so brave or is it because in Southern California flowers is so cheap and plentiful that one funeral more or less don't figure at all?'[81]

In much the same spirit, the *Los Angeles Times* accompanied an item announcing that Los Angeles had one of the lowest death rates in the country with a cartoon showing a group of motorists conferring and saying to each other, "Well, men, we've got to do something about it." "Yes sir! We've got to improve our marksmanship!"[82]

Touring Topics published much in the same vein, clearly intended to be funny and presumably considered so, though it seems remarkably crude by present-day standards. By now the lives of most people have been touched in some unpleasant, perhaps in some tragic, way by at least one automobile accident. In the Nineteen-Twenties, the phenomenon was still a comparative rarity. This made it somewhat easier to joke, for example, about the art of running down pedestrians, as George Pampel did in an article of 1926:

> To get the pedestrian and quickly . . . you need the panther type of low, crouching, swift and silent motor car. Why, one . . . driver ran

down three tiny tots, an old woman, and a street cleaner in one
day. 'I could have done much better,' the local paper quoted the
young man, 'but I was developing a cataract in one eye.' An
efficiency expert is working up what seems to have been a desul-
tory interest in the new game of 'Driver and Pedestrian,' getting
up contests between cities with individual prizes of brass-studded
bumpers for the highest records.[83]

Similarly Leepson Brownes suggested that a pedestrian-chasing contest ought to be included in the next Olympic Games. He pointed out,
however, that the relative agility of the pedestrians would have to be
taken into consideration:

> It would obviously be unfair for one contestant to pursue and run
> down an unsuspecting Middle-West pedestrian while his opponent
> was forced to combat the uncanny wariness of the typical Los
> Angeles or San Francisco pedestrian. There are people in these
> California cities who have crossed the street daily for five or six
> years and have never suffered anything worse then a compound
> skull fracture.[84]

Rob Wagner's California Almanac for 1924 included the prediction that
"Pedestrianism will decline while undertakers will establish branch
mortuaries at all crossings," and further informed the reader that
"There is an automobile in California for every 3½ persons, the ½
persons being the victims of automobile accidents" and that "When
automobile prices drop, hospital dividends rise."[85] What these various
writers seemed to be saying was that "automobile accidents are a
terrible thing, but there seems to be nothing we can do to prevent
them, so we might as well try laughing about it."

Macabre humor was by no means peculiar to the Nineteen-Twenties,
but it seemed during that period to attach itself with particular delight
to the motorcar. Los Angeles almost prided itself on its designation as
"the city of the quick or the dead."[86] Its motorists laughed when they
heard a safety zone defined as "the isle of lost souls,"[87] and jingles like
the following were frequently printed on magazine joke pages:

> Here lies the body of John H. Black
> Whose car went dead on the railroad track
> And when the engine gave it a jar
> John H. "went dead" with the rest of the car.[88]

> There was a young lady named Eleanor
> Whose auto turned over and feloner
> 'Twas ten minutes or so
> Ere she seemed to know
> The things that the people were 'teleanor.[89]

Even more significant, perhaps, were the Hollywood film comedies, in which the automobile became firmly established during the Nineteen-Twenties as a standard comic prop. Audiences never seemed to tire of seeing cars colliding, overturning, falling apart, tumbling over precipices, being squashed by trains, flattened by steamrollers, or simply pulled to pieces by angry men. As one example, take the highly successful Laurel and Hardy silent comedy film "Two Tars." In one sequence the two heroes are caught in a traffic jam and become involved in arguments with the other drivers. The arguments soon proceed from words to an almost ritualistic demolition of the cars involved. The Boys methodically set to work pulling off doors, fenders, headlights, wheels, and roofs; they ram into cars, turn them upside down, and roll them off the road. The climax comes when the Boys in their car are chased by a large group of other cars into a railroad tunnel, just as a train is entering the tunnel from the other end. All the pursuing cars are forced back out by the train, but the Boys' car emerges at length from the other end, still in one piece, but squeezed to half its original width.

In another famous Laurel and Hardy sequence, the Boys escape from prison by pretending to be painters. A suspicious policeman follows them, and so they have to continue their pretense, painting everything they see. When they come upon a car parked at the curb, they proceed to paint it with great finesse, not omitting its headlights, windshield, and motor.[90]

What was it that made such scenes so popular? Did Hollywood comedies of this era really "celebrate the motor-car" as Gilbert Seldes claimed,[91] or did they often prefer rather to celebrate its destruction? If the latter, was this simply one aspect of a general destructiveness upon which slapstick comedy must, by its very nature, always rely; or was there something about the automobile and its general relationship to society in the Nineteen-Twenties which particularly lent itself to abusive treatment? Might it not be, in fact, that much of the destructive automotive humor of the time was a kind of concealed protest against the ever-increasing encroachments of this new machine (albeit that many of them were supposed to be beneficial) upon the life of the ordinary man?

Movies and Cars

There are a number of interesting comparisons to be made between the social effects of automobiles and motion pictures. Both appeared on the American scene at about the same time. Both have peculiarly strong associations with Southern California. Each is capable of giving human beings a sense of escape and of tremendously enlarged experience. Each has profoundly affected ways of life and thought all over the world in the twentieth century. Each has given rise to huge industries and vast fortunes. Each has been hailed as a great social benefit and blasted as a great social evil.

Even more interesting is the way the two phenomena have interacted with each other. Movies publicized cars, and cars enabled more people to go and see movies. Movies conveyed many ideas and attitudes about cars and driving to the public at large, and cars aided tremendously in the actual making of movies. Eventually there was to come a complete marriage of the two great social influences in the form of the drive-in movie theater; but this the Twenties did not see. (The drive-in movie, eventually to become a very common feature of the American landscape, was actually invented and patented by one man, Richard M. Hollingshead of Camden, New Jersey, in 1932. But there were fewer than one hundred such theaters in the entire country until after World War II.[92]) Only the fact that, at our present stage of automotive development, there still has to be a driver, who must not be unduly distracted while driving, has limited the same marriage in another form—automotive television—the theater in the car instead of the car in the theater.

Mr. Floyd Clymer of Los Angeles created what amounted to a small industry of his own, publishing books about automotive history and specializing in the "scrapbook" type of publication in which old automotive advertisements, illustrations, and other oddments are reproduced in more or less random fashion simply for their curiosity value, or for the sake of whatever nostalgia they are capable of evoking in the reader. Clymer brought out, in 1954, a "scrapbook" of this type called *Cars of the Stars and Movie Memories* which demonstrates very well the influence which cars and movies had upon each other in the Nineteen-Twenties. An introduction by Cecil B. DeMille compared the two as both reflecting "the love of motion and speed, the restless urge toward improvement and expansion, the kinetic energy of a young, vigorous nation."[93]

The most potent association between Hollywood and Detroit, however, seems to have been less along the lines of motion and speed than along those of wealth and prestige. One of the commonest types of publicity photograph appears to have been that of a star posing beside or inside a luxurious automobile. In any case, the denizens of filmdom were as much hampered in the expression of their restless kinetic urge

as were all other Southern Californians by the increasing restrictions
upon freedom of movement which paradoxically attended the advent of
the mass motorcar. Once again, Jan and Cora Gordon saw the irony
which others missed. They wrote of the cars of the movie population
proceeding along Hollywood Boulevard "block by block as the automatic traffic signals permitted, progressing thus to or from the set or
the sea in much the same spasmodic manner as their films were
made."[94]

In the actual making of those films, the automobile was highly
important both off-stage and as a participant in the action. As early as
1915, a popular book on film-making devoted an entire chapter to
"Using Autos in the Movies;"[95] and by 1920, *Touring Topics* could
boast that "excepting for the typical western drama . . . the motor car
is the most generally used method of transportation in modern screen-
plays," and that "in the matter of reaching remote and wilderness areas
where a romantic background is sought . . . automobiles usually take
the actors and actresses on such journeys."[96] It was early realized that
cars were "Simply great . . . for producing thrills,"[97] and they came to
be relied upon more and more as "the main accessory for speedy and
exciting action."[98] Stunt men made specialties of such feats as leaping
from top to top of cars in busy streets,[99] but filmgoers were assured
that dummy cars and passengers were used in scenes of cars tumbling
over cliffs.[100]

The production of thrills was greatly assisted by the fact that a
motion picture camera could actually be mounted upon a moving motor
vehicle, capturing and heightening action in a way that would never
otherwise have been possible. The famous chariot race in the 1926
production of *Ben Hur*, for example, depended for much of its effect on
the fact that the camera could actually race around the track with the
participants. The film audience, instead of simply witnessing the race,
was thus enabled to feel that they were actually taking part in it (see
Figure 14).

But it was in comedy films more than in any other kind that (in more
senses than one) full advantage was taken of the new machine. As has
already been indicated, violence, inflicted both by cars and upon cars,
formed a large ingredient of automotive film humor. In more general
terms, film audiences appear to have found it easy to laugh at nearly
every aspect of the motor age which in real life filled them with fear,
anxiety, and frustration. The Harold Lloyd comedies provide many
illustrations of this. "Only fifty-nine more payments and it's ours," says
Harold as he presents the family's first car to his wife. The first family
drive inevitably causes a traffic jam, with poor Harold vainly cranking

his car in the middle of it; and equally inevitably there is an eventual smash, with Harold's brother-in-law concerned, not about the wrecked car, but about his watch which was also damaged. Naturally, the naive driver is bedevilled by traffic cops who are always giving him tickets, and traffic regulations which he doesn't understand. At one point, an angry policeman rebukes him for making a left turn without going around the outside of a round turning-marker which is set in the middle of an intersection. Shortly afterwards, he sees what he thinks is another turning-marker. It is actually a hat which someone has dropped that is only a few feet from the curb; but Harold conscientiously goes around it, though in order to do so he has to drive up onto the sidewalk.[101]

Much humor of this kind could perhaps be expected to accompany any great social and technological innovation, no matter in what period such a change might occur. Jokes based on ignorance of the new phenomenon and a tendency to regard it in the now unreliable terms of previous experience were, in fact, extremely common. Of such a type was, for example, the stunt which Harry L. Wilson's Merton Gill performed in one of his comedy films: Merton rides up in a car; the car stops and he throws out an iron weight on a rope attached to the car.[102] Such a joke could be appreciated only by people who remembered that this was one way a driver of a horse-and-buggy had anchored it when he stopped where there was no available hitching post.

On the other hand, there was a certain quality to many of the things people were prepared to laugh at which seems peculiarly relevant to the spirit of the particular era we are discussing. When Harold Lloyd steals cars, causes accidents, and outrageously ignores all traffic rules in order to accomplish his particular "good" objective (e.g., to arrive in time to prevent a scoundrel's wedding to an innocent girl), the sympathies of the audience are clearly intended to be with him. Modern film makers do not present their audiences with so severe a conflict of values, especially where driving is concerned. As a particularly vivid illustration of this change, the following contrast might be pointed out. In one Harold Lloyd film the hero, in a hurry to get somewhere, manages to slip from one car into another while both are in motion on a busy street. He sits down beside the astonished driver, who of course wants to stop the car and get rid of his uninvited passenger. Harold prevents him from doing so by pressing the driver's foot with his own, down hard on the accelerator, forcing the driver to steer with desperate skill in order to avoid disaster.[103] This, of course, was intended to be funny, and presumably Harold Lloyd knew the kind of things which the audiences of that day liked to laugh at. A generation later, in a

Hollywood film of the 1950's ("Julie"), the same device is employed—someone sitting beside the driver and forcing his (her, as it is in this case) foot down on the gas pedal while driving along a dangerous road. But this film is no comedy; this time the device is used to create a mood of high suspense, and the sympathies of the audience are entirely with the driver.

Even more significant were the attitudes of drivers towards policemen, particularly as depicted in comedy films. In general, policemen were always fair game. Mack Sennet's "Keystone Cops," who flourished in the Twenties, virtually embodied ridicule of the law. Both heroes and audience howl with glee in a Laurel and Hardy film when a traffic cop's motorcycle is squashed very flat by a steamroller. The policeman practically bursts into tears.[104] Another motorcycle cop tries to make Harold Lloyd come to a halt, but Harold just keeps driving straight at the man, forcing him to keep riding in order to escape and causing him finally to ride into a lake, where a little boy comes up to him and says, "Hey, don't you know swimmin' ain't allowed here?"[105]

The lawless attitudes thus represented were not confined to the screen, although even off the screen Hollywood personalities played their part in creating the anarchic automotive image of the Nineteen-Twenties. In 1921, for example, movie star Bebe Daniels was found guilty of exceeding the speed limit in Orange County, where speed laws were enforced much more strictly than in adjoining Los Angeles County. She was sentenced to serve a few days in the Santa Ana Jail. The inclination of public opinion, forced to choose between a glamorous celebrity and the majesty of the law was, however, soon clearly manifest. Miss Daniels' jail cell, according to the *Los Angeles Times*, was comfortably refurnished for her. Her meals were brought from the best hotel in town by a "French waiter in full-dress outfit," and the miseries of her first day of incarceration were relieved by fifty visitors, who brought such gifts as large bouquets and boxes of chocolates with the star's initials engraved on each bonbon.[106]

The Driver and the Law

The tendency of Hollywood to hold such figures as traffic policemen up to ridicule was only one aspect of a multifaceted conflict between the freedom loving motorist and those forces which appeared as a threat to his freedom. In some respects, traffic laws tended to be regarded as being in the same category as Prohibition laws—ostensibly enacted for the public safety, but in reality unwarrantable infringements upon personal liberty. As far as the motorist was concerned, the policeman was less a guardian than a menace. A tradition of hostility between motorist and policeman grew up in the Twenties which has in many ways poisoned relations between them down to our own time and made the coming of the motor age a much more difficult process than it might otherwise have been. The editors of *Touring Topics*, for example, apparently saw no inconsistency between their constantly reiterated pleas for an aroused sense of personal responsibility as the only guarantee of "real safety,"[107] and an advertisement which their magazine carried for a rear view mirror (made, incidentally, by Herger and Company, a Los Angeles firm) which sold under the trade name of "Cop-Spotter."[108] The public found the term so apt that it was soon apparently being applied to any rear view mirror regardless of manufacturer.[109] The same magazine once carried as its cover design a gleeful picture of a traffic policeman whose motorcycle had a flat tire shouting and gesticulating vainly after an (unseen) speeding car[110] (see Figure 16). "It must be a dreadful thing," reflects a character in Upton Sinclair's *Oil!* "to be a 'speedcop' and have the whole human race for your enemy."[111]

The fact nevertheless remained that the motorist, however innocent his intentions, was in control of a potentially deadly weapon, a "mechanical axman" as one writer on the legal aspects of motoring put it[112], which must therefore be brought under strict control. Bailey Millard complained in 1921 that "The position of the motorist before the law is at times one of the most anomalous and equivocal in which a well-meaning individual can be placed."[113] But the very fact that this kind of feeling on the part of motorists was intense and widespread made the position of those whose job it was to administer and enforce the law equally anomalous and equivocal. Attempts to regulate the new automotive deluge brought about a situation, for example, in which the idea of "talking back" to a police officer had become almost respectable and was certainly far from criminal. The problems raised were so novel that it was easy to feel justified in arguing with those in authority as to the best way of dealing with them. And this was one area in which women had plenty of opportunity to assert themselves. Marie R. Ullman, writing in 1924 of women's growing influence upon automotive developments, was evidently proud that "it's the women who go right past the traffic officer when his sign says 'stop,'" and held that "it may be the women who awaken us to the fact that much of the stopping is unnecessary. Many a progressive change has been made in the direction of traffic . . . because women were not afraid to argue out points when they felt they were right!"[114]

Policemen were now in fact confronted with the problem of dealing with a whole new class of lawbreakers, a class which soon embraced a very large proportion, if not the majority, of the population. For almost every driver was sooner or later guilty, wittingly or not, of some traffic offense. Yet people who had never before come into conflict with the law tended to react very strongly against being suddenly confronted as offenders. Sometimes the reaction was one of intense anger. In 1926 Charles Reade, a California state traffic policeman of long experience, wrote that he had often been threatened by the drivers he had arrested. "Some of them sit in the car and tell you they're going to get your job, or have you disciplined by your superiors. . . . Plenty of others will start to climb out of the car, telling you they are going to beat you up, or kill you."

Such threats, however, according to Officer Reade, were nearly always mere empty expressions of rage. The more common response was to admit one's offense but to claim some highly suspect, patently mendacious, or simply absurd justification. The most frequently heard stories were that somebody's wife was dying, that the baby was sick, that the driver "didn't know you were an officer or didn't hear your siren, or didn't know it was sounded for him." Some drivers would claim they were doctors on their way to attend a case, or deputy sheriffs going to arrest somebody. Many actually carried as "evidence" specially prepared fake telegrams summoning them somewhere urgently. But many others could only resort in desperation to what had already become known as "the classic excuse of them all," that the gasoline was low and the driver was hurrying to reach a filling station before it ran out.[115]

The continual battle of wits between the driver and the law had to be conducted according to rules of some kind. Until 1923 the rules of the game permitted policemen to check a car's speed from concealed positions by the roadside, only revealing themselves to arrest violators of the speed limit. This device was known as a "speed trap" and was opposed from many quarters as being ineffective in its ostensive purpose of inducing motorists to obey the speed laws. It was, however, recognized on all sides as being a very effective method of utilizing the motoring public as what one writer has called "a lucrative instrument to cut down local taxes."[116]

In September 1923 the protests, which were of course particularly strong from motorists, won out to the extent that the new California Vehicle Act stated that traffic officers were not to be allowed to testify as to the speed of a vehicle if their information had been obtained by the use of a speed trap.[117] Three months later, however, the editors of

Touring Topics were complaining that this new rule was frequently being ignored, that there were some communities where "what is virtually a program of nullification" of the anti-speed trap provisions was being carried out. This gave occasion for a sanctimonious outburst on the evils of disregarding a law, highly ironic in view of the fact that the magazine had never taken a similar stand against all those drivers who habitually treated traffic laws with contempt. "There is danger in such an attitude," warned the Auto Club editors, "Disrespect for some provisions of a law tends to weaken the whole law and disrespect for one law engenders disrespect for all law."[118] One cannot help but remark upon the similarity between the sentiments thus expressed and those which at the same time were (often hypocritically) being uttered all over the country in censure of those who were violating the prohibition laws. It seemed indeed, as E. J. Hopkins wrote some years later, that three kinds of lawlessness were abroad in the land, "the lawlessness of the criminal, the lawlessness of the average man, and the lawlessness of the law-enforcing authorities."[119]

Under such conditions, with traffic offenses being, in the words of one investigator, "shared, in various degrees and quantities by all vehicle owners and drivers,"[121] those who were seriously concerned with the enforcement of the law found themselves hard-pressed and subject to severe demoralization. Writing in September 1922, Captain of Traffic, Cleveland Heath, who then commanded the 30 speed motor-cycle officers, 76 traffic or crossing officers, 6 mounted police officers, and two traffic investigators of the Los Angeles Police Department, admitted that with so small a force, his division was "unable to enforce all the traffic laws," but claimed that nevertheless "we manage to get quite a few of the traffic violators." By "quite a few," he explained, he meant "about one out of every ten."[122]

One of the big hindrances to enforcement was the fact that, as cars and motorists multiplied, there came to be a general public presumption in favor of the driver, resting on a kind of axiomatic principle that driving was a *right* to which everyone was entitled until proved otherwise. Some people let their sense of judgment in this matter run away with them to such an extent that they began to depict the victims of motor mania as acting in obedience to some sort of higher law. The Bogardus study, for example, quoted one youth worker as claiming that the desire of boys "to drive a great high-powered machine at breakneck speed" was only a manifestation of "the developing man inside of them . . . crying for release," that it was "a natural physical proposition just as eating and getting fresh air is."[123] Such opposition as appeared in the Twenties to this kind of viewpoint came not so much from those interested in "safety," whose emphasis always tended to be upon private responsibility rather than public control, as from those whose economic interests were threatened by the advent of mass private motordom. Thus we find George B. Anderson, Manager of Transportation of the Los Angeles Railway, arguing in 1928 that driving should be regarded not as a right but as a privilege, and that there ought to be some controlling body having power "to allocate the use of the streets for the highest economic welfare of the city as a wealth-producing unit."[124] This, however, was definitely a minority opinion, and the problem of those charged with administering the law remained primarily, not one of determining who was to be permitted to drive, but of bringing home to all those millions who *were* permitted to drive the serious nature of the responsibility which driving involved.

One method of approaching the problem of dealing with novel offenses on a mass scale lay in the employment of equally novel techniques of punishment. Southern California was particularly fruitful with ideas for dramatizing the chastisement of offenders. In the month of November 1926 alone, for example, the *Los Angeles Times* carried three different items on radically new suggestions for handling traffic violators, two of which had already been put into effect.

Officials in Inglewood, apparently reasoning that swiftness of retribution would in itself have a chastening effect upon wrongdoers of the road, inaugurated a mobile traffic court. In a system which the *Times* dubbed "court-a-la-carte," the judge and bailiff, together with table, chair, and lawbooks, were installed in the back of a light truck which "parked unostentatiously near the motorcycle officers' beat" and waited for the telltale sound of the siren, signifying that an arrest was about to be made. The truck then rushed to the site of the arrest and confronted the presumably dumfounded driver with the full majesty of the law. The only disadvantage of the system from the judge's point of view was that the "business" was not always as brisk as it might have been.[125]

Meanwhile, in Huntington Park, another judge, Louis Budway, was sentencing drivers who failed to obey the signals of traffic officers at intersections to spend an hour on a street corner watching an officer in his signalling.[126] And down in San Diego the Mayor, John C. Bacon, came out with the suggestion that every driver convicted of a violation should have to display on his car a sign reading: "An erratic driver is operating this automobile. I am under police observation." The latter idea, however, was not adopted, at least in part because of the fear that it might create panic in the streets. As one city official put it, "Who wouldn't make for the nearest drug or cigar store when he saw such an animal coming?"[127]

San Diego, in fact, had until 1928 a higher number of traffic fatalities per thousand population than any other American city of its class. In that year a new police chief, Joseph V. Doran, inaugurated, apparently for the first time anywhere in the country, a bold new approach to the problem of traffic law enforcement. Since it was clearly impossible to apprehend all delinquent drivers, Doran decided to concentrate on catching and punishing those who had actually caused accidents. He ordered his men to shift the emphasis of their work from looking for violators of speed and other traffic laws to making a careful, detailed investigation of every accident which occurred, in order that the exact cause might be fixed as definitely as possible. In effect, drivers were now being told, "You may drive any way you like, within reason, but heaven help you if you have an accident." The pronounced success of this new policy may have done much to influence future thinking on the whole subject of accident prevention.[128]

But the problems raised in the Twenties are still far from solution. At a 1963 conference, Dr. Irma West of the California Department of Public Health pointed out that only $2.68 was spent for the investigation of each death in automobile accidents. "We have only scratched the surface in looking into the causes of automobile accidents," she said. As for the idea of driving as a right, the continuing strength of that conviction was illustrated by the fact that about 27 percent of California's eight million licensed drivers consisted of physically handicapped people, problem drinkers, epileptics, narcotic addicts, and former inmates of state mental institutions.[129]

The Driver and His Machine

In a 1924 editorial, *Touring Topics* expressed fears that driving had already become too easy: "In the old days when it was tremendously hard work to drive, the very fact that it was difficult to handle the machine kept the driver constantly on the alert to meet emergencies. The very simplicity of operation of the modern car tends to lull the driver into a false sense of security."[130] The process of learning to drive was, however, still something of a challenge; and the actual business of getting about in a car and maintaining one in good running order was in many ways considerably more demanding than it has since become. There was in any case the fact that, while "driving" may theoretically have become easier, drivers as a class had become far less competent.

In the "old days" driving had after all been the preserve of a comparatively few enthusiasts. Now it was the common property of the masses. For millions of people the introduction of an automobile into their lives was their first experience of deep personal involvement with any complex piece of machinery; and the operating of this machine required of them the development of certain skills of a kind which they had never before needed to exercise. Yet for many years the amount of instruction and training which most beginning drivers received before they ventured out alone upon the public highway was extremely rudimentary. Such things as professional instructors or organized driving schools were rare.

It was hardly surprising, therefore, that people who had been driving for less than a year, although in 1926 they constituted only 8 percent of the drivers in California, were found to be responsible for 40 percent of all the automobile accidents in the state.[131] Naturally, under such conditions many people who would have been eager to join the great car rush tended to hesitate before flying, possibly, to other ills that they knew not of. Nor, in all likelihood, were they wholly reassured by such disquieting exhortations as the following by Bailey Millard:

> Nobody should be deterred from owning and driving an automobile because he doesn't like the looks of the traffic and is dubious about taking a chance in it. If he is fairly able-bodied, has common-sense, is not flighty or fidgety, and has that real love of motoring which in itself makes for efficiency, he can readily learn to drive an automobile in the heaviest traffic. But . . . he must, above all things, learn and constantly practice the life-saving art of dodging.[132]

Some writers even tried to make a case for the idea that cars were in some ways safer than houses. In an article called "There's No Place Like the Automobile," for example, Frederick Russell pointed out that whereas "If a baseball strikes the window of a residence, glass is shattered and someone is apt to be cut," the introduction of non-shatterable glass in automobile construction was rendering the occupants of cars quite safe from that particular hazard.[133]

Nevertheless, the incentives eventually became, for most of those who considered becoming motorists, stronger than the fears. The more one saw one's friends and neighbors buying cars, the less difficult it seemed to take the step oneself. And after all, from one viewpoint, to become personally involved with a machine which was taking over one's civilization was a means of defending rather than losing one's individual integrity. A more recent visitor from South Africa expressed the idea in terms which apply almost as well to the period we are considering: "To have a car in California was not to surrender to the mechanization around one, but rather to take the first step towards mastering it," wrote Dan Jacobson in 1957. "Social communication became possible. . . . One no longer felt dwarfed, clumsy, out of place. . . . Buying a car, driving a car, was altogether to become more human, not less so."[134]

And so, sooner or later, the majority of Southern Californians found themselves sitting at the controls of what often seemed at first an incredibly complicated machine. Fortunately for most of them, there was no need to understand the various mechanical, electrical, and chemical principles according to which the vehicle functioned in order to be able to operate it. It was not even absolutely necessary to know or remember the names of the various controls which the driver had to manipulate. All that was strictly essential, assuming that the machine was in good running order, was for the driver to know the right things to do with his hands and feet at the right times. There was thus something more than sheer humor in J. W. Livingstone's passing on to the uninitiated the benefits of his own automotive education in 1922:

> To those unfamiliar with an automobile, let me explain that there is a key-board above with pegs which you pull out as an organ-player does the 'stops' on his instrument. . . . Sometimes you use the feet alone, or one foot; again, you may need to employ one or both hands and one foot or both feet and one hand. Occasionally you bring into play both hands and both feet. . . . The first three stops I play on are the differential, the preferential, and the essential. I named these myself. I don't know what they do, nor what they are for. I was told, but have forgotten. The west side of the keyboard contains the pestilential, the referential, and the providential. . . .[135]

But regardless of initial instruction, learning to drive was for many people largely a matter of trial and error, with the educational process often punctuated by costly mistakes. It was necessary, as Livingstone put it, to "get out and straddle a few telegraph poles and eucalyptus trees . . . mop up one or two wayside markets, [and] knock out a brace or two of other cars" before one could "really be in the way of finding out something about driving."[136]

It was frequently observed that new drivers tended, once their initial trepidation had been overcome, to go to the opposite extreme and apparently to lose all sense of caution. They quickly became victims of what Edward Bellamy Partridge called "flivver-complaint," cutting corners, pushing ahead of other cars whenever possible, refusing to yield an inch.[137] Often they seemed deliberately intent upon frightening pedestrians as much as they themselves had been frightened before they started driving.[138] They soon acquired an exaggerated sense of pride in their machines,[139] and in fact often ruined them by testing them as rigorously as possible before the motor had even been "broken in." Car dealers complained, according to an article of 1923, that the inclination of the average new car owner was to pay no attention whatsoever to the instructions he had been given about the care of his car, but to "run blithely home, load the boat to the gunwales with all the family, most of the neighbors, and an assortment of miscellaneous luggage and rush out for a wild ride to the mountains or the beach 'stepping on her' most of the way just to see what she'll do, and making a side trip to try to climb the Grand Avenue Hill [since cut through] in high gear or some other equally foolhardy feat."[140]

Since driving was for most people a totally new and absorbing kind of experience, it tended frequently to be the subject of editorial comment, often of a type which seems rather silly and overdrawn by today's more sophisticated standards—another aspect of the motor mentality. A *Los Angeles Times* editorial of October 1925, for example, dragged in some great figures of the past in order to illustrate its contention that driving ability was not "a matter of intellect but of fitness to the task":

> One wonders what kind of automobile driver Emerson would have made, or Montaigne or Samuel Johnson. It would seem, from what has been told of them, that Montaigne, the alert and agile Frenchman, might have made a very good one, but one can hardly 'see' the sedate and deliberative Emerson or the phlegmatic and ill-tempered Johnson shining at the wheel. Emerson would have been getting in everybody's way and would have been 'bawled out' by traffic officers along his route, while the testy Johnson would have been disputing rights with other drivers at every crossing[141]

Even sillier was an article by Eugene Brown in 1926 called "Dancing Drivers" which devoted itself to demonstrating that the younger generation made good drivers because their dancing experience was somehow good training for the exigencies of the road:

> Just as they instinctively take the right step at the right time when they are cavorting over the polished floor, so can they be depended upon to do the right thing at the right time when they are driving a highly spiced motor car through the glut of city traffic. In the moment of emergency, they can find the brake with the precision of a stop-watch. Shifting gears is deft and certain as the next step in the trot.
>
> One of these flappers who puts fresh fever into the Charleston could drive a bus through Broadway with her eyes shut. Her little muscles would co-ordinate with the movement of the traffic round

about her. The entanglements of the dance floor have equipped her mind with mental fenders. She can be free of the jam and yet in the heart of it.[142]

It seemed indeed that automobiles and "flaming youth" always made good copy, no matter what the connection.

According to Merrill Denison[143] there are two principal reasons why the Nineteen-Twenties have always been known to many automobile historians as "The Golden Age." First, the decade was one which saw the costliest luxury cars ever produced. The automobile as a symbol of wealth and prestige never again reached the pinnacle it attained in the era when Cadillac could advertise one of its creations as "an emerald, platinum mounted, a possession to prize, to adore."[144] It was a time when, as a Los Angeles reporter put it, as far as cars were concerned, "the term de luxe [had] attain[ed] a new and more potent meaning."[145] Second, the period was remarkable as one in which the motorcar underwent its most rapid development, and every aspect of this process seemed to represent a spirit of dynamic progress.

Interesting though the luxury aspect may be to the historians of cars as cars, it is far less important to the student who is primarily concerned with the broader aspects of social history. For contemporary observers were much more impressed with the ubiquity of car ownership than by the outlandish display of the ultra-rich. Some, in fact, made a point of the apparent absence of status consciousness among the car-owning population as a whole. Fremont Rider, for example, in the introduction to his Baedeker-like guidebook to California published in 1925, commented: "That the cars are hard worked is self-evident in town or city, wherever a row of them are parked. The majority are toil-worn, travel-stained, dusty or mud-caked, for there is scant time for cleaning between trips, and the Californian philosophically regards his car as a tool to be used, not a possession to be snobbishly displayed."[146]

But there was one respect in which the trend towards what was then considered luxury signified more than a sheer love of ostentation in an economy of abundance. This concerned the extent to which the changes which were being made reflected the feminine influence. Discussing the Los Angeles "Closed Car Salon" in 1926, Olive Gray noted that "Scarcely a feminine requisite is not installed, . . . Vanities, . . . card-cases, key-tainers, clocks, vases, perfume cases . . . mirrors, not merely to use as 'cop-spotters,' but rouge-reflectors and lip-stickers . . ." She commented also on the fact that color appeared to be playing a more prominent part in automotive design than previously and hypothesized that "it may be that the makers of motor cars hope to engage attention of the feminine clientele by enabling her to match her costumes."[147] On a more basic level, Marie Ullman was convinced that it was the growing interest of women in cars which had been responsible for the introduction of the self-starter, the improved turning radius of cars, the easier clutches and shorter shift levers. In her view, it was a case of women bringing about the improvements "which man, not having time to consider, regarded as necessary evils. . . . Woman takes the wheel and says 'Good heavens, isn't there a better way of doing this?' " Writing in 1924, Mrs. Ullman predicted that woman's influence would continue to make itself felt. Some of her predictions, such as increased automotive luggage space and the eventual predominance of the closed car, proved valid. Others, however, such as that the car's working parts would have to be made more accessible so that women could make their own repairs, because "a man will ruin a new suit of clothes if it is necessary to get under the car, but a woman won't stand for such contortions regardless of how she is dressed," were pretty far off base.[148]

In accordance with the developing importance of the new female factor, manufacturers and advertisers began to emphasize the idea that the car was merely an extension of the home. The "Neville More-Room Steering Wheel" which was advertised in *Touring Topics* in 1922, for example, was a special steering wheel made so that it could slide up out of the way. "You wouldn't stand for the inconvenience in your home," read the advertisment, "—a table just inside the door that you have to squeeze past every time you go in or out . . . then why tolerate it in your car?"[149] In view of such developments, it was quite appropriate that when the Ford Motor Company in 1927 ceased manufacture of its Model T "Tin Lizzie," (after producing 15,000,000 of them) the advent of a somewhat more genteel Model A was celebrated with a popular song called "Henry's Made A Lady Out Of Lizzie."[150]

It was not only in the design and appurtenances of automobiles that the dynamic spirit of the "Golden Age" manifested itself. Around the new institution of automotion a whole complex of related businesses, industries, and services began to develop. When the Goodyear Tire and Rubber Company opened a branch plant in Los Angeles in 1919, it was quickly followed by Goodrich, Firestone, and the U.S. Rubber Company. Next came automobile assembly plants, and accessories and parts manufacturers.[151] According to Margaret S. Gordon, 15 percent of the total rise in factory employment in California in the Nineteen-Twenties was in those industries most directly affected by the expanding use of the automobile.[152]

The Los Angeles used car business was already, by 1921, described as having reached "vast proportions."[153] And by 1926 the *Times* was able to report that "The disabled auto [had] dignified the junk business" to the extent that 'the wrecking of automobiles and the salvaging of parts has become an established industry in Los Angeles. . . . There are 66 automobile wreckers in this city, and 32 of them are on South Main Street."[154] Garages, of course, abounded in all parts of town, as Thomas Murphy noted in 1921, "from the most palatial and perfectly equipped to the veriest hole-in-the-wall."[155] Even parking became a big industry, with the opening in 1928 of the huge thirteen-story Hills Brothers "Skyscraper Garage" on South Spring Street in downtown Los Angeles. Built at a cost of $1,250,000, this remarkable edifice could hold up to 1,000 cars which were raised and lowered by means of fast elevators, and was claimed, shortly after it opened, to have "already materially reduced the critical traffic situation in that section of Los Angeles."[156] As usual, however, the continuing influx of cars soon cancelled out whatever gain had been made.

In view of the ever-widening ramifications of this expanding automotive economy, it is not surprising to find our old booster friend Ernest McGaffey trying, in 1928, to reassure those who were becoming worried about what might happen if ever the market for cars reached a "saturation point." This "fantastic gabble" was no more justified, he maintained, than would be the expectation that a saturation point might be reached in bread, meat, or milk: "The constant use of automobiles . . . wears them out, the constant increase in population makes a demand for more cars, and the constant increase in business of all kinds compels a volume of automobile manufacturing that will no more come to a saturation point than any other recognized, vital, and imperative necessity demanded by our modern civilization."[157] Yet, according to Professors Galbraith and Leuchtenburg, the fact that production of industrial products, of which automobiles were by then one of the most important, had indeed, at least temporarily, outrun demand was one of the key factors in the precipitation of the "Great Crash" of 1929.[158]

One of the favorite devices for stimulating demand was the auto show, a big annual event in Los Angeles. As one might expect in Southern California, such shows often employed bizarre techniques to attract the interest of the public. The promoters of the auto show held just after the war in February 1919, for example, apparently decided that they wanted to get as far away from war themes as they possibly could—so they chose an oriental theme, and the shining new contraptions of occidental ingenuity were displayed to a car-hungry public amid "more than $100,000 worth of Chinese tapestries, paintings, lanterns, teak-wood chairs, and carved mahogany furniture."[159]

Ten years later a disaster struck the annual show which gave Southern California a chance to demonstrate the phenomenal energy which is another of its outstanding characteristics. Four days after it had opened, the entire show, which was being held at the Biltmore Hotel, was completely burned out in a fire caused by a short circuit, which did $1,250,000 worth of damage. Yet only twenty-seven hours after the fire, a new duplicate show was opened at the Shrine Auditorium.[160] There could surely be few more dramatic demonstrations of the importance attached, both by the exhibitors and by the public they sought to reach, to this annual display of new cars, and thus in a wider sense to everything which it had come to represent in the life of the community.

One reason for the popularity of the auto shows was that the public had come to expect constant improvements. There was good reason to hope for improvement, both in the cars themselves and in many other aspects of driving. For the motorist of the Nineteen-Twenties was confronted by a variety of problems which he had a right to feel ought not really to exist. Some of these were purely technical matters, of which by far the most frequent and the most bothersome had to do with the air-filled rubber tires which formed the rims of his vehicle's wheels. Progress in the development of satisfactory tires had not kept pace with other automotive advances. A car which was in perfect running order in every other respect could be completely incapacitated by a single small sharp object lying in its path. "Tire troubles you will have," warned a Ford manual of 1924, "and you must be prepared for them."[161] The "balloon" or low-pressure tires nicknamed "rubber doughnuts" which began to become popular in 1924,[162] provided a more comfortable ride, but were no less subject to punctures and blow-outs. Demountable rims had taken much of the work which had earlier been required out of changing tires, but it was still an irksome business, especially in bad weather.

More particularly related to the weather was the problem of how to see through the windshield when it was raining. Although mechanical wipers existed by 1926, they were still uncommon, and a popular motoring book published in that year recommended "a sliced onion rubbed over the surface of the glass" or "a moistened plug of chewing tobacco" to "prevent the gathering of moisture upon it."[163]

Another and even more dangerous problem of this kind, which existed in its most acute form until 1925, concerned the blinding glare from the headlights of opposing vehicles when driving at night. Judging from a *Touring Topics* editorial of 1922, the only satisfactory means then known of dealing with this problem was the practice, when two cars met on the highway at night, of both drivers switching off their headlights and lighting their way only by their small "curb lights" until they had passed each other. But even this custom, it appears, while widely observed "Back East," was "seldom if ever practiced in California."[164] Not until 1923 were laws passed specifying headlights which would cast a minimum of glare into the eyes of oncoming drivers and a maximum of light upon the roadway. But the new equipment, which still provided only a single fixed beam of light, did not become mandatory for all cars until the beginning of 1925,[165] and even then only a very small step had been taken towards solving the very complex problem of road lighting—which later involved the introduction of multiple-beam headlights, enabling the driver to choose from two or more different beams according to road conditions.

Another problem which assailed the motorist of the Twenties was that of losing attachments or parts of his car on the roadway. The lost-and-found columns, early in the decade, frequently advertised for the return of such items as a "rim of King car lamp," a "tire and rack," or an "auto cover in white sack" which had been lost while driving.[166] But as the automobile became less and less of a platform to which things were attached and more and more of a container within which everything was enclosed, such losses became less frequent; and by the end of the decade, advertisements of this type had entirely disappeared from the newspapers.

One consequence of the rapidly increasing complexity of motorized life, which created new problems of its own for the motorist, was the growing specialization in the automobile service industry. Satirizing this trend in 1929, Joe Mears wrote that recently when he had had a flat tire, he had called garage after garage for help, only to be met with replies like these: " 'We only do generator work' . . . 'The manager said the Universal Joint Association would fine him if he worked on any other part of the car, even on his day off'. . . . 'We only repair pinion gears. We couldn't work on anything else, not even for our own grandmother. Besides, I doubt very much if any of our mechanics could repair anything but pinion gears. They can't even replace ring gears. Our foreman is president of our local Pinion Gear Luncheon Club.' "[167]

Apart from the problems directly connected with his vehicle, the most serious difficulties confronting the motorist concerned road conditions. Driving conditions were always better in Southern California than anywhere else in the world, but they have probably never yet been, in general, as good as a majority of motorists thought they ought to be. The very fact, for example, that roads were constantly being improved during the Nineteen-Twenties meant that there had to be frequent detours over inferior surfaces, which were one of the biggest banes of driving at the time. One of Harold Lloyd's comedy film sequences illustrated the jarring effects often produced by this kind of inconvenience. Harold, driving pleasantly along a good highway, is forced to leave it and take a long and extremely bumpy detour. When at last he returns to the highway, his car still cannot stop bumping. When he gets out and tries to walk, even *he* is unable to stop bumping as he walks![168] Many detours were so unpleasant that the very knowledge that a detour existed on a particular road would cause many drivers to avoid that road altogether. Hence, for example, we find the secretary of the Santa Barbara Chamber of Commerce, in 1926, actually requesting the California`Highway Commission to delay making improvements on the highway between Ventura and Santa Barbara until after the end of the tourist season.[169]

Another major problem to the motorist was that of finding his way. Although compared with the rest of the country, the roads of Southern California were unusually well-marked with directional and warning signs, there was apparently still, at least as late as 1920, need for such publications as the annual *Automobile Blue Book,* which guided the motorist from place to place with detailed verbal descriptions of the routes to be followed. In order to make effective use of the book, it was necessary to keep careful watch on the car's odometer (the instrument showing distance travelled), and it was almost essential to have a passenger to act as navigator. The following extract, describing the beginning of the route from Los Angeles to San Bernardino, "one of Southern California's most popular highways," will illustrate the method employed by this valuable guide:

Total Mileage	Distance between points	
0.0	0.0	LOS ANGELES Broadway and 7th St. Go northeast with trolley on Broadway. Thru irregular 4 corners, just beyond tunnel 1.1, keeping ahead on N. Broadway.
2.3	2.3	3-corners; bear right with trolley across long concrete bridge over L.A. River.
2.6	0.3	3-corners; bear left with trolley onto Pasadena Ave.
3.1	0.1	Diagonal 4-corners. Bear left with trolley and Pasadena Avenue.
4.2	1.1	3-corners; bear right with trolley

		and Pasadena Ave. Pass Sycamore Park on right 4.8. Thru Highland Park 5.9. Cross RR 6.3.
6.6	2.4	Right-hand diagonal street at small green; bear right along same—still on Pasadena Ave. Cross RR 6.7. Pass Cawston Ostrich farm on right 7.2.[170]

Where necessary the book warned the driver of dangers ahead with phrases like "*Caution* for curves on upgrade. . . . *Caution* for narrow winding road. . . . *Caution* for another wash."[171]

Helping to make such meticulous manuals unnecessary, and indeed assisting and advancing the interests of drivers in numerous ways, was the remarkable organization known as the Automobile Club of Southern California. This powerful independent body (it had withdrawn from the American Automobile Association in 1913 because of jurisdictional controversies, and did not re-affiliate until 1946) was by this period, as pointed out earlier, in no sense a social or sporting club. For a number of years in its early years it had sponsored automobile races, but by 1920 such activities had been entirely eclipsed by the principle of service to the expanding motoring public. This service embraced, among other activities, the mapping and sign-posting of roads, the providing of insurance at rates much lower than those generally prevailing in the rest of the country, the arrangement of emergency road service for cars in distress, and the waging of a constant campaign for better roads. The correspondence files of the California Highway Commission, preserved in the State Archives, bear witness to an extremely close collaboration between the Club and the Commission. Complaints by Club members even about such minor matters as the need for a single tree to be trimmed in order to improve drivers' visibility at a particular point were officially forwarded by the Club's engineers to the Commission, which usually promised speedy attention to the matter. When "safety" became an important concern, the Club sponsored elementary and junior high school safety committees, juvenile traffic schools which delinquent drivers between the ages of fourteen and eighteen were required to attend, and a "Safe Drivers' League" whose members signed pledges and were provided with windshield emblems.

The Club was the largest of its kind in the world, and its activities extended far beyond the boundaries of Southern California, including, for example, the vast project begun in 1920 of charting most of the then-existing transcontinental highway system.[172] Work of this kind was, of course, closely tied in with the desire to attract more and more people to Southern California. For as the importance of the automobile increased, the Automobile Club of Southern California came to be regarded less as representing one particular interest group, and more as what one booster publication of 1929 called "a great public institution."[173] It was thus to be found taking a lead in such public-spirited endeavours as the campaigns to "Save the Redwoods" and to preserve or restore the Spanish missions and other historical monuments. And its monthly magazine revealed, during the decade, a notable shift in emphasis from the more technical and practical aspects of automobiles and driving to the wider interests of the general public in the literature, history, and wildlife of California and the West.

Nevertheless, the Club was always first and foremost, in the minds of most motorists, a means of helping them to avoid trouble or of rescuing them from it. As early as December 1922, a regular daily Automobile Club radio program was being broadcast from KHJ, the *Times* station, giving information on road conditions and news about stolen cars.[174] The rescue type of service became particularly important in 1924, when the Club inaugurated its own Highway Patrol (not to be confused with the California State Highway Patrol established in 1929) and negotiated contracts with garages to provide emergency service on call and without cost to its members only. The Patrol consisted of a fleet of light trucks operated daily along fixed routes by drivers specially trained in giving first aid to cars and (if necessary) to people, and instructed to remove road hazards and obstructions where possible, *e.g.*, by sweeping up broken glass. Originally its services were offered free to all motorists in trouble who were encountered, regardless of whether or not they were Club members. Ernest McGaffey, who rode in a Patrol truck to observe its work soon after the system began, wrote of it as representing "the true spirit of automobiling freemasonry. . . . the example of the Good Samaritan translated to modern days," and described how "men and women in automobiles saluted our car" and everyone seemed happy to see it.[175] But the charitable aspect of the Patrol appears to have been soon curtailed, with assistance being subsequently offered only to Club members.

PART IV

LAND

In this third section our emphasis is going to be on the dynamics of the relationship between the mass automobile and the artificial and natural setting within which it made its appearance. Cars were invented to carry people over the land. In order for them to be able to do so effectively, it was necessary for people to change the face of the land by building roads and providing all the other facilities required by the cars and the people who travelled in them. Having then made it easy for large numbers to reach places previously accessible only to a few, people changed the land further by playing on it, living on it, and working it for profit. But meanwhile, the land thus opened to their wheels and feet was having its own influence upon their lives and attitudes. This sort of process, of course, took place in many different regions. Its effects upon Southern California, however, are universally acknowledged to have been particularly striking. This strange "metropolitan area," as Carey McWilliams points out, could be characterized neither as urban nor as rural, but was everywhere a combination of both.[1] With its attractive climate and expanding economy luring more and more settlers, with its paucity of natural advantages requiring the human mastery of nature on a scale hitherto unheard-of, with its comparative geographical isolation and its regional peculiarities creating a sense of separatism which was only enhanced during the Nineteen-Twenties by the revelation of the census of 1920 that its inhabitants now constituted a majority of the state's population— Southern California transformed the image of the great American melting pot into that of a pressure-cooker. Los Angeles, as the famous architect Richard Neutra pointed out, was the only metropolis in

America whose major expansion occurred entirely within the automobile era[2] and was, therefore, able to incorporate the automobile more completely into its highly artificial landscape than could any already well-established city. That incorporation was not, however, achieved without challenging many of the values upon which older concepts of what constituted a good life and an attractive environment had been founded.

Roads

The roads, which crossed the "rurban" landscape of Southern California, and funnelled tourists and settlers from all over the country into the region and turned Southern Californians themselves into tourists on a massive scale, were one of the features of the land which most frequently impressed visitors. This was true to a certain extent of the state as a whole. Numerous motor travellers wrote of the tremendous improvement they found in road conditions as soon as they crossed the border, especially from Nevada, into California: "California, where the motorist's troubles are ended" wrote one in 1920, ". . . the roads are smooth as marble, with no dust, and the signs read 'Smile at Miles,' 'Miles of Smiles.'"[3] But it was the Southland which more particularly had by the beginning of the Nineteen-Twenties earned the designation of being "easily the motorist's paradise."[4]

The great era of road building, however, was then really only just beginning. The nationwide movement for "good roads," which had won its first major victory in the Federal Highways Act of 1916 and found its most dramatic expression in the activities of the Lincoln Highway Association formed in 1912, had reached an early and peculiar intensity in Southern California, largely because of the very active part taken in it by the Automobile Club of Southern California. As early as 1909, the Club had taken the initiative in procuring for Los Angeles County F. H. Joyner, the best road-building engineer available in the country.[5] By 1920 an authority on California roads could write quite definitely that "in Southern California . . . road improvement has outstripped all other sections of the state."[6]

The excellence of the region's roads was, however, only comparative and was, in general, confined to main thoroughfares and well-populated areas. Thomas Murphy, who was particularly fervent in his enthusiasm for its motoring advantages, nevertheless felt obliged to point out, in 1921, that Southern California still had many unimproved country roads, with "stretches of 'adobe' . . . miles of heavy sand . . . rough stone-hewn trails hardly deserving to be called roads at all . . . many primitive bridges and oftener no bridges at all."[7]

In desert areas, conditions were particularly bad. The average desert road, according to a government publication, consisted of "a pair of wheel ruts," and travellers were advised that ". . . in sandy places it is essential to stay in these ruts. Leave them only to pass another vehicle and then keep two wheels of the car in a rut if the sand is bad."[8] There was a somewhat more acceptable road connecting El Centro with Yuma via Holtville, but it consisted only of wooden planks bolted together and could be kept open only by the constant employment of maintenance crews with scrapers to remove the sand.[9] An eastern traveller of 1926 described this road as containing

> . . . just room enough for one car. . . . At intervals of about 100 feet stand posts with discarded automobile tires dandling as sentinels to warn one to look for an approaching car. At the foot of these posts are wooden islands to allow one to draw off the main road. . . . If a car once falls off there is no hope of retrieving it. We passed many cars dug into the sand mutely waiting to slowly disintegrate.[10]

Throughout the Nineteen-Twenties the building and improvement of roads proceeded on an unparalleled scale. Aided by a decline in building costs, by a plentiful supply of cheap labor including convict labor,[11] and by what Merrill Denison has called the "the epochal discovery" that both the car and its fuel could be taxed to help provide the necessary funds,[12] the road-building program of California alone was probably the largest ever undertaken anywhere up to that time.[13] The pages of *California Highways*, the official monthly magazine of the state Highway Commission, which began publication in January 1924, clearly demonstrate the feverish pace of this program with tremendous and spectacular feats of engineering—bridges, tunnels, cuttings, widenings, straightenings, smoothings—occurring in such rapid succession as to become commonplace. Yet each major accomplishment was marked by appropriate public ceremonies of a type that F. L. Paxson characterized as a new form of "American ritual." The ordinary celebration of this kind, as Paxson described it, consisted of a civic parade over the new pavement, "the cutting of symbolic ribbon with official shears, a little crowding by politicians to get near the center of the picture, oratory reminiscent of that which poured over the completed Erie Canal and the junction of the Union and Central Pacific railroads, and the pretty girls for the newsreels."[14] Southern California, however, liked to do things in a big way. The official opening of the Mulholland

Highway in 1925 was marked, among other things, by an aerial display, a rodeo starring Tom Mix, a costume carnival and street dance on Vine Street between Hollywood and Sunset Boulevards, a parade of armed forces and civic leaders, a celebration in Hollywood Bowl with a galaxy of movie stars showered with roses from a fleet of airplanes, and "the most brilliant street lighting and searchlight display ever seen in Southern California."[15]

But such achievements were not made without encountering difficulties and set-backs, sometimes very costly ones. Road building had been more or less a lost art for a very long time, and besides, the fact that roads were now being built for a new and different kind of traffic meant that there were many new lessons to be learned. One of the chief troubles was that, even after motor vehicles had arrived on the scene, those responsible for building the roads had difficulty in making allowances for the constantly increasing volume and weight of traffic. By 1921 the roads which the state had been building since its program officially got under way in 1912 had already become so inadequate that the Automobile Club of Southern California, in cooperation with the California State Automobile Association, which was its northern counterpart, instituted an engineering study of all the paved State highways, the most extensive and comprehensive study of its kind yet made in the U.S.[16]

The report that resulted flatly charged the Highway Commission with "building inadequate roads, and persisting in such construction when it was evident even to the layman that the roads would not serve the increasing traffic and loads to which they were subjected."[17] Not surprisingly, it was found that the southern part of the state had suffered from the highest percentage of what was known as "highway failure."[18] But it was not private automobiles, the report alleged, which were primarily responsible for the rapid deterioration of the new road surfaces. Rather, it was the increasing number of heavily loaded motor-trucks: "The evidence shows that in the rebuilding of one old road [the builders] destroyed with their own trucks more roads than they repaired."[19] This report was probably an important factor in the defeat, in 1922, of the incumbent governor William D. Stephens by Friend W. Richardson, followed shortly by the appointment of a new Highway Commission; and it was certainly influential in securing important changes in highway specifications.[20]

The tremendously increased expenses of highway building and maintenance entailed by increased road use brought about much controversy as to just how they were to be apportioned among the private motorist, the "commercial motorist," and the general taxable public.

Until the end of the nineteenth century, the theory had prevailed in California that the maintenance of roads was a local matter and a responsibility shared by all the inhabitants of the locality, to be fulfilled either by performing the work themselves or by the payment of a poll tax. As the Good-Roads movement got under way, with its stress upon the economic advantages of better roads, emphasis came to be placed on the primary responsibility of the property owners. It was under this theory that the State Highway Bond Issues of 1910, 1916, and 1919 were passed. The growing number of motor vehicles, however, brought about a wholly new theory—that the principal expense of highway construction and maintenance should be borne by the people who made most actual use of the roads. Acting in accordance with this new doctrine, the legislature of 1923 enacted a two-cent-per-gallon tax on gasoline and a four percent gross receipts tax on transportation operators, thus setting a pattern which, with modifications, was to form the basis of all future highway fiscal policy.[21]

The question of road finance in the Nineteen-Twenties is particularly interesting from the point of view of the present study in that it occasioned the first and only serious sectional conflict between the organized motorists of Northern and Southern California. The two-cent gasoline tax of 1923 had been designated as being solely for the purpose of highway maintenance and was not to be used for new construction. By 1926, however, it had become apparent that existing funds were not going to be sufficient to complete the building of the state highway system first begun in 1912. It was, therefore, proposed that the gasoline tax be increased by one cent in order to pay for the new construction. Since by that time Southern California had over 50 percent of the state's population and 57 percent of the registered motor vehicles, while 62 percent of the new road construction was to take place in the lagging northern section of the state, it appeared to many Southern Californian motorists, led by their Auto Club, that they were to be taxed in order to benefit "foreigners." *Touring Topics* spoke of "another attempt to gouge the motorist" having appeared "out of the north."[22] North and South supported rival highway initiatives aimed at protecting their respective interests in the election of 1926, but both were defeated. Eventually in 1927 Southern California accepted the new gasoline tax, after what was known as the Breed Allocation Act had provided for a more equitable distribution of new highway mileage as between the two sections.[23] In general, however, as pointed out earlier, gasoline taxes, as long as they were applied entirely to road construction and maintenance, were among the least unpopular taxes ever introduced anywhere.

Another problem with which the road builders had to contend concerned the selection of routes. From the short-term strictly commercial point of view, roads meant traffic, which meant business, which meant prosperity. The Highway Commission was, therefore, constantly being presented with petitions to route its new roads in such a way as to benefit some particular local interest. Thus the inhabitants of the little desert community of Hesperia requested in 1919 that the new state highway from Cajon Pass to Barstow should go through their town, even though this would make the route two miles longer than if the town were by-passed. Their petition stated frankly that "we believe that in constructing highways, attention should be given to building up the county through which they pass."[24] The request was unsuccessful, however, which perhaps in part accounts for the fact that Hesperia is still one of Southern California's more charming settlements.

There was one problem encountered by the road men of the Nineteen-Twenties which they had not really bargained for at all, and which was entirely a product of the automobile age. It was not a major problem, but it has a certain symbolic aspect which makes it particularly interesting in a discussion of the relation of the automobile to the land. The difficulty concerned a certain weed known to botanists as *Tribulus Terrestris* which became unpleasantly familiar to motorists as the "puncture vine." The spiked seed pods of this plant were found to be a great menace to the tires of automobiles; they could puncture thin tires and weaken the fabric even of good ones as they got worked in. The remarkable thing was that the Puncture Vine had not been at all common in California until the advent of the Mass Automobile. Then it was found to be spreading rapidly all over the state, growing especially profusely along the highways. The reason was, of course, that it was the automobiles themselves which were spreading the pest, transporting its seeds on their tires from one area to another. As an article of 1925 in *California Highways* put it, "the rapid spread of puncture vine in California during the past few years is directly traceable to the improvement of highways and the resulting increase in motor vehicle traffic."[25] There does not appear to have been any contemporary comment on the symbolic irony of a situation in which the automobile spread its own misfortunes. Perhaps only a later generation could appreciate it. The question at the time was, what to do about it. The best known method of combating the pest, according to a Highway Commission Report of 1926, consisted of spraying it with diesel fuel. To be effective, this required several applications at a cost per application of 2¼¢ per square yard. But even then, unless all the land adjacent to the public right-of-way could also be controlled, there was a danger, as the report put it, that "our work will avail nothing, as these areas will be reseeded from outside faster than we can eradicate."[26] No really satisfactory answer to the puncture vine problem appears to have been found until tires became less vulnerable. In some aspects, it was only part of the much broader problem of the control of roadside vegetation in general, a problem whose aesthetic and ecological aspects are still very much a matter of controversy.[27]

On the whole, however, with a backing of almost unparalleled public enthusiasm, the California highway program surmounted most difficulties easily. By the end of the decade the state could boast of what one writer called "the finest and most expensive network of smooth paved roads that ever tempted a motorist."[28]

Touring and Motor Camping

Good roads and reliable cars created, among other things, the phenomenon of mass motor touring. "The extent to which the good roads system [in Southern California] has been developed," said a guidebook of 1930, "enables motorists to reach most of the prominent points of interest by one road and return by another, ensuring fresh views both ways." In more senses than one, the new mobility provided opportunities for "fresh views both ways."[29] For it brought tourists to Southern California in previously unheard of numbers, while residents of the region themselves became one of the most significant groups of tourists in the country. Southern California had 658,594 tourists when it began to count them in 1928, of whom a large proportion had come in their own cars.[30] The number of motorized tourists entering California nearly doubled between 1920 and 1923, and doubled again by 1929.[31] Yet there were two-thirds more Californians travelling in other states than there were residents of other states travelling in California. By 1929, California cars outnumbered all others in the national parks of the West, except cars locally registered.[32] Motor tourists from other parts of the country frequently remarked on the number of California cars they encountered outside of California, and on the irrepressible tendency of their occupants to boast of the good roads, climate, scenery, and "live" towns of their own state.[33] There naturally arose the question of why Californians chose to venture beyond their own state at all. One booster-bored traveller could only speculate that "possibly it is a desire to prove by personal investigation the complete supremacy of their own commonwealth."[34]

Motor touring was more than a new means of travel. For many it became a new way of life. Since it was now possible to to carry without effort all the equipment one needed to make wilderness comfortably habitable, and since there were still plenty of open spaces available close to the roads for camping, the phenomenon of "auto-camping" became widespread and respectable among all classes during the Nineteen-Twenties. A great deal of romanticism tended to become associated with this new type of recreation. Auto-campers liked to regard themselves as "nomads" or "gypsies," and possibly for the first time in modern history, peregrination and self-sufficiency became characteristics for society at large to admire rather than to regard with suspicion. We sense much of the flavor of this new outlook in one of the first books on motor-camping:

> In the old days, none of us followed the open road in the care-free manner of the gypsy himself. . . . That was a thing we only wistfully dreamed about. Then came . . . a modern miracle. The motor car appeared upon the scene. On the heels of its magic-like development followed motor touring. Here was the nomadic instinct within us popping out in a brand-new form. It was a distinct step in the direction of the real gypsy way but still something of a compromise. We were now following the open road, to be sure, but the smouldering camp fire in front of the silent tent was notably lacking from the picture. We were gypsies in the daytime but evening found us back in the turmoil of city streets. . . . In due time a happy and quite obvious solution sprang up in the West and quickly spread throughout the country. This was motor-camping. . . . It is the real gypsy way. The motor car has become a gasoline caravan.[35]

A Los Angeles booster publication of 1920 showed a photograph of a family beside their car and tent with the caption, "The Californian's Weekend Home. He has as many of them as there are beautiful camping sites around the bend of a paved road a few hours' ride from his home. He needs no cabin. He is sure nine-tenths of the year that his plans are not to be upset by rain."[36] Rider's guidebook of 1925 graphically described the new phenomenon:

> One of the biggest instruments in making the Californian live so large a share of his life out-doors is the automobile. . . . All along the main highways, at all seasons, a notable feature is the droves of excursionists, picknickers, and campers. Whole families on the move, in autos piled high with luggage and bedding, adults and children perched where they may, and sometimes a sleeping baby strapped securely to a narrow mattress on the running-board. Thanks to the ubiquity of . . . automobile camps . . . frequent woodland and mountainside vacations are within easy reach of a large social class whose outdoor life on the Atlantic coast would be mainly limited to dusty city parks.[37]

It was not until 1926 that the first establishment which called itself a "Mō-tel" appeared in California, at San Luis Obispo (the usual halfway stopping place between Los Angeles and San Francisco on the old "Royal Highway"), providing detached accommodations both for guests and for their cars, with a central restaurant and coffee shop.[38] Similar establishments calling themselves "motor inns" had already appeared, including one in Los Angeles which a national motor camping manual of 1926 described as "one of the most complete" examples of this "new development in motor touring." This place consisted of a community building containing cooking and dining facilities surrounded by a group of bungalows.

It was thus possible, as the manual put it, "to be a camper, but a camper with hotel conveniences."[39] Such hostelries became increasingly common, but in general the decade was remarkable as the heyday of open air motor-camping, with a multitude of devices being advertised to convert one's car into a portable home, for example, "auto kitchenettes"—large cases containing spaces for food, dishes, and cooking equipment, which fitted onto the back or side of the car.[40] Commercially manufactured house-trailers did not begin to appear until the end of the decade,[41] though some adventurous souls had begun installing their own mobile homes upon the chassis of converted trucks at least as early as 1920.[42]

According to Frederic Van de Water, who motored with his family across the country from New York and wrote a delightfully entertaining book about the trip in 1926 (a book which, incidentally, had great effect in persuading people that transcontinental auto travel was no longer difficult or dangerous),[43] the institution of the organized motor camp, which had originated on the West Coast, had also reached its highest development there. One could "tour from Vancouver to Tia Juana comfortably and cheaply," camping every night in a place where laundry, kitchen, shower-bath, and restroom facilities were provided.[44] California had nearly twice as many motor camps in 1926 as the next leading state which was Colorado.[45]

There were many municipal camps which at first offered free facilities to all motorists, presumably on the theory that motorists were a source of potential wealth for a community. But it was soon found that in this new age of the Mass Automobile, some motorists might actually turn out to be a parasitical drain upon a community's bounty, and so the camps began making a charge, generally of about fifty cents a night, to keep undesirables away.[46] These undesirables, often consisting of whole families of impecunious people wandering in their cars over the land, formed a striking element in the colorful new pattern of highway

life, about which J. B. Priestley commented in the following decade
that "a contemporary American *Don Quixote, Gil Blas,* or *Tom Jones*
could be written."[47] They became known as "motor hoboes," and were
a sort of backwash of the great motor-migration to Southern California
which Mildred Adams described as being "like a swarm of invading
locusts. . . . For wings they had rattle trap automobiles, their fenders
tied with string, and curtains flapping in the breeze; loaded with
babies, bedding bundles, a tin tub tied on behind, a bicycle or a baby
carriage balanced precariously on top. Often they came with no funds
and no prospects, apparently trusting that heaven would provide for
them."[49] Many who could not find work became drifters. As Frederic
Van de Water saw the motor hobo, "he finds that he can earn or beg or
pilfer enough to live and so drifts along from town to town. . . . Up and
down the West he wanders, a new type of Weary Willie who drives an
asthmatic rheumatic car and expects the open-handed West to aid him
should he and his family run out of gasoline, oil, or food."[49] A Los
Angeles Juvenile Court official went so far as to suggest, in 1927, that
future historians might find in this phenomenon the most telling indication of "disintegrating family life" and the destruction of the home.[50]

Motor hoboes were only one of the many fascinating features of
motoring life to be encountered in the days when the Mass Automobile
was still young. Another, frequently commented upon by victimized
travellers, was the "road liar" who seemed to delight in purveying
exaggerated misinformation about the road perils he had come through
to which the motorist going in the other direction might look for-
ward.[51] In general, however, the auto camps provided a warmth of
human experience which appears to have been one of the most attractive features of car life during the decade. There was still enough
novelty in long-distance motoring to enable all those participating in it
to feel that they were sharing a common adventure. The free-and-easy
atmosphere of the motor camps was a delight to those who had been
long in city pent. D. D. Stephenson's poem, which we cited earlier,
conveys this atmosphere splendidly:

> Goal for all who seek refreshment
> After many a vanished mile
> Here is balm for man and motor
> Gratefully they rest awhile
> Walk right up to any body—
> Cards or introductions? Nix!
> Where you been and where you going?
> How'd you find your new twin-six?
>
> . . . .
>
> Oklahoma's son is flirting
> With a peach from Alabam'

Georgia's neighboring with Utah,
Borrows aspirin and ham.
Texas smokes a pipe with Kansas
Swaps a joke with Tennessee
Here's no place for cold aloofness
Water, air and speech are free . . .[52]

Even at the time, however, it was realized by some that the best features of what was known as tin-can touring, since they were only a product of its newness, were inevitably ephemeral. Frederic Van de Water penned a prediction which proved only too insightful:

> Tin-can tourists are too new to the craft to have developed skepticism and suspicion of their fellows. They are friendly, generous, kind-hearted folk exceedingly easy to impose upon. There are no traditions behind them to warn them to beware. . . . As time goes on, sophistication will creep in. As the comforts of auto camping increase and the enterprise becomes more formalized, the campers . . . will grow warier, more vigilant against imposition, less openly, eagerly friendly. And when that happens, the pleasantest most endearing element in tin-can touring will have evaporated.[53]

Nevertheless, it was good while it lasted; and fortunately there were those who were able to extract and convey to others a full measure of appreciation of what it meant to go out into the land in those brief years of the motor camper's frontier. Since the relationship between Americans and their cars in the Nineteen-Twenties has often been likened to a love affair, the title of the following poem, a beautiful evocation of the affirmative values of motoring, by Mary Carolyn Davies, which appeared in *Sunset* magazine in 1925, seems doubly and ironically appropriate. It is called "Motor Honeymoon":

We shall sleep yet beneath star-broken skies;
And wake with winds of morning in our eyes.
We shall discover worlds and fields and ways
To make adventures out of quiet days.

Out of your days and mine, that we have vowed
To join together for the little while
Of life. We'll leave the cities and the crowd
To take the world of roads, grey mile on mile.

We shall drive yet into the setting sun;
And feel the dusk and feel the dewy night;
And make, like God, a world from nothingness
And say 'let there be dark,' 'let there be light.'

The only ticking clocks we must obey
Will be your heartbeats and my heartbeats too
And we will listen to the words they say
And do the things they order us to do.[54]

Unfortunately, the co-authors of the handbook on motor-camping already referred to did not see things in quite the same rosy light. "We would not advise a newly married couple to try motor camping," they counselled. ". . . The infinite variety of experience that motor camping offers is likely to bring some things that will tend to cloud the honeymoon, and the young couple had best have a year or two of experience in trying out the problem of living together before undertaking camping."[55]

Cars on the Land

A contemporary American social critic has complained that the automobile and all its appurtenances have so completely overrun the American scene that a point has been reached where "any place an automobile can go is probably not worth visiting," and that "it is now possible to drive across the face of the nation without feeling that you've been anywhere or done anything."[56] Such wry comments make the present age seem a far cry indeed from the days of the Nineteen-Twenties, when there really was an element of fun and adventure in motoring and for a brief period the automobile seemed to hold more promise of bringing man back to nature than threat of removing him ever further from it.

Yet even in the literature of the time one detects a certain ambivalence with regard to the interrelations of mass motorization and the pre-existing landscape. As an interesting example, we may take a little book called *Our Araby*, written in 1923 by J. Smeaton Chase, an English social worker and amateur botanist who had made his home in what was then the small desert settlement of Palm Springs, which was also the subject of his book. The peak winter population of the town was then about 550, including 40 or 50 Indians. Chase loved the wildness of the area, and delighted in the primitive conditions which then prevailed in the village: "Rural free delivery does not entice us: we prefer the daily gathering at the store at mail-time. . . . Nothing seems so homelike . . . as . . . a good kerosene lamp . . . Telephones? No thanks: we are here to possess our souls and live all day in the open. . . . Cement sidewalks to us would be a calamity. . . ."[57] He realized that if the region became "too much peopled, its charm would be lost," and claimed, therefore, to be interested only in attracting "people of the right kind . . . the discerning few."[58] Nevertheless, he could not help emphasizing with apparent enthusiasm how easily accessible the area had now become by motorcar:

To breakfast late at the beach or 'in town,' to lunch leisurely at the Mission Inn at Riverside (which is strictly the *comme il faut* thing to do) and lounge for an hour afterwards among the famed groves and avenues of the citrus belt, and then, by mid-afternoon to be arriving at our little oasis in time for a cup of tea and a desert sunset—this ought to be easy enough and spectacular enough for even the sophisticated tourist of the nineteen-twenties.[59]

And even though he rejoiced that "the State highway, which threatened to bring an ever-increasing roar of automobile travel through our quiet streets, has been diverted—averted is the better word—to the north side of the valley,"[60] he seems scarcely to have been aware that the increased accessibility provided by the motorcar would in itself do much to change the area almost beyond recognition. (Its winter population increased about seventy-fold over the next 40 years, and the land owned by the "40 or 50 Indians" and their descendants was by 1963 worth about $41,000,000.[61] Somewhere in the interim the Palm Springs community appears to have had a change of heart about the introduction of such amenities as telephones and cement sidewalks.)

From a short-term point of view, it did, indeed, appear that there was something essentially salutary about the fact that men and women were now able to venture out with safety into what had formerly been considered a hostile wilderness. It was only natural that for some travellers feelings of admiration began to replace the fearfulness with which such areas had hitherto been regarded. As the editors of *Sunset* expressed it in 1926, "Once it was customary to speak of the desert regions of the West as 'the country God forgot.' But as we become better acquainted with the awe-inspiring grandeur and beauty of these waste places the conviction grows upon us that here, after all, we are in the very presence of God."[62] Yet it was equally possible for sudden new mastery over a forbidding environment to produce a certain disdain for obstacles which could now be so easily overcome. Rockwell Hunt conveyed some of this feeling when he described how "motorists may now go with ease and comfort . . . where the pioneers suffered and died. . . . Death Valley, . . . now but a diversion to many seeking to experience a new thrill, . . . [is] visited in luxury today."[63] The process was already under way whereby it would eventually become difficult to find any truly wild area left in Southern California. As a contemporary authority on the geographical aspects of the region has observed:

Although large areas of wild landscape remain on mountains and in some desert areas, the mark of urban man is heavy upon it. Nearly 8 million strong, he jams its roads and highways. He hikes through it, camps in it, and gets lost in it. In season he skis down its slopes and breaks his bones on them. He burns it and litters it, until the wild landscape, too, is in a sense urbanized.[64]

But it was not only by facilitating the access of man that cars and roads helped to change the landscape. In fact, they themselves became important features of the landscape in their own right. In 1921 a motor-traveller who had come over the Tioga Pass commented that in so rugged a setting "Alpenstock and the picturesque Swiss mountaineers might appeal to the more romantic as less out of place . . . than a modern motor car;"[65] but this consciousness of the incongruity of the new machines with natural objects was quick to disappear as the automobile became a more and more common sight everywhere in California. The rotogravure section of *Touring Topics* seemed to specialize in photographs contrasting the hard angular lines of motor cars with the flowing shapes of trees and hills. Its cover illustrations often depicted a car in some kind of natural setting, but there was an interesting evolution during the decade from pictures in which the car itself was the dominant feature to those in which it was often made to appear merely as part of a landscape. Finally in 1929 the magazine's covers, for the first time, abandoned the automobile itself altogether and instead depicted nothing but car-less landscapes. Perhaps the automobile had already become too common on the land to be considered pictorially interesting.

By the end of the decade, there were children living in Southern California who could not remember a time when the streets had not been full of parked and moving cars. Cars for them were more or less a part of the natural scenery, a constant temptation to be played with, as one would play upon rocks or climb trees. The children in Peter Viertel's novel *The Canyon* lived in an area close to the beach where the curbs were often solidly lined with parked vehicles. "Keetcheye and Jimmy once had a contest to see who could walk the farthest along the streets without touching the ground. They went quite a way, climbing from one car to the other until Keetcheye put all of his weight on the hood of an old Cadillac and it caved in. There was a man sitting inside who made quite a fuss about it."[66]

Roads were perhaps even more prominent features of the new "rurban" landscape than the cars themselves. Dirt roads had, by no means, entirely disappeared by the end of the decade, especially those that had come to be known as "recreational roads." The State Highway Commission was, in 1928, still recommending the application of oil to these roads two or three times during the summer as the best known "dust palliative."[67] (It is interesting to note the many varied capacities in which oil served the new motor age—not only by fueling and lubricating its vehicles, but also by surfacing its roads and smothering its puncture vines.) But as early as May 1919 the Los Angeles *Evening Express* was commenting on the fact that dirt roads were becoming a rarity in Southern California and quoting one regretful motorist to the effect that, as much as the efficiency of motoring might be improved by the addition of artificial surfaces, there was something about a natural surface that he was sorry to lose:

> I've been a consistent booster for all of our good road bond issues . . . but I still have to confess to a sneaking fondness for an occasional trip over a good dirt road, and actually it's getting to a point where you have to hunt a good while to find a dirt road of any length anywhere near Los Angeles. In fact, about the longest stretch of dirt road that I know of begins just the other side of Temecula and leads out to Aguanga and Oak Grove. But that is about a hundred miles from L.A., and it is pavement all the way there.[68]

A much stronger expression of the same kind of feeling was given utterance by the motor-hating English philosopher C. E. M. Joad who, seeing the same process going on his own country, protested that the "improvement" of roads was one of "the horrors of the countryside," that every time a country lane was paved for the benefit of cars, "another weal left by the whiplash of civilisation seams the face of the land."[69] Not only the paving of roads but also their straightening meant a certain loss of values in the minority of minds not entirely motorized. In 1925, an organization called the California Outdoor Art League went rather heroically on record as being concerned about the threat to picturesque scenery represented by the state engineers' constant program of curve-cutting on hitherto winding highways. The Los Angeles *Daily News* gave such protests short shrift. "Too many curves are death curves, where lives of whole families are sometimes snuffed out," it argued. "And, too, the straight line has its beauty in which the driver of the car can share, which is something he cannot do when he must constantly negotiate hairpin turns."[70] It is interesting to note that some modern critics of highway design are now arguing that a straight road can be less safe than one with curves, since "it is monotonous and fatiguing [and] it encourages excessive speeds, since the driver tries to get it over with."[71]

But despite touches of nostalgia, most Southern Californians did not hesitate to agree with Thomas Murphy that in order to "get the best of this wonderful country . . . surrounding Los Angeles," automobiles and good paved roads, running "into the deep recesses of hill and valley, to unfrequented nooks along the seashore, and above all to the slopes and summits of the mountains [were] surely the nearest approach to the ideal."[72] And even Dr. Joad felt obliged to admit that he himself had a fondness for the railroads which the sensitive souls of an earlier generation had seen as desecrating the landscape.[73]

Aesthetics and Conservation

But even if steel cars and concrete roads could, in time, come to be accepted as quasi-natural features of the land, there are many other aspects of the process of motorization in Southern California that were much more difficult to incorporate into any new aesthetic scheme. Since it was now so much easier for people to spread themselves over the land, the "deep recesses" and "unfrequented nooks" soon lost much of their charm. The land began to undergo what Dr. Joad called a transition from a land of beauty to a land of beauty spots.[74] The highways began to change from links between communities to actual extensions of them, provoking one of the most interesting intellectual controversies of the era. For even among the most ardent enthusiasts of the new automotive age, there were those who were not altogether sure to what extent they ought to approve of the process whereby commercial urban civilization pushed itself out along the roadsides in the form of advertising signs, eating establishments, gasoline stations, and numerous other types of enterprises. After all, one of the great delights of motoring had supposedly been that it enabled one to get out into "the country." But unless the use of roadsides was somehow controlled, there would be no "country" for the automobile traveller to see. Ogden Nash once put the problem very succinctly:

> I think that I shall never see
> A billboard lovely as a tree.
> Perhaps unless the billboards fall,
> I'll never see a tree at all.[75]

On the other hand, of course, the fact that constantly increasing streams of people were now travelling in their own vehicles in numerous well-channeled routes over the land meant that there now existed vast new areas of human needs, desires, and susceptibilities which it was only natural for other people to wish to take advantage of. The more motorists used the roads, the more roadside businesses and billboards sprang up which threatened that sense of escape which had been one of the major appeals of the automobile. Complicated questions of aesthetics, economics, and ethics were involved. Was it more important for a road to be "scenic" or commercially functional? Where did the public interest really lie? To what extent ought aesthetic considerations be allowed to impinge upon the rights of property? The decade of the Twenties saw the problem itself in full flower, but the matter of how best to deal with it was only beginning to be seriously discussed.

As early as 1922, the Biennial Report of the California Highway Commission called attention to the fact that convenience and safety were no longer the only factors involved in the maintenance of "good roads." There was also a matter of beauty, hitherto more or less taken for granted, but now something which would have to be actively defended: "It would seem that the creation of a public sentiment against the nightmare of futuristic advertising that litters up the landscape and renders unsightly the vicinity of state and county highways might be a matter worthy of the attention of newspapers, women's clubs, and civic bodies generally."[76] Such public sentiment did gradually find organized expression; but in the meantime, some indignant individuals had their own ways of making their feelings known. The President of the American Civic Association, while reporting with satisfaction, in 1924, that the courts "particularly in California have spoken of the necessity of recognizing the aesthetic as a factor in life," seemed equally pleased to report that he knew of a man

> who carries in his car a short crowbar, with which he regularly tears down signs erected during the day along the pleasant highway that takes him home in the evening. Further, he has equipped several of the trucks he uses with proper lengths of wire rope, and in some way these seem to get entangled with the larger signs so that they do not stay up! This man declares that he has a right to see the beauty of the landscape.[77]

In 1927, the California State Director of Public Works, Bert B. Meek, argued that the state highways needed wider rights of way in order that their borders might be protected "against disfigurement by 'hot dog' stands and unsightly shacks," an appeal which moved even the *Press* of sleepy El Centro to fiery eloquence: ". . . away with the whole blooming mess of them! The State . . . should . . . show . . . compassion on . . . the human eye, and protect it from this epidemic of jazzomania that affronts 'El Camino Real' and all the lesser 'reals.' "[78] In an effort to combat this particular form of roadside blight on a national scale, the Art Center of New York conducted a national beauty contest for hot-dog stands in 1928, with $1,000 in prizes being offered by Mrs. John D. Rockefeller, Jr. Seven hundred competitors submitted photographs and designs, and it was a source of considerable local pride that two of the top prizes were won by Southern California establishments, Young's stand outside of Ontario, and The Hut near San Diego—the latter "a ground-hugging little nook with palm-leaf thatched roof which the judges said harmonized admirably with the surrounding scenery."[79]

Thus did the automotive age set about establishing its own new aesthetic standards. For if there were going to be commercialized roadsides at all, certain minimal standards of good taste ought at least to be encouraged. A similar process was taking place with regard to the housing of the private automobile. At first little consideration had been given to the appearance of the structure in which a car owner kept his vehicle. Usually it was a detached shed of some kind. During the Twenties, however, with all the emphasis upon the car as a mere extension of one's home, it became fashionable to give this concept literal meaning by incorporating the garage into the general design of one's house. As *Touring Topics* commented on a page illustrating how aesthetically this was now being done, the motorcar could "no longer . . . be relegated to a converted woodshed or a renovated stable."[80]

There were two notable instances of response to public opinion in the matter of roadside aesthetics during the decade. First, in 1924, the Standard Oil Company of California made the following remarkable announcement:

> Convinced that highway advertising signs detract from the natural beauty of the great routes of travel of the Pacific coast, this company has decided that it will immediately remove all of its signs of this nature now standing. Hereafter, the company will confine its use of signs to commercial locations.[81]

This significant decision, the first of its kind to achieve any publicity, meant the removal of 1,100 large billboards which the company had been maintaining, leaving the field wide open for its competitors. It was based, according to the National Council for the Protection of Roadside Beauty, on the sound argument that, "The more beauty, the more travel; the more travel, the more gas."[82] It does not, indeed, appear to have damaged the profits of the company; but on the other hand it did little to alleviate the problem. Other firms did not follow the Standard Oil example, and the removed signs were soon replaced by thousands of others.

The second important action, though equally futile from the agitators' point of view as it turned out, was the appointment, in 1929 by the state legislature, of a committee "to investigate and make recommendations concerning the possibility of regulating and controlling the locations of gasoline stations, hot-dog stands, advertising signs, and other structures of a commercial nature along scenic roads and highways."[83] This Committee did not report until 1931, and when it did, the report turned out to be an almost complete exoneration of the commercial interests, with no recommendation for any further legislation, and a general conclusion that, if there was any problem at all, "the matter is righting itself under present laws and conditions in an intelligent and effective way."[84]

Critics of this report alleged that nearly a third of its general text had been taken bodily from, and that much more was based largely upon, two booklets issued earlier by Foster and Kleiser, at that time and to this day California's largest outdoor advertising firm.[85] As a firm specializing in publicity, Foster and Kleiser were particularly adept at advertising themselves and the right of their industry to exist and prosper. The legislative committee's report stated, "Our investigation revealed that not one signboard regularly maintained by a standard up-to-date company had been so located that it marred the view of any highway."[86] But a counter-report issued by the National Council for the Protection of Roadside Beauty flatly challenged this conclusion, giving many examples and photographs, including one showing a large roadside billboard almost obliterating a country hillside view, bearing only this legend:

FOSTER AND KLEISER

*THIS NAME DISTINGUISHES OUTDOOR ADVERTISING
PLACED AND MAINTAINED WITH RESPECT TO THE
PUBLIC'S BEST INTEREST*[87]

While denying that the beauty of the landscape was in any danger, the committee maintained that highways were "just the extension of commercial city streets,"[88] and that roadside businesses ought to be regarded, not as a blight on the land, but as "pioneers of future industry."[89] In any case, aesthetics were a very individual matter. Even a forest fire, especially when seen at night from a distance, might seem scenically grand to some people (the implication here apparently being that proponents of roadside control who were alleged to be largely motivated by unspecified selfish interests[90] were just the kind of fanatics who would enjoy the aesthetic satisfaction of seeing a forest burn.)[91] On the other hand, certain artificial roadside objects might acquire enhanced beauty when there was no "scenery" to be seen:

> The scenic wonder by daylight becomes a foreboding and darkened pathway 'after dark.' Welcome indeed would be the beacon of a well-lighted gasoline station or artistic signboard. Such would do

more to relieve the uneasy feeling of [the] traveller and be of greater value than would the commensurate dissatisfaction that might be suffered by the aesthetic sense of some purely artistic individual.[92]

The National Council for Protection of Roadside Beauty called this report an "amazing and amusing document,"[93] and professed to be astonished at the extent to which commercial interests had gained control of the situation:

Californians, if anyone, should recognize the wiles of the adver-tiser, but they seem strangely credulous. Given extra lattice-work around the panels, so-called gardens in front of a few boards . . . and free posters for philanthropic projects—and they are willing to forget that the highways of California are being cheapened and uglified. They shudder at the thought of 'interfering with business' and ignore the fact that the tourist business, which depends upon scenic beauty, is almost the leading business of the state. . . . They even accept at its face value the outrageous claim that the organ-ized billboard industry is beautifying the landscape.[94]

With battle of interests so sharply joined, no outcome other than some ungainly form of compromise seemed possible. The first comprehensive attempt at a settlement of the problem on a statewide basis was advanced in 1929 by the California Development Association, subse-quently to become the State Chamber of Commerce. It was known as the California Scenic Reserve Plan, and proposed, in effect, that the roads of the state should be classified either as scenic or as commercial, with commercial activity, particularly advertising, being confined to the roads so designated. This scheme was to be carried out on a voluntary basis, with owners of the land bordering scenic stretches signing promises not to rent their land for advertising purposes. The National Council for Protection of Roadside Beauty objected to this plan, protesting that the roads designated as scenic were usually those used only by tourists and vacationers, "whereas the public clamors for beauty along the everyday highways, beauty which may be enjoyed as we pass to and fro in our daily affairs." Knowing that the alleged public clamor was not likely to be satisfied while the individual profit motive was given free rein, the Council called for legislation and zoning as the only satisfactory solution.[96]

It ought not to be supposed that the men responsible for building and maintaining the state's highway system were themselves entirely blind to aesthetic considerations. Where they had power, they often did what they could to preserve the beauty of the roadsides; but this power was very narrowly circumscribed. A division engineer like S. V. Courtelyou could see to it that an application to remove seven eucalyptus trees on Foothill Boulevard "which hide our two places of business— the oil station on the corner and our florist stand" was turned down on the grounds that "these trees are fine, large specimens, located in a practically unbroken row of eucalyptus trees extending along the highway for over a mile. To permit even the beginning of the cutting of these trees would be injuring one of the finest drives in the highway system."[97] But these men had no power to check roadside "development" beyond the state's right-of-way, which accordingly proceeded at a feverish pace, especially in Southern California. Foothill Boulevard, which was the main highway between Pasadena and San Bernardino, was, in fact, one of the worst examples of rampant commercialism. In 1921, Thomas D. Murphy had described it as probably the most beautiful roadway in the world with palms, roses, and groves of oranges and olives in the foreground and snow-capped mountains in the background.[98] Ten years later, the 44 miles lying between the 13 towns on this road were found to be lined with 324 signboards, 74 filling stations, 9 garages, 117 food stands, inns, and roadside markets, 8 real estate offices, 33 stores, 4 industries, and one junkyard.[99]

Jan and Cora Gordon described in a graphic passage the dismal "rurban" sprawl which mass motorization had made of Los Angeles by the Late Twenties:

> We were able to take longer excursions in our old car. . . . Northward we had to drive twenty miles to be free of the interminable succession of raw villages, towns, bungalow courts, real estate promoters, and gasoline stations. Westward, through twelve miles of almost continuously inhabited areas, we reached the sea. . . . Southward for thirty miles . . . small villa holdings were alternated with oil-wells and petroleumized desolation; south-eastward, along the flank of the Sierra Madre, one could drive for almost sixty miles among raw towns and hot-dog stalls. Even beyond the town limits advertisements on farms and houses showed the commercial spirit. Oranges—Figs—Home-Made Soups—Rhode Island Red Chicks—Peppers—Puppies—Encino Watch It Grow— Pruning and Tree Surgery—Eggs—Honey—Concord Grapes— See Movie Animal In Person—cocoanut Ice—Mahjong Teacher— Voice Placement—Grape Juice—Prunes—and a petrol station every five minutes without intermission. In fact no one who had only an hour or two to spare could possibly shake himself free from the city, with its crude eye-aching newness.[100]

But it was not only the abstract and somewhat debatable aesthetic values of natural or rural scenery which the new "Octopus" of automobility appeared to threaten with extinction. The flora and fauna of the land itself were exposed to danger in numerous new ways. A newspaper columnist, for example, pointed out, in 1924, that "since the advent of the automobile . . . in California . . . it is so easy now to reach the mountains and forests that the chances for conflagrations have increased many fold."[101] But a bill which passed the State Assembly, in 1929, which would have required "receptacles to receive and extinguish cigar and cigarette stubs" as standard equipment in all automobiles was apparently subsequently defeated on the grounds that it was only an attempt to boost the sale of auto accessories.[102] There appears to have been a general prejudice against any "freak law" which would have the effect of increasing the cost of motoring.[103]

The more organized process of forest destruction known as lumbering was, of course, facilitated by motor vehicles but reached a peculiar kind of compromise with the champions of roadside beauty. Agreements were worked out between lumber companies and the State Highway Department whereby enough trees were to be left standing on the land adjacent to the highways ("timber fringes" was the term employed) "to give the impression of uncut forest as one travels along the highway."[104] The happy but not too inquisitive motorist might thus enjoy the sense of being surrounded by virgin timber, oblivious of the fact that the timber fringe was itself a kind of artificial screen maintained merely to protect his aesthetic sensitivities.

In the case of the wild flowers the problem was somewhat different; for here it was the highway travellers themselves who were generally the culprits and the roadside areas which were most immediately in danger of spoliation. *Touring Topics* began to warn its readers in 1922 that since "with the extension of the highway system and the increase in the number of motorists, the wild blossoms of mountain, valley, and desert are becoming yearly more accessible to an increasing number of motorists. . . . there is real danger that the wild flower glories of California will be dimmed and diminished."[105]

It is worth noting that the problem of litter, which in subsequent decades has become a major concern of those interested in highway aesthetics, does not appear even to have been recognized as a problem during the decade of the Twenties. To throw rubbish out of one's car was simply a matter of keeping the car's interior clean and tidy. The notion that things discarded by human beings could actually deface the landscape took time to make headway against the earlier idea that open land was simply a natural dumping ground.

But it was the mass assault upon animal life that began in the Nineteen Twenties which owed most to the motor car. "It is but too certain," wrote J. Smeaton Chase in 1923, "that since the appearance of the automobile (the worst foe of wild game everywhere) on the desert, the [wild big-horn] sheep have fallen victims to illicit shooting to a terrible extent. Parties of 'sports' . . . lolling at ease in high powered cars, now invade every part of the desert . . . and blaze away at anything that moves, in mere intoxication of blood-lust."[106] Leslie T. White described how one Los Angeles millionaire amused himself by sitting in his parked car in a wooded area at night, leaving the headlights on, and shooting deer which were attracted by the lights— without even having to get up out of his seat.[107] By 1926, a writer in *Sunset* was complaining that "the West's biggest and best trout streams" were becoming "barren of fish because they are accessible by motor."[108] And in 1929 H. C. Bryant described the hunters of California as a "mobilized" and "wonderfully equipped . . . army": "Its reconnoitoring is easily accomplished at a great distance from its base; a few hours puts a company on the firing line and routs the enemy from its most secret hiding places."[109]

Southern California in the Twenties thus saw the intensification of a process which has been characteristic of the relation of Man to Land in America since the earliest white settlements: the unregulated or under-regulated exploitation of apparently limitless resources. By one of the many paradoxes with which automotive social history abounds, the very beauty and bounty of the land, with the aid of the motorcar, was hastening its own undoing.

The Changing Metropolis

The automobile effected an amazing transformation in the Los Angeles metropolitan scene within an amazingly short space of time. The boom of the Twenties saw the city extending its boundaries almost monthly, and the pattern of expansion bore very little relationship to existing transportation facilities. Development came to be postulated upon the idea that people would travel mostly in their own cars and that there would somehow be enough adequate roads and other facilities to take care of all the traffic. The electric railway system went into a decline from which it never recovered, and while serious discussion of the need for what was called "rapid transit" began as early as 1923,[110] the private motorcar took such a firm grip upon the consciousness of the community that the solution of traffic problems always tended to be seen primarily in terms of more space for more cars. This occurred despite what appears to have been the prevailing assumption that, as one writer put it, "A comprehensive subway system will, in time, be inevitable."[111]

From this point of view, Los Angeles was seen to be at a distinct disadvantage as compared with most other cities. Investigators of the traffic problem soon discovered that the city which had the country's greatest number of automobiles per 1,000 inhabitants also had "one of the lowest percentages of street areas of any of the major cities of the U.S."[112] There were "surprisingly few streets of generous width." The main business district devoted only 21.5 percent of its area to street space, as compared with 34 percent in Pittsburgh and 44 percent in Washington D.C.[113] It was easy to come to the conclusion that if only there were more and wider streets the problem of congestion would be eliminated.

Accordingly, a massive program of city road building and improvement was embarked upon, possibly the greatest in scope since Baron Haussmann's face-lifting of Paris, though much more piecemeal in nature. That this was not the answer, however, soon became abundantly clear. As George B. Anderson, Transportation Manager of the Los Angeles Railway, wrote in 1928, "In Los Angeles . . . where many miles of existing streets have been widened and straightened and where some new thoroughfares have been built, it has been shown that, the more street room is provided, the greater the use of automobiles. A newly opened . . . or widened street immediately becomes glutted by the access of cars that hitherto have reposed more in their garages than they have utilized the streets."[114]

Besides the insufficiency of street space, another alleged cause of congestion was what Paul G. Hoffman of the Los Angeles Traffic Commission called "the promiscuous mixing of various types of traffic."[115] Attempts to relieve this, particularly in the form of pedestrian tunnels and grade separations, led to further changes in the face of the city. A book of photographs celebrating its achievements in municipal architecture, which the city published in 1928, revealed the civic pride attaching to such projects.[116] Despite lack of public enthusiasm, the County of Los Angeles did manage to separate some thirty railroad-highway grade crossings during the decade, largely through the work of a non-official civic group known as the Los Angeles County Grade Crossing Committee, which published an interesting report on its progress in 1930, showing that although the structures erected to keep cars and trains from running into each other often added little to the aesthetic value of the urban landscape, they could, occasionally, especially if constructed of reinforced concrete rather than of raw steel, have quite a striking beauty of their own.

Moreover, this was becoming a factor of increasing importance in the design of such projects. "The public at large are demanding that such structures be pleasing to the eye," wrote one engineer. ". . . Good architectural treatment of the grade separation . . . adds to the pleasure of the travelling public and acts as an advertisement of the charm of the locality."[117] The problem of eliminating all grade crossings was enormous, however, for new ones were continually being created in the process of building new roads. Between 1915 and 1930, 2,000 new grade crossings appeared in California, while only 100 were separated.[118] But the need, felt the Committee, was imperative, not only because of the tremendous inconvenience and economic loss involved in making cars wait for trains to pass, but also because, despite all the protective devices such as wig-wag signals, warning lights, gates and flagmen, cars and trains continued to collide, largely because there were always some drivers who would neglect all warnings or who simply seemed bent upon denying the possibility of any obstacle in their path. There were in fact "a surprisingly large number of . . . collisions . . . where automobiles plunge head-on into the side of a standing or passing train."[119]

The influence of motorization was becoming as visible in patterns of housing and shopping as upon the streets and highways. Automobility enabled separate single story homes on large lots to become the characteristic type of Southern California dwelling, since land was still plentiful and there was no need to crowd in close to the metropolitan center or to the rail lines which radiated from it.[120] At the same time the interurban and intracity lines, which had hitherto served the region so well, failed to extend their services to these new residential areas or to establish ring routes connecting the outlying areas with each other rather than solely with the urban center.[121] This happened partly because of rising commodity prices and partly because there was no assurance (so deeply and rapidly had the private automobile become entrenched) that patronage from the newly settled areas would be sufficient to cover even the cost of operations.[122] This, of course, in turn created an even greater need for every home owner to have his own means of transportation. And it explains why Daisy C. Breeden, writing the following poem in 1928, saw the twilight hour in Los Angeles primarily in terms of weary automotive commuters returning through the din of heavy traffic to quiet suburban homes, only apparently to be off again somewhere in their cars as soon as the evening meal was over.

TWILIGHT IN LOS ANGELES

The hills of Hollywood, turned purple-gray
Against the gold sky of a waning day

Seem, like a wall'd fortress, to enclose
The city of the Angels in repose.

Afar across the city's wide expanse
A thousand twinkling lights begin to dance;
And then, a thousand more, while as you gaze,
The whole horizon seems to be ablaze!

The eager, roaring traffic homeward pours,
Emptying its weary burden at the doors
Of hill-side home or Spanish bungalow
Italian villa, cottage, studio.

Too brief the magic hour of twilight, soon
Aloft the sky appears the yellow moon;
Too soon the spell is gone, again the blare
Of traffic rends the stillness of the air.[123]

The lights of moving automobiles at night in the city appear, incidentally, to have constituted one of the most impressive visual features of the new motor age. One writer described them turning wet streets into "rivers of molten gold."[124] Another likened them to "animated stars or enlarged fireflies, each adding its bit to the beauty of the night-time spectacle."[125] With typical Southern Californian love of display, the motorists of Los Angeles went to great lengths to heighten the spectacle. Many cars bore, in addition to the regulation lights, "red or even triple spots, blue side runners, red yellow and white tail lights, beacons on their hoods, and smaller eyes under the fenders."[126]

Naturally each bungalow, villa, and cottage needed a place for its vehicle(s), and, as already indicated, what was known as "the inside garage," whereby "one can depart from or arrive at home at any time without obliging the driver to pass from the protection of the home roof"[127] was becoming increasingly popular. By 1925, Southern California builders were incorporating garages with space for two cars in nearly all better-class homes.[128] A survey of advertisements of houses for sale in the classified section of the Los Angeles Times shows an interesting change with regard to garages between 1919 and 1929. On January 5, 1919, for example, 293 houses were advertised for sale, of which 106 were specified as having a garage, including 18 with double garages. On October 20, 1929 (both dates chosen at random) there were 270 houses for sale, but only 49 of the advertisements mentioned garages. Presumably garages had by then become so common that it was taken for granted that the house would have one, and it would tend to be mentioned only if larger than average. For of the 49, 20 were double garages, 10 were three-car, and 2 were four-car.

The interior of the home itself was also changing in response to the new motorized way of life. In an article of 1924 on "The Automobile and the Home of the Future," John F. Harbeson commented that, "With the automobile at the curb, the home needs to be less a place to live in because it is so easy to get away from." The spacious old-fashioned kitchen and dining room were, accordingly, on the way out. Bedrooms, too, were becoming smaller, more like "the pullman car compartment or the stateroom on a steamer, comfortable enough for the few hours we spend in them." The spare room would also soon be a thing of the past, since guests would just as easily be able to lodge at "a nearby inn."[129]

With a car at nearly every family's disposal, business development no longer had to locate itself along streetcar lines. The first significant departure in this direction occurred in 1922 when a few business blocks were experimentally erected on Western Avenue, a broad residential street which had no streetcar line. The experiment proved so successful that the bungalows and apartment buildings which formerly lined the street were soon being moved away to less valuable sites as land values along Western Avenue sky-rocketed.[130] The modern supermarket, a kind of store catering especially to customers who could provide their own transportation home for bulky purchases, was born in Los Angeles during the Nineteen-Twenties.[131] The transition in shopping practices which was taking place is indicated, for example, by the fact that, in 1925, the ten Markets of the Ralph's chain, while offering free home delivery for all purchases amounting to over $1.00, also offered price reductions on many heavy items like sugar, flour, grain and potatoes if the customer would carry them away himself.[132] The huge downtown Hills Brothers garage, already mentioned, afforded its patrons the convenience of a system whereby their shopping purchases in the downtown stores might be delivered directly to the garage.[133]

Most remarkable of all commercial adaptations to the automotive way of life, however, was the planning and building during this decade of an entire shopping center at a spot in western Los Angeles which was virtually uninhabited, but which was within easy driving range of a number of well-established residential areas. The man responsible for this imaginative and highly successful scheme was a realtor named A. W. Ross, and his project was given the name of the "Miracle Mile." At some time in the early Twenties, Ross decided that he was going to build what was probably the world's first business district designed especially for the motor age. Calculating that people with cars would be willing to travel at least four miles to go shopping, he sought a location rich in potential automotive hinterland. He selected a spot far out on Wilshire Boulevard, then occupied by nothing but bean fields but within four miles of some of the most exclusive residential districts in Southern California, including Hollywood, Beverly Hills, and West Adams Heights.[134]

The idea was not unopposed, particularly by those whose concern for the land went beyond the question of its market value. One group of opponents, fearing that the realization of Ross's plan would mean the end of Wilshire Boulevard as a street of beautiful homes, published an advertisement which showed a large octopus with tentacles encircling those homes beside a line of billboards bearing such messages as "This home to be wrecked—splendid locations for filling stations, garages, hot-dog stands . . . etc.—Greed & Grab, agents."

Ross won out, however, and the Miracle Mile became one of the commercial showplaces of Southern California. One notable feature of its planning was that ample provision was made for customers to be able to park their cars in lots off the street in the rear of the buildings. The rear entrances to the buildings from the parking lots were, therefore, actually the main entrances, and were made more elaborate than those facing Wilshire Boulevard itself.[135]

Although streets, houses, and shops underwent tremendous changes as a result of the automotive revolution, there was one kind of facility which appeared upon the urban and urbanized landscape in response to the Mass Automobile which was as new, in essence, as the motor car itself. This was an institution variously known as the filling station, gas station, or service station. In the form it assumed in the Southern California of the Nineteen-Twenties, it can hardly be said to have evolved out of the hardware store or the smithy where autoists in the early days of motoring customarily procured fuel, lubricants, and the possibility of mechanical aid; but those were its closest lineal antecedents. As motoring became a mass activity, the supplying of gasoline and oil to motorists became a lucrative and highly competitive business. Great chains of gasoline stations were established, often associated with particular oil companies.

Because of the intense competition and the many new needs which mass motoring produced, these stations had to appeal to the public in a variety of ways. As usual in things automotive, Southern California went the limit in outlandish celebration of the new institution. When a new Calpet gas station was opened in Los Angeles at Washington and Crenshaw in 1926, for example, the spot, according to a *Times* account, was marked by a giant captive balloon carrying a cutout banner illuminated by a spotlight. Pennants were strung from all corners of the station; "a 325 hp. generator from one of the motion-picture studios furnished an elaborate display of arcs and colored lights," while "Comely girls in Calpet costumes with silk shoulder streamers and chic Calpet caps pass out cigars to men, confections to women, and balloons to the children."[136]

It was recognized that the appearance of such stations was an important factor in their ability to attract patronage. "Proper landscaping," for example, was to be considered "a business asset," according to a manual for prospective service station proprietors published in Los Angeles in 1927. "Women especially favor the station which has been made inviting through the generous use of growing things but men also appreciate beauty, though they may not speak of it."[137]

It was during this period of "hurly-burly commercial growth," as one modern architectural authority puts it, that Los Angeles, "Seeking some cultural touchstone . . . harked back to its early heritage. The Spanish style was revived for many distinguished residential, religious, and institutional buildings."[138] Among the buildings thus designed (which also incidentally included the new headquarters of the Automobile Club of Southern California at Adams and Figueroa, opened in 1923) were gasoline stations that steeped themselves in the Spanish tradition, as well as in a number of other traditions equally dubious. The manual cited above recommended a "type of building [which] looks substantial and permanent and encourages a good class of trade . . . It may be fashioned over Moorish lines or may follow the attractive Mission type of architecture with its arcades, iron grills, and simulated balconies."[139] (An appearance of substance and permanence was of course particularly to be desired in a city which, as Matt Weinstock recalled, had at that time so decided an air of impermanence that there was a popular expression, "Don't buy anything you can't put on the Santa Fe Chief.")[140] With Southern California in the lead, the whole country was soon blossoming out in "Old English," "Georgian," and "fairy-tale cottage" gas stations.[141] (See Figure 20)

Equally as important as attracting the customer with visual artifice was the matter of providing facilities for his personal convenience. Filling station proprietors were advised that "many a sale is made" through the provision of toilet and washing facilities, universally known as "restrooms,"[142] or sometimes jocularly as "emptying-stations."[143] California gas stations, especially those controlled by the larger companies, were remarked upon by cross country travellers as having unusually clean and well-furnished restrooms.[144] Drinking fountains, telephones, and directional information, often in the form of free maps, also came to be expected by the gas station customer.

In addition, of course, there was the car to be taken care of. One

Southern California couple driving eastwards found that "a service we are so accustomed to at home . . . the courteous cleaning of your windshield and glass by service station employees" was not nearly as common in other parts of the country.[145] California station men were cautioned that . . . "The car owner expects instant service. He is impatient if he has to wait even a few moments. He is restless until he gets his car back on the road." He must, therefore, at all times be provided with "peppy service."[146] This service was coming to mean far more than the mere providing of gasoline and oil.

Many service stations were evolving into "super-service stations" where different departments offered a wide variety of automotive services, such as lubrication, washing, polishing, tire service, brake service, and mechanical repairs, all on one lot. Those thinking of establishing such stations were told that "Splendid profits . . . are possible [since] every car that drives onto the lot is a prospect for every department of super-service at one time or another." But in the matter of selecting sites, they were warned to "avoid subdivisions that are too new. Even if they are built up, the people who live in such neighborhoods are usually saddled-up with heavy trust-deeds on their places and, with other payments, have little to spend on keeping up automobiles."[147]

The type of urban landscape which the low-density housing, monster commercialism, and various motor needs of the new auto age combined to produce was one which sensitive observers like Jan and Cora Gordon found an affront both to the eye and to one's sense of individual human dignity, especially for someone who simply wanted to take a walk for pleasure:

> The large rectangular monotony of the town . . . gave [one] almost a horror of venturing on foot in the streets. There was, indeed, small pleasure in such exercise. At a pedestrian pace the eye could feast only on endless repetitions of low houses, green lawns cut with pavements and set with fern palms, long lines of boardings plastered with huge and garish posters, crude square open shops made from raw bricks, garages and gasoline stations, and numberless street-crossings which one was not allowed to pass over unless the signal lights permitted.[148]

AFTERMATH

"Until 1929," wrote Matt Weinstock in 1947, "Los Angeles kept abreast of its problems. Since, it has fallen far behind in its planning. It may never catch up."[1] Just how such factors are to be measured may not be clear, but the investigation which produced the foregoing pages would seem to suggest that, at least as far as matters automotive in the Nineteen-Twenties were concerned, Mr. Weinstock may have been too kind to his city. But then, he was probably thinking in the terms in which most Southern Californians, and by now most Americans, regard problems connected with the automobile. Such thinking tends to go along the following lines: There are inevitably going to be more and more cars, and this is in itself a good thing. Our problem is to provide sufficient space for them, space for their movement and for their repose. Los Angeles thus "kept abreast" of its car problems in the Twenties by making more room for more cars, and it has since "fallen far behind" simply because cars have been multiplying faster than space could be made available for them. Traffic engineering has become a highly specialized science, and the man who can make two cars fit where only one could fit before is one of the heroes of the age.

The Los Angeles Traffic Commission probably thought it was being exceptionally thorough when it devoted several pages of its 1929 annual report to the parking problem; and indeed, by the standards of the time, it was. It even went so far as to differentiate between "long time parkers," "short time parkers," and "live parkers" (cars parked while still containing a driver).[2] But a glance at a book like Burrage and Mogren's *Parking* (1957) will illustrate the complexity which this particular subject later attained. The coin-operated parking meter, for example, which, together with the automatic traffic signal, may be considered the most remarkable regulatory mechanism which the mass motor age has yet produced, did not even make its first appearance until 1935.[3]

Road building underwent a similar metamorphosis, in which a fantastic system of special motor roads called "freeways," free of all cross-traffic, spread itself over the face of Southern California. Even the cars, to a certain extent, improved from the Twenties onward, although there were social critics like John Keats who insisted that "our automobiles are overblown, overpriced monstrosities built by oafs for thieves to sell to mental defectives,"[4] and although the safety factor in automotive design, which was being emphasized at least as long ago as 1940 in a book written by a Californian who had lost his wife in a motor accident,[5] has only in recent years been a primary consideration in the minds of American manufacturers. All these developments, however, growing out of the motor mania of the Nineteen-Twenties, may have been, in the eyes of later thoughtful observers, seriously misguided as far as true social progress was concerned. Wilfred Owen, for example, pointed out that "after all the roadbuilding, parking lots, street-widenings, traffic-lights, parking meters, one-way streets, and other measures designed to keep us moving, we have ended in a bigger jam than when we started. We have tried to adapt ourselves to the automotive age through improvisation when the task required fundamental changes in the whole urban environment."[6] Just what form those changes should take, however, continued to be a matter of considerable controversy.

In a 1962 interview, California architectural and urban critic Allan Temko, after blasting the automobile as "an economic waster, a space eater, and a psyche ruiner," went so far as to say that "if we got rid of all the cars, if someone put them all in a huge crate and dumped them into the ocean, the relief would be magnificent. Of course, we would be left with our sprawling civilization and the problems of communication. How would we do it? Well, I think we would have to rebuild our cities."[7] Jane Jacobs, however, was of the opinion that cities, rather than undergoing mass redesigning to accommodate the motor age, should simply change their attitude towards the tyranny of cars and begin to fight back against them:

> Possibilities for adding to convenience . . . and cheer in cities, while simultaneously hampering automobiles, are limitless. . . . If we fail to stop the erosion of cities by automobiles . . . we Americans will hardly need to ponder a mystery that has troubled men for millenia: What is the purpose of life? For us, the answer will be . . . indisputable: The purpose of life is to produce and consume automobiles.[8]

Lewis Mumford stigmatized the Los Angeles of the 1960's as "the *reductio ad absurdum* of the belief that space and rapid locomotion are the chief ingredients of a good life," suggesting that, with so much of the land already given over to the "grotesque facilities" which the automobile requires, the time is approaching "when there will be every facility for moving about the city and no possible reason for going there."[9]

There have been, of course, voices heard on the other side, but their tone has had a clearly defensive ring. When John Dykstra, president of the Ford Motor Company, spoke at the 60th annual meeting of the American Automobile Association in 1962, his speech was devoted to replying to such indictments of urban motordom as those cited above. Any cure for traffic congestion based on eliminating personal motor travel, he argued, is sure death for a city. "The city lives on traffic, as any retail merchant can tell you. I have yet to hear a merchant complain because the aisles of his stores are crowded with customers." If certain traffic problems yet remain to be solved, "perhaps the most fruitful field of inquiry will be to find ways of making more use of the automobile rather than less, to take greater advantage of the ability it gives people to spread out farther from the center city and still be a part of it." As to the aesthetics of the modern roadopolis, "highways and freeways are frequently more attractive than the construction they have replaced," and, in any case, "we have to assess them in the light of new needs."[10]

But it is not only the surface of the land which was seen by many as suffering from a vast automotive blight. The very atmosphere has fallen victim to the motor age. With an irony almost too tragic to be true, the clear blue sunny skies which more than any other factor have been responsible over the years for attracting people to Southern California and for making it a "motorist's paradise," became discolored and poisoned by the waste matter emitted daily by millions of motor vehicles. To compound the irony, the "smog" thus created had the notable effect not only of reducing visibility, damaging and killing plants, and irritating eyes, but also of cracking the tires of automobiles.

This special kind of air pollution first came to public notice in Los Angeles in 1943, though old-timers like Jackson Graves had been complaining about an unpleasant change in the urban atmosphere since at least as far back as the early 1930's.[11] But it was not until about 1954 that the exhaust gases of automobiles began to be identified as a major source.[12] There has since been no question that "the chief cause of smog in Los Angeles is the automobile."[13] Meanwhile, as with many other automotive phenomena which made their first significant appearance in Southern California, the smog problem has appeared in many other parts of the world.[14]

"Los Angeles is a city," wrote an anonymous observer in 1931, "where sorrow and joy are strangely interwoven, and where thousands of . . . people, overcome with a delirium of enthusiasm, have paid the penalty for their lack of wisdom and in the end contributed to the heartrending tragedies of the city's abnormal growth; . . . a city . . . where all . . . human endeavours are tragically overdone. . . . AND THE WORST IS YET TO COME."[15] He was referring in particular to the real estate situation, but the words might equally well be taken as an appropriate epitaph for the first decade of mass motordom in Southern California, which was, after all, very closely connected with the real estate frenzy. Jan and Cora Gordon's minds had

> staggered with horror at the vision of the real-estate salesman's ideal, when every plot shall have been bought up, and the whole area packed with a monotonous mass of undistinguished dwellings . . . when every block shall have its 'drive in' grocer's shop and . . . every corner shall have bred its gasoline station, though each may strive for the prize offered by the city for the most beautiful.[16]

Such expectations were more than fulfilled in the years which followed and the "WORST" which was yet to come has, perhaps, already been seen. But then again, in view of the perversity with which the automobile seems so far to have resisted true social control, one may be permitted to fear that perhaps it has not.

Conclusion

It seems impossible to generalize about the overall effects upon human life and thought of a phenomenon with as many diverse facets as the Mass Automobile, even when we are referring to a relatively limited geographical area during a relatively limited period of time. What can be said with reasonable certainty is that the automotive deluge hit Southern California earlier and harder than anywhere else, that this led in the short run to unusually chaotic conditions and produced long-range problems which have yet to find satisfactory solutions. On the other hand, Southern California's head start in the process of motorization enabled the region to acquire a certain automotive sophistication and to develop a kind of individual-mobility civilization which, judged entirely by its own standards, must be acknowledged as highly impressive. What is most striking about the Los Angeles of the Nineteen-Twenties is not the frequency with which people were accidentally or deliberately done to death with the aid of automobiles, but the fact that the entire community did not, so to speak, drive itself into the ground. Somehow people made adjustments, and life, in its strangely altered context, went on.

Los Angeles today may be smog-ridden, congested, and disfigured by auto urbanization almost beyond belief, but it is also a place where visitors from other parts of the country, and even more so those from foreign countries like Italy and Japan, which have suffered their own virulent forms of auto-mania, are impressed by the many courtesies extended by motorists both to pedestrians and to each other. Drivers actually stop for pedestrians in their path. If a car has difficulties in the street, the driver can nearly always find another driver to give him a push. When any kind of automobile accident does occur, help usually comes with astonishing rapidity and is administered with equally impressive efficiency. Moreover, most drivers habitually obey most traffic laws, such as the law that a car must stop at a "boulevard stop" sign, even though there may almost certainly be no officer of the law present to enforce it. Having made its fatal commitment to individual internal combustion as a way of life, Southern California at least deserves some measure of credit for doing its bewildered best to render such a kind of life liveable.

Illustrations

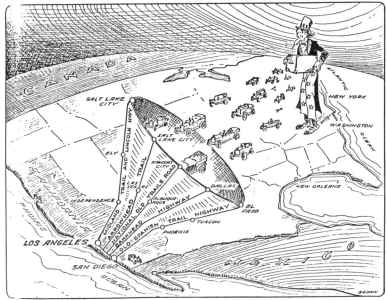

Figure 1. The Great Funnel

This cartoon from *Touring Topics* of February, 1920, rejoices in the vast new influx of auto tourists to Southern California. Notice that highways still had names rather than numbers. Numbers were assigned later in the decade after the multiplicity of names had become too confusing. Note, too, that most of the cars are depicted as being open models.

Figures 2A and 2B. The Status Symbol Par Excellence (Pages 158, 159)

This two-page spread from the August, 1924, edition of *California Sports*, published in Los Angeles, a magazine clearly intended for people of wealth, leisure, and "good taste," shows the extent to which the motorcar had come to be regarded as an article of fashion, reflecting its owner's individuality while at the same time conforming to certain social norms. The captions are worth careful study, especially in view of the fact that this was *not* an advertisement which might be expected to attempt to instil false values into prospective customers, but rather a, presumably, genuine reflection of the values which already existed among those who liked to think of themselves as belonging to the "smart set." Notice that the inferior social status of the chauffeur was emphasized by making him ride out in the open while his passengers rode behind in an enclosed section—a vestige, of course, of the earlier horse-drawn coaches on which the coachman had to ride outside in order to be able to control the horses. The expression "somewhere west of Laramie" in the caption beside the Jordan Eight refers to a famous car advertisement of the time. Note the general emphasis upon *appearance*. Fenders were still known as "mud guards," a term retained today in British usage.

WHAT THE SMART SET SELECTS IN MOTORS

HERE ARE THE THOROUGHBREDS OF CALIFORNIA HIGHWAYS

Drawn for California Sports by Byron Bruce

Making an appeal to the red-blooded sportsman in that its sheer beauty and rakishness of line are indicators of its vital endurance and swift superiority on the open road, this new Kissel Enclosed Speedster may be seen wherever one goes—at the polo games, tennis tournaments, golf clubs and other places at which discerning sport devotees foregather.

This Rolls-Royce town car—the "Salamanca"—is a new carriage of Continental lines, originally designed by Count Salamanca, of Madrid, for Rolls-Royce. In it is developed a happy combination of privacy and comfort, together with an atmosphere of extreme smartness. The rear quarter collapses, if desired, converting the passenger compartment into a perfectly wind-screened open motor carriage.

The new Cunningham Town Cabriolet has many new and distinctive features characteristic of Cunningham coach work. Among the exquisite interior appointments a mahogany compartment is provided for "milady's" jewels and for sundry small packages. There is a vanity case of sterling silver inlaid with French enamel. Tiffany reading lights are provided in the rear corners of the tonneau. The color scheme of both the interior and exterior are optional.

The new Speedway Six Sportbrohm recently offered by Stutz is a decided departure from the old Stutz in lines and coach work. Balloon tires and four wheel brakes are optional. For outside color the purchaser has the choice of Brewster green, maroon, Fleetwood blue and old wine color. This fascinating model shows the effect of European automotive fashions.

Figure 2A

Designed by the Custom Built Department of the Locomobile Company, this roadster is the latest creation of the Locomobile line. Flexible brass exhaust pipes brought out from the motor through the side of the hood add a dignified racy touch. Trimmings are of brass, nickle plate being optional.

The rakish top, the sweeping lines of the rear section which enclose the concealed emergency seat for two and the roomy compartment for luggage, the graceful curves of the fender lamps are distinctive details in the standard Pierce-Arrow roadster. The owner may express his taste in a wide choice of exterior color finish.

Murphy of Pasadena designed and built this exquisite four-passenger Phaeton on a Packard small eight chassis for E. J. Miley. Seven inch balloon tires under extra wide mud guards and the long wheel base add considerably to the outside appearance. Color is dragon fly blue striped with old ivory. The top is imported English Burbank and the upholstery is special hand buffed Spanish leather.

'A new thrill'—Jordan gave it when his Playboy Six first hit out for somewhere west of Laramie, 'n now he's promised another—the kind that made Bill Jones, motorcycle cop at Pumpkin Center, who traded a pinch of lester for a ride, say—'you ain't been nowhere and you ain't done nothing until you've driven the new Great Jordan Line Eight.

The striking contour of the standard Lincoln roadster suggests a rugged note which appeals to the motorist fond of the open road and its bevy age of doors. Exterior finish is the color of cobalt blue. Rumble apron, crushed calf or dull gray. Khaki top and gray leather upholstery are standard with the dull gray finish.

Figure 2B

Every Man: "I Wish I Had a Bus of My Own'

Figure 3

And He's in High Gear!

Figure 4

We Must Keep the Radiator Full!

Figure 5

Figure 3. A Bus of One's Own

A political cartoon from the *Los Angeles Times* of November 8, 1926. The artist, in emblazoning the car with the royal coat of arms and its motto, *"Honi soit qui mal y pense"*—"Evil be to him who evil thinks," did not, presumably, mean to imply that it was evil for people to wish to have cars of their own and that such a wish might in turn bring evil down upon them, but such an ironic interpretation adds an apt touch to the significance of the cartoon.

Figure 4. Carranza's Clutch.

The *Los Angeles Times* published this elaborate example of the Southern Californian love of seeing even international events in automotive terms, on April 25, 1920. The cartoonist has not only been able to play upon the words and expressions *Ca*rranza, *Car*-amba, revolutions, clutch, being in high gear, and keeping one's foot down, but has even managed to make the automobile parts involved resemble Mexican sombreros.

Figure 5. Keeping the Radiator Full.

There could be no more compelling imagery for reminding the Angeleno of the Nineteen-Twenties of his growing city's need for water than a comparison with his car's need for the same fluid. Los Angeles, in this cartoon from the *Los Angeles Times* of June 1, 1925, is as usual depicted as a rather gaudy Hispanic female, a representation which to Carey McWilliams very appropriately bespoke the harlot.[1]

[1] Carey McWilliams, "Los Angeles," *Overland Monthly*, Vol. LXXXV, No. 2 (February, 1927), p. 135.

Figure 6

Figure 7

Figure 6. Traffic Chaos.
This photograph, from *Nation's Traffic* magazine of August, 1928, was taken at a Los Angeles downtown intersection in 1919, before there were any traffic signals or rules prohibiting left-hand turns. Streetcars, cars, pedestrians, and horse-drawn vehicles wallow in hopeless confusion. Somewhere in the middle stands a rather forlorn policeman.

Figure 7. Traffic Discipline.
The same intersection as in Plate 6, nine years later. (Same source.) There is just as much traffic—in fact, probably a good deal more—but now it is more carefully regulated than any traffic in history. In the center of the intersection stands a little sign informing drivers that they may not turn left there even though they may wish to do so. In addition, all vehicles and pedestrians are now required to obey automatic signals directing them when to stop and when to proceed. Like all human systems, however, this one has its imperfections. The semaphore signal at the lower right-hand corner already says "GO," but there are still pedestrians in the opposing croswalk.

A CALIFORNIAN HOLIDAY   Figure 8

Figure 8. The Open Road: Artist's Conception.

This is one of the illustrations which appeared in *Star-Dust in Hollywood*, by the English couple, Jan and Cora Gordon. Should the reader suspect that these rather unsympathetic visitors to Southern California were presenting a ridiculously exaggerated caricature of the actual situation, he is advised to turn immediately to *Figure 9*.

Figure 9. The Open Road: Reality.

The California Highway Commission used this photograph as the frontispiece to its biennial report for the year 1928. The coastline has become a car line. Such a spectacle makes it easy to understand the protest of a coastal property owner who wrote to a member of the Commission in 1924, concerning one section of a proposed new coast road south of Los Angeles: "My argument on this point is that one of the reasons for building the road along this coast is to open up a senic Coast route, but I must confess that I am unable to understand what would be the advantage of making a road to show off the seenery, and then destroy the seenery [sic] in making the road."[1]

[1] J. S. Thurston to N. T. Edwards, August 12, 1924, California State Archives, Division of Highways, Dept. of Public Works, Correspondence, D127, 28, F 1387.

Figure 9

Figure 10. Confused Images and Values.

It would be hard to find a more vivid illustration of the uncertain status of motoring which resulted from the rapid social change of the early Twenties than this page from the *Los Angeles Sunday Times* of March 14, 1920. Here, virtually side by side, are articles condemning and exalting reckless driving. This was the first page of a regular section of the Sunday paper devoted to news of sports. It was still felt that automobile news belonged in this section, even though, as the "VIGILANTES TO HALT RECKLESS" article indicates, the tendency of city motorists to drive in the streets like the BLOODTHIRSTY BUGS" whose photographs are featured was becoming a major social problem.

Figure 11. Los Angeles Children Go Underground.
(From *Sunset* magazine, March, 1926.) These schoolchildren stand at the entrance to one of the new pedestrian tunnels, built primarily to protect them from cars on their way to and from school.

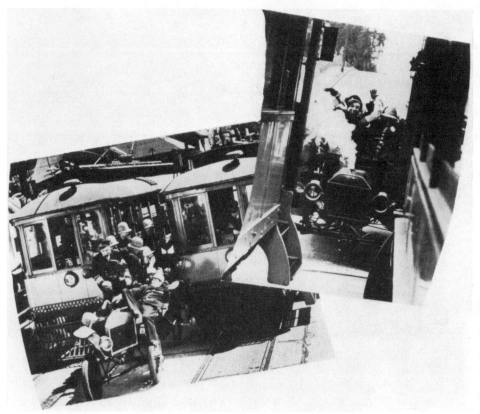

Figure 12. Comedy on Wheels. (Sequence runs from right to left.)

Many a driver would have liked to be able to avoid disaster by squeezing his car to half its width, but only in the movies was it possible. These pictures, from Floyd Clymer's *Cars of the Stars and Movie Memories*, show the Keystone Kops with a special "folding" Model T Ford used in many comedy films. There was something both ludicruous and endearing about the Model T which gave it a special place in American folklore. Partly the explanation probably lay in its ungainly and vaguely anthropomorphic features which tended to distinguish it, especially during the 1920's, from more style-conscious models; but, more importantly, it was probably a matter of simple familiarity breeding both love and contempt. For the Model T was by far the most common of all cars. Fifteen million of them were produced between 1908 and 1927. During most of that period, "Ford" and "automobile" were to many people almost synonymous terms. A good example of the affection in which these machines were held, and symbolic, in a broader context, of some of the more pathetic aspects of the man-machine relationship, was the story of the man who insisted on having his Ford buried with him when he died "because I never have got in a hole yet but what my Ford couldn't pull me out."[1]

[1] Floyd Clymer, *Henry's Wonderful Model T* (New York: McGraw-Hill, 1955), p. 169, and Reese, *op. cit.*

Figure 13. The Humor of Violence.
A scene like this was funny to the movie goers of the Nineteen-Twenties.
(Also from Clymer's *Cars of the Stars*.) Today most of us are too familiar with
scenes of actual horror to find such a burlesque very amusing.

Figure 14. Action Captures Action.
Side by side, as symbolized in this photograph from Benjamin B. Hampton's
A History of the Movies, the movie industry and the automobile raced into
glory beneath the Southern California sun.

Figure 15. Cars and Stars.
Hollywood press agents found that motor themes always interested the public, even if the effect was sometimes rather preposterous. The original caption to this publicity photograph read: "Dan, Blanche Sweet's clever canine, is a motor enthusiast. With the dainty Pathe star as a companion, who can blame him?" (From Frederic Thrasher's *Okay For Sound: How the Screen Found Its Voice.*)

Figure 16. Law and Order.
This is only one of a number of "humorous" covers to be found on editions of *Touring Topics*, the monthly magazine of the Automobile Club of Southern California, during the Nineteen-Twenties, which conveyed the idea that some kind of a war was going on between motorists and traffic policemen. Another cover (Feb., 1926) depicted a huge cop on a gigantic motorcycle writing a ticket over a frightened, almost microscopic motorist in a car so tiny it scarcely reached the lawman's ankle. A third (April, 1927) found the same quivering little motorist in court facing a monstrous judge and policemen, whose heads actually bore horns.

By 1929, the organization of state traffic officers first established in 1923 had reached what the California Crime Commission described as a condition of "general demoralization."[1] But this was a result not so much of public hostility in itself as of an administrative conflict between state and county authorities, subsequently resolved with the institution of the California State Highway Patrol entirely under state control.[2] Lawmen's techniques and *esprit de corps* improved, but motorists' attitudes of hostility had had a good head start.

[1] California Crime Commission *Report*, p. 34.
[2] Reese, *op. cit.*

Figure 16

Figure 17

Figure 17. Hazards of the Road.

(From Bellamy Partridge: *Fill 'Er Up.*) Cars and roads of the Nineteen-Twenties were much improved over their previous condition, but certain hazards still existed which the modern motorist hardly has to worry about. The Automobile Club of Southern California employed people to go around sweeping up broken glass, a major menace to automobile tires, and offered rewards for the arrest and conviction of persons caught throwing glass in the streets.

Figure 18. Commercialization of the Roadsides.

When a special Committee of the California Legislature appointed, in 1929, to investigate the question of the "scenic preservation of state highways" reported that it had been unable to find a single signboard "regularly maintained by a standard up-to-date company . . . so located that it marred the beauty of any highway," the National Council for Protection of Roadside Beauty, from whose own report on the Roadsides of California this and the following photograph are taken, frankly doubted just how honest and extensive their investigation had been. The view of Mount Shasta, alleged the Council, was scarcely improved by this very well-maintained and up-to-date sign.

Figure 19. Road Rivalry.

Just west of Beaumont, where a choice of routes towards Los Angeles confronted the motorist, one route passing through the town of Riverside, the other through Redlands, the commercial interests of these two communities erected huge displays competing for the Los Angeles bound traffic. "Neither gains," alleged the Council for Protection of Roadside Beauty, "and the roadside suffers doubly."

Figure 18

Figure 19

Figure 20.

"It is no longer painful and depressing," rejoiced Battelle's manual on *Building A Profitable Super-Service Station Business* in 1927, "to look down the vista of the modern business street, but rather a pleasure to contemplate the handsome store fronts with their artistic grills, balconies, leaded windows, tapestry brickwork and many other beauties. The super-service station at its best is not to be outdone. Many truly striking examples of artistic architecture may be seen in this field."[1] Here, taken from this manual, are two "striking examples" of the type of architecture to which the new machine gave rise in Southern California. Just what the toadstool-like structure in the upper photograph was meant to represent is not clear, but presumably it was intended to exert some kind of charm upon the passing motorist. The huge and bizarre sign silhouetted majestically against the Los Angeles sky was no doubt considered among the "many other beauties" of the establishment.

At the other extreme, the lower picture illustrates the lengths to which some architects of gasoline stations went to disguise the actual function of their creations altogether, investing them with the phony "dignity" of a largely spurious tradition.

[1] Battelle, *op. cit.*, pp. 14–15.

NOTES

PART I: INTRODUCTION

[1] George R. Stewart, *U. S. 40* (Boston: Houghton Mifflin, 1953), p. 24.

[2] Nancy Barr Mavity, "The Woman at the Wheel," *Sunset*, Vol. LVIII, No. 4 (April, 1927), p. 31.

[3] David L. Cohn, *Combustion on Wheels: An Informal History of the Automobile Age* (Boston: Houghton Mifflin, 1944), p. 4.

[4] Howard J. Nelson, "The Spread of An Artificial Landscape Over Southern California," *Annals of the Association of American Geographers*, Supplement, Vol. XLIX, No. 3, part 2 (Sept. 1959).

[5] Stewart, *op. cit.*, p. 20.

[6] John W. Caughey, *California* (Englewood Cliffs, N. J.: Prentice-Hall, 1953), p. 352.

[7] Mel Scott, *Metropolitan Los Angeles: One Community* (Los Angeles: The Haynes Foundation, 1949), p. 28.

[8] Ben Blow, *California Highways: A Descriptive Record of Road Development by the State and by such Counties as Have Paved Highways* (San Francisco: by the author, 1920), pp. 14–16.

[9] Rockwell D. Hunt and William S. Ament, *Oxcart to Airplane* (Los Angeles: Powell Publishing Co., 1929), pp. 206–207.

[10] William H. McGaughey, *American Automobile Album* (New York: E. P. Dutton and Co., 1956), pp. 34–35.

[11] Robert Glass Cleland, *California In Our Time (1900–1940)* (New York: Alfred A. Knopf, 1947), p. 105.

[12] Frank Norris, *The Octopus* (New York: Doubleday, 1901), p. 127.

[13] Caughey, *op. cit.*, p. 266.

[14] Marshall Breeden, *California—All of It* (Los Angeles: Kenmore Publishing Co., 1925), p. 189.

[15] Carey McWilliams, *California: The Great Exception* (New York: A. A. Wyn, 1949); *Southern California Country: An Island on the Land* (New York: Duell, Sloan, and Pearce, 1946).

[16] Harold W. Fairbanks, *Southern California, The Land and Its People: A Reader for Beginners in Geography* (San Francisco: Wagner, 1929), p. v.

[17] McWilliams, *Southern California Country*, p. 114.

[18] Scott, *op. cit.*, p. 35.

176   THE GREAT CAR CRAZE

[19] Phil Townsend Hanna, "The Wheel And The Bell: The Story of the First Fifty Years of the Automobile Club of Southern California," *Westways*, Vol. XLII, No. 12 (Dec. 1950), p. 41.
[20] McWilliams, *California, The Great Exception*, p. 210.
[21] Fairbanks, *op. cit.*, p. 1.
[22] William E. Leuchtenburg, *The Perils of Prosperity, 1914–1932* (Chicago: University of Chicago Press, 1958), p. 271.
[23] Security Trust and Savings Bank, Los Angeles, *Industrial Summary of Los Angeles for Year, 1924*, (Los Angeles, 1925), p. 3.
[24] Oliver Carlson, *A Mirror For Californians* (New York: Bobbs-Merrill, 1941), pp. 122–3.
[25] McWilliams, *Southern California Country*, p. 136.

PART II: MAN

[1] Ethel Imogene Salisbury, *Boys' and Girls' California* (Boston: Houghton Mifflin, 1925), p. 49.
[2] Alice M. Williamson, *Alice in Movieland* (New York: Appleton, 1928), pp. 16–17.
[3] Fremont Rider (ed.), *Rider's California: A Guide-Book for Travellers* (New York: Macmillan, 1925), p. lii.
[4] Edward Hungerford, "California Takes to the Road," *Saturday Evening Post*, Sept. 22, 1923, p. 27.
[5] Jackson A. Graves, *California Memories: 1857–1930* (Los Angeles: Times-Mirror Press, 1930), p. 293.
[6] McGaughey, *op. cit.*, p. 29.
[7] Hanna, *op. cit.*, p. 43.
[8] Cohn, *op. cit.*, p. 58.
[9] Christopher Tunnard and Boris Pushkarev, *Man-Made America: Chaos or Control—An Inquiry Into Selected Problems of Design in the Urbanized Landscape* (Yale University Press, 1963), pp. 162, 165.
[10] Julia M. Sloane, *The Smiling Hill-Top and Other California Sketches* (New York: Scribners, 1919), p. 72.
[11] Mark Lee Luther, *The Boosters* (Indianapolis: Bobbs-Merrill, 1923), pp. 255–256.
[12] U.S. Bureau of Public Roads and California Highway Commission, *A Report of Traffic on State Highways and Country Roads in California* (Sacramento: 1922), p. 7.
[13] Hunt and Ament, *op. cit.*, p. 213.
[14] e.g., *California Digest*, Vol. 1, No. 1, Sept. 18, 1922.
[15] Hunt and Ament, *op. cit.*, p. 210.
[16] Leon Mirp in *Los Angeles Citizen*, Aug. 29, 1924.
[17] Ernest McGaffey, "The Automobile Transforms Business," *Southern California Business*, Vol. II, No. 7 (Aug. 1923), pp. 17, 40.
[18] Los Angeles *Illustrated News*, July 13, 1924, p. 16.
[19] Frederick Lewis Allen, *Only Yesterday: An Informal History of The Nineteen-Twenties* (New York: Bantam, 1959), p. 115.
[20] Hendrick Willem Van Loon, *Man, The Miracle Maker* (New York; H. Liveright, 1928).
[21] Los Angeles *Times* (hereafter cited as *Times*), June 18, 1926, pt. II, p. 4.

22 *Ibid.*, Feb. 13, 1927, Sunday Magazine Section, p. 11ff.

23 Paul H. Blades, "Amazing Tide of Travel," *Times*, July 17, 1921.

24 Lincoln Steffens, *The Autobiography of Lincoln Steffens* (New York: Harcourt Brace and Co., 1931), p. 26.

25 Ernest McGaffey, "Living in the Age of Motorization," *Southern California Business*, Vol. VII, No. 2 (March, 1928), p. 34.

26 Jan and Cora Gordon, *Star-Dust in Hollywood* (London: George G. Harrap, 1930), p. 35.

27 Emory S. Bogardus, *The City Boy and His Problems: A Survey of Boy Life in Los Angeles* (Los Angeles: Rotary Club of Los Angeles, 1926). Bessie Averne McClenahan, *The Changing Urban Neighborhood: From Neighbor to Nigh-Dweller* (Los Angeles: University of Southern California, 1929).

28 Robert S. and Helen M. Lynd, *Middletown: A Study in Contemporary American Culture* (New York: Harcourt Brace & Co., 1929).

29 *Ibid.*, p. 94.

30 McClenahan, *op. cit.*, p. 70.

31 *Ibid.*, p. 68.

32 *Ibid.*, pp. v–vi.

33 *Ibid.*, p. 38.

34 *The Community*, Riverside, Vol. I, No. 1 (April 9, 1927), p. 48.

35 Bogardus, *op. cit.*, pp. 69–70.

36 Lynd, *op. cit.*, p. 279.

37 Ray U. Brouillet, *Objections and Answers* (San Francisco: by the author, 1925), p. 17.

38 Bogardus, *op. cit.*, pp. 28, 22, 75, 69–70.

39 Bogardus, *op. cit.*, pp. 69, 73.

40 Peter Viertel, *The Canyon* (New York: Harcourt Brace and Company, 1940), p. 163.

41 Graves, *op. cit.*, p. 283.

42 Southern California Conference on Modern Parenthood, *Proceedings of the Southern California Conference Held in Los Angeles, California, December 15th, 16th, 17th and 18th, 1926* (Los Angeles: 1927), p. 284.

43 Gordon, *op. cit.*, pp. 272–273.

44 George Harmon Knoles, *The Jazz Age Revisited: British Criticism of American Civilization During the 1920's* (Stanford University Press, 1955), p. 34.

45 Southern California Conference on Modern Parenthood, pp. 156–157.

46 Lynd, *op. cit.*, p. 258.

47 Upton Sinclair, *Oil!* (Long Beach: by the author, 1926), p. 205.

48 *Times*, Oct. 22, 1921, pt. II, p. 1.

49 *Ibid.*, Feb. 20, 1925.

50 Bogardus, *op. cit.*, pp. 74–75.

51 Caryl Chessman, *Cell 2455, Death Row* (New York: Prentice-Hall, 1954), p. 37.

52 The expression itself may be traced back at least as far as 1909. See Mitford M. Mathews (ed.), *Dictionary of Americanisms* (Chicago: University of Chicago Press, 1951).

53 Kilpatrick Smith Jr., "The One-Way Street," *Overland Monthly*, Vol. LXXV, No. 2 (Feb., 1927), p. 42.

54 *Times*, Dec. 7, 1926, pt. II, p. 5.

55 Mark Sullivan, *Our Times* (New York: C. Scribners Sons, 1923–1935), Vol. VI, p. 398.

[56] Joseph H. Pound, "Civilization and the Motor Car," *Rice Institute Pamphlet*, Vol. XI, No. 1 (January 1924), p. 66.

[57] Emily Post, *Etiquette* (New York: Funk and Wagnalls, 1923), p. 293.

[58] See Dorothy Canfield's novel, *The Homemaker* (New York: Harcourt Brace and Co, 1924), for one of the most imaginative contemporary discussions of this situation.

[59] *Times*, September 30, 1925.

[60] *Ibid.*, July 31, 1926.

[61] *Hollywood Daily Citizen*, October 4, 1922.

[62] William A. Robson, "American Glimpses, viii—Automobiles," *English Review* (June, 1925), p. 814.

[63] H. B. Ross, "Cupid in the Fog," *Touring Topics*, Vol. XIV, No. 10 (October, 1924), pp. 24 ff.

[64] Mavity, *op. cit.*, p. 31 ff.

[65] *Touring Topics*, Vol. XVI, No. 7 (July, 1924).

[66] Los Angeles Police Department, *Annual Report, 1920–1921*, p. 4.

[67] David R. Faries, "Crimes Involving the Automobile," *Touring Topics*, Vol. X, No. 12 (Jan. 1919), p. 17.

[68] William P. Gratton, Public Safety Department, Automobile Club of Southern California, to author, April 25, 1963.

[69] California Crime Commission, *Report* (Sacramento, 1929), p. 44.

[70] Gordon, *op. cit.*, p. 145.

[71] Harold J. Fitzgerald, "Auto Bloodhounds," *Sunset*, Vol. XLVI, No. 1 (January, 1921), p. 33 ff.

[72] *Times*, January 5, 1919.

[73] *Touring Topics*, Vol. XIV, No. 7 (July, 1922), p. 48.

[74] Los Angeles *Examiner, California, Its Opportunities and Delights*, 1920, p. 126.

[75] *Times*, September 26, 1926, pt. VI, p. 13.

[76] *Ibid.*, January 7, 1927, pt. II, p. 10.

[77] Fitzgerald, *op. cit.*, p. 36.

[78] Bogardus, *op. cit.*, 73.

[79] *Times*, August 8, 1926.

[80] California Crime Commission, *op. cit.*, p. 51.

[81] *Times*, June 1, 1925, pt. I, p. 15; pt. I, p. 1; pt. I, p. 6; pt. II, p. 11.

[82] Robert O'Connor, "Don't Try to Use Your Car as a Brewery Wagon," *Touring Topics*, Vol. XII, No. 8 (August 1920), p. 19.

[83] California Crime Commission, *op. cit.*, p. 35.

[84] Don Ryan, *Angel's Flight* (New York: Boni and Liveright, 1927), pp. 23, 110, 126.

[85] Craig Rice (ed.), *Los Angeles Murders* (New York: Duell, Sloan, and Pearce, 1947), p. 51.

[86] J. Francis McComas (ed.), *The Graveside Companion: An Anthology of California Murders* (New York: Ivan Oblensky, 1962), p. 64.

[87] *Ibid.*, pp. 61–90.

[88] Ursula Spier Erickson and Robert Pearsall Erickson (eds.), *The Californians: Writings of Their Past and Present*, (San Francisco: Hesperian House, 1961), p. 55.

[89] Los Angeles Police Department, *Annual Report, 1928–1929* (Los Angeles: 1929).

[90] *San Francisco Chronicle*, January 28, 1923, p. 71, col. 2.

[91] Anonymous, *Sunshine and Grief in Southern California: Where Good Men Go Wrong and Wise People Lose Their Money: By An Old Promoter Forty Years in the Field of Real Estate* (Detroit: The St. Claire Publishing Co., 1931), p. 55.

[92] Frank Thompson Searight, *The Doomed City* (Chicago: Laird and Lee, 1906), p. 40.

[93] Ryan, *op. cit.*, p. 249.

[94] Los Angeles *Examiner, California: Its Opportunities and Delights*, p. 23.

[95] Williamson, *op. cit.*, p. 88.

[96] Hungerford, *op. cit.*, p. 113.

[97] D. D. Stephenson, "Tourists' Motor Camp," *Touring Topics*, Vol. XIX, No. 1 (January, 1927), p. 11.

[98] *Times*, October 20, 1926, pt. II, p. 1.

[99] Upton Sinclair, *op. cit.*, p. 80.

[100] *California Sports*, Vol. II, No. 6 (August 1926), pp. 38–39.

[101] *Times*, October 20, 1926, pt. II, p. 1.

[102] Gordon Gassaway, "Scooting Stars," *Touring Topics*, Vol. XIII, No. 4 (April, 1921), pp. 18–20.

[103] Carl Van Vechten, *Spider Boy* (New York: Alfred A. Knopf, 1928), p. 87.

[104] Harry Leon Wilson, *Merton of the Movies* (New York: Doubleday, Page and Co., 1923), pp. 165–66.

[105] *Touring Topics*, Vol. VIII, No. 2 (March, 1916), p. 30.

[106] Sloane, *op. cit.*, p. 83.

[107] Towne Joseph Nylander, "The Casual Laborer of California," (unpublished Master's thesis in Economics, University of California, 1922), p. 33.

[108] *Times*, November 27, 1926.

[109] *Ibid.*, Feb. 20, 1919, pt. II, p. 7.

[110] *Times*, March 25, 1925, pt. VI, p. 14.

[111] Bogardus, *op. cit.*, p. 71.

[112] *Ibid.*, p. 72.

[113] *Ibid.*, p. 70.

[114] Syl McDowell, "Highway Hikers vs. Asphalt Turtles," *Touring Topics*, Vol. XV, No. 2 (February, 1923), p. 22.

[115] *Ibid.*, p. 21.

[116] Anonymous, "Do You Give the Tramp a Lift?" *Sunset*, Vol. LIV, No. 5 (May, 1925), p. 15.

[117] McDowell, *op. cit.*

[118] *Anonymous, "Do you Give the Tramp a Lift?"*

[119] *Joseph K. Hart, "The Automobile in the Middle Ages," The Survey*, Vol. LIV, No. 9 (August 1, 1925), p. 102.

[120] Chessman, *op. cit.*, pp. 35–36.

[121] Leo C. Ward, "A Plea For Light Harness," *The Catholic World*, Vol. CXXVII, No. 761 (August, 1928), p. 562.

[122] Allen D. Albert, "The Social Influence of the Automobile," *Scribner's Magazine*, Vol. LXXI, No. 6 (June, 1922), p. 685.

[123] *The Christian Century*, "Our Motorized Society," Vol. XLI, No. 41 (October 9, 1924), p. 1298;

[124] Hart, *op. cit, pessim.*

[125] *Abraham Cronbach, "Motors and Morality," The Survey*, Vol. LV, No. 2 (October 15, 1925), p. 102.

[126] Edmund de S. and Mary V. Brunner, *Irrigation and Religion: A Study of*

180   THE GREAT CAR CRAZE

Religious and Social Conditions in Two California Counties (New York: Doran, 1922), pp. 30–31.

[127]James J. Coole, "Influence of the Automobile on the City Church," in American Academy of Political and Social Science, *The Automobile: Its Province and Its Problems* (*Annals* Vol. CXVI, Nov. 1924), p. 80.

[128]Lynd, *op. cit.*, p. 153.

[129]John D. and J. C. Long, *Motor Camping* (New York: Dodd, Mead and Co., 1926), p. 129.

[130]Warren H. Nelson, "What the Automobile Has Done to and for the Country Church," in *The Automobile: It Province and its Problems*, p. 83.

[131]*The Citizen's Advocate*, March 5, 1921, p. 1.

[132]*Times*, November 16, 1926, pt. II, p. 4.

[133]Leonard Brown and Phillip Selznick, *Sociology: A Text with Adapted Readings* (Evanston, Ill.: Row, Peterson and Co., 1956), p. 258.

[134]Lynd, *op. cit.*, p. 251.

[135]Ward, *op. cit.*

[136]Quoted in Cohn, *op. cit.*, p. 24.

[137]Larry Freeman, *The Merry Old Mobiles* (New York: Century House, 1949), p. 200.

[138]Sloane, *op. cit.*, pp. 160–161.

[139]*Times*, June 7, 1925.

[140]*Times*, March 11, 1926.

[141]*Ibid.*, November 8, 1926.

[142]*Ibid.*, April 25, 1920.

[143]*Ibid.*, June 21, 1925.

[144]*Times*, June 1, 1925, pt. I. p. 5.

[145]*Ibid.*, Sept. 5, 1926, pt. II, p. 9.

[146]Ryan, *op. cit.*, p. 29.

[147]Southern California Conference on Modern Parenthood, *op. cit.*, p. 163.

[148]Quoted by John C. Long, "The Motor's Part in Public Health," in *The Automobile: Its Province and Its Problems*, p. 18.

[149]Brouillet, *op. cit.*, p. 10.

[150]John C. Long, "The Motor's Part in Public Health," p. 18.

[151]*Times*, November 3, 1923, pt. I, p. 2.

[152]*Times*, September 26, 1926, pt. II, p. 7.

[153]e.g., McGaughey, *op. cit.*, p. 82.

[154]Lynd, *op. cit.*, p. 256.

[155]Brouillet, *op. cit.*, pp. 10–11.

[156]John Chynoweth Burnham, "The Gasoline Tax and the Automobile Revolution," *Mississippi Valley Historical Review*, Vol. XLVIII, No. 3 (December 1961), p. 435 ff.

[157]Richard M. Zettel, *An Analysis of Taxation for Highway Purposes in California, 1895–1946* (Sacramento: 1946), p. 31.

PART III: MACHINE

[1]Bellamy Partridge, *Fill 'Er Up: The Story of Fifty Years of Motoring* (New York: McGraw-Hill, 1952), p. 212.
McGaughey, *op. cit.*, p. 93.

Merrill Denison, *The Power to Go: The Story of the Automotive Industry* (New York: Doubleday and Doran, 1956), pp. 205–207.

[2] Denison, *op. cit.*, p. 207.

[3] Gordon, *op. cit.*, p. 138.

[4] See A. M. Low, *It's Bound to Happen* (London: Burke, 1950).

[5] Lewis Mumford, *The City in History* (New York: Harcourt Brace and World, 1961), pp. 218–219.

[6] Jane Jacobs, *The Death and Life of Great American Cities* (New York: Random House, 1961), pp. 340–342.

[7] *Times*, April 25, 1920, pt. VI, p. 1.

[8] *Ibid.*, April 21, 1920.

[9] Times, April 25, 1920, pt. VI, p. 1.

[10] *Touring Topics*, Vol. XII, No. 5 (May, 1920), p. 9.

[11] "Los Angeles and Its Motor Jam," *Literary Digest*, Vol. LXXI, No. 4 (April 26, 1924), p. 68. Walter V. Woehlke, "Traffic Jams," *Sunset*, Vol. LVI, No. 3 (March, 1936), p. 40.

[12] Mumford, *op. cit.*, p. 510.

[13] Irma Armand, "The Pedestrian," *Los Angeles Times*, January 3, 1919, pt. II, p. 2.

[14] *Touring Topics*, Vol. XII, No. 5 (May, 1920), p. 24.

[15] James Montgomery Flagg, *Boulevards All the Way—Maybe* (New York: George H. Doran, 1925), p. 149.

[16] Daniel Smith Crowningshield, *The Jolly Eight: Coast to Coast and Back* (Boston: Richard G. Badger, 1929), p. 94.

[17] R. W. Read, "From The Front Platform," *Touring Topics*, Vol. XIV, No. 4 (April, 1922), p. 16.

[18] Ernest C. Johnson in *Times*, November 18, 1926, pt. II, p. 4.

[19] *Touring Topics*, Vol. XIV No. 7 (July 1922), p. 17.

[20] *Ibid.*, Vol. XIV, No. 6 (June, 1922), p. 32.

[21] Gordon, *op. cit.*, p. 137.

[22] Automobile Club of Southern California to author, April 25, 1963. See also Appendix C.

[23] Freeman, *op. cit.*, p. 111.

[24] Hanna, *op. cit.*, p. 44.

[25] *Times*, Sept. 26, 1926, pt. VI, p. 20.

[26] Partridge, *Fill 'Er Up*, p. 47.

[27] *Los Angeles Citizen*, May 7, 1920.

[28] *Ibid.*, September 15, 1922.

[29] *Ibid.*, October 28, 1921.

[30] "Gale," in *Touring Topics*, Vol. XV, No. 5 (May, 1923), p. 17.

[31] *Times*, March 23, 1920.

[32] Tom Connor, "His Majesty, the Pedestrian," *Touring Topics*, Vol. XIV, No. 5 (May, 1922), pp. 16–18.

[33] *Times*, November 2, 1926, pt. II, p. 7.

[34] Mrs. Helen Lucille Holt, "California Women on the Firing Line for Safety," *Nation's Traffic*, Vol. II, No. 3 (May 1928), p. 36.

[35] *Touring Topics*, Vol. XVII, No. 4, (April, 1925), p. 26.

[36] *Times*, March 8, 1920, pt. II, p. 4.

[37] J. C. Furnas and Ernest H. Smith, *Sudden Death and How to Avoid It* (New York: Simon and Schuster, 1935).

[38] *Times*, March 18, 1920.
[39] *Times*, March 14, 1920, pt. VI, p. 1.
[40] *Ibid.*, March 8, 1920.
[41] *Ibid.*, May 4, 1920.
[42] *Ibid.*, May 16, 1920.
[43] *Times*, March 8, 1920.
[44] *Times*, July 8, 1927.
[45] *Ibid.*, August 10, 1929.
[46] *Ibid.*, May 14, 1926.
[47] Alfred I. Tooke, "Festina Lente . . .", *Touring Topics*, Vol. XVIII, No. 6 (June, 1926), p. 22 ff.
[48] William Gilmore Beymer, "Talion," *Los Angeles Times*, Sunday Magazine Section, February 13, 1927, p. 11 ff.
[49] *Touring Topics*, Vol. XII, No. 5 (May, 1920), p. 18.
[50] *Ibid.*, Vol. XIV, No. 9 (September, 1922), p. 17.
[51] Hanna, *op. cit.*, p. 49.
[52] *Touring Topics*, Vol. XII, No. 7 (July, 1920), p. 20.
[53] Paul G. Hoffman, "The Traffic Commission of Los Angeles—Its Work on the Traffic Problem," in *The Automobile: Its Province and Its Problems*, p. 246.
[54] J. Allen Davis, former General Counsel of Automobile Club of Southern California, to author, November 5, 1963.
[55] Woehlke, "Traffic Jams." *Sunset*, Vol. LVI, No. 3 (March, 1926).
[56] *Times*, November 14, 1926, pt. VI, p. 6.
[57] Connor, *op. cit.*, p. 18.
[58] Woehlke, "Traffic Jams." *Sunset* Vol. LVI, No. 3 (March, 1926), p. 40 ff.
[59] Los Angeles Traffic Commission, *Annual Report* (Los Angeles: 1929), p. 9.
[60] Lee McCrae, "Traffic Control in Los Angeles," *Nation's Traffic*, Vol. II, No. 6 (August, 1928), p. 13.
[61] T. N. Koenig, Sacramento Chief of Police, in California Crime Commission *Report*, p. 44.
[62] See Hanna, "The Wheel And the Bell . . ."
[63] *Harper's*, Vol. CXXV, No. 705 (June, 1917), p. 70, cited in Mathews.
[64] Montague Glass in *Touring Topics*, Vol. XIII, No. 18 (August, 1921), p. 32.
[65] J. Allen Davis, "Shall Everyone Be Allowed to Drive?" *Touring Topics*, Vol. XVI, No. 12 (December, 1924), p. 22.
[66] E. L. Johnson, "Our Traffic Problem as an Officer Sees It," *Touring Topics*, Vol. XV, No. 9 (September, 1923), p. 29.
[67] J. Allen Davis, "New Rules For the Motorist," *Touring Topics*, Vol. XVII, No. 7 (July, 1925), p. 29.
[68] *Times*, May 4, 1920.
[69] *Los Angeles Citizen*, October 29, 1920.
[70] *Touring Topics*, Vol. XV, No. 9 (September, 1923), p. 13.
[71] *Times*, December 12, 1921, pt. II, p. 8.
[72] *Ibid.*, October 24, 1926, pt. II, p. 6.
[73] *Touring Topics*, Vol. XIV, No. 5 (May, 1922), p. 28.
[74] *Times*, June 3, 1926, pt. II, p. 14.
[75] Willard G. Thorpe (Police Commissioner of Los Angeles), "Teaching Safety with Radio, Song, and Movies," *Nation's Traffic*, Vol. II, No. 1 (March, 1928), p. 15.
[76] Holt, *op. cit.*, pp. 36–37.

[77] *Times*, November 2, 1926, pt. II, p. 7.

[78] *California Highways*, Vol. I, No. 9 (September, 1926).

[79] *Times*, June 1, 1925, pt. I, p. 10.

[80] R. H. Bacon, "Plans for Pedestrian Subways," *The Municipal Employee*, Vol. I, No. 10 (August, 1925), p. 27.

[81] Abe Potash in Los Angeles *Examiner, California: Its Opportunities and Delights*, p. 167.

[82] *Times*, September 19, 1926, pt. II, p. 1.

[83] George Pampel, "Motoring's Infant Days," *Touring Topics*, Vol. XVIII, No. 9 (September 1926), p. 18.

[84] Leepson Brownes, "Motorizing the Olympic Games," *Touring Topics*, Vol. XVI, No. 9 (September, 1924), p. 17.

[85] Rob Wagner, *Rob Wagner's California Almanac, 1924* (Los Angeles: Times-Mirror Press, 1924), pp. 9, 35, 52.

[86] Woehlke, "Traffic Jams," *op. cit.*

[87] *Touring Topics*, Vol. XVII, No. 4 (April, 1925), p. 26.

[88] Ibid., Vol. XIII, No. 6 (June, 1921), p. 23.

[89] *California Highways*, Vol. III, No. 3 (March, 1926).

[90] "The Golden Age of Comedy" (film), Hollywood, 1957.

[91] Gilbert Seldes, *The Movies Come From America* (New York: Scribners', 1937), p. 36.

[92] John Durant, "The Movies Take to the Pastures," *Saturday Evening Post*, October 14, 1950, p. 24 ff.

[93] Cecil B. DeMille in Floyd Clymer, *Cars of the Stars and Movie Memories* (Los Angeles: by the author, 1954).

[94] Gordon, *op. cit.*, p. 132.

[95] Ernest A. Dench, *Making the Movies* (New York: Macmillan, 1915).

[96] *Touring Topics*, "Coruscating Constellations in the Automobile Club of Southern California," Vol. XII, No. 10 (October, 1920), p. 18.

[97] Dench, *op. cit.*, p. 62.

[98] Touring Topics, "Coruscating Constellations . . ." *op. cit.*

[99] e.g., Clymer, *Cars of the Stars*, op. cit., p. 51.

[100] Dench, *op. cit.*, p. 62.

[101] "Harold Lloyd's World of Comedy," (film) Hollywood, 1962.

[102] Wilson, *op. cit.*, p. 258.

[103] "Harold Lloyd's World of Comedy."

[104] "Golden Age of Comedy."

[105] "Harold Lloyd's World of Comedy."

[106] *Times*, April 16, 1921, pt. II, p. 1; and April 17, 1921, pt. I, p. 9.

[107] *Touring Topics*, Vol. XIV, No. 3 (March, 1922), p. 15.

[108] *Ibid.*, Vol. XII, No. 8 (August, 1920), p. 1.

[109] E.G., Olive Gray in *Times*, October 20, 1926, pt. II, p. 1.

[110] *Touring Topics*, Vol. XX, No. 1 (January, 1928).

[111] Upton Sinclair, *op. cit.*, p. 9.

[112] James Harvey Braffet, "Vicarious Liability and the Family Purpose Doctrine" (unpublished Juris Doctor thesis, University of California, 1924), p. 36.

[113] Bailey Millard, "Traffic Perils and the Law," *Sunset* Vol. XLVI, No. 4 (April, 1921), p. 33.

[114] Marie Russell Ullman, "Women Make A Difference," *Touring Topics*, Vol. XVI, No. 10 (October, 1926), p. 29.

184   THE GREAT CAR CRAZE

115 Charles Reade, "Pull Up By the Side of the Road," *Sunset*, Vol. LVII, No. 6 (December, 1926), p. 15.
116 Paul Francis Reese, "The California Highway Patrol: Its History, Organization, and Work," (unpublished Master's thesis in Political Science, University of California at Berkeley, 1940), pp. 2–3.
117 David R. Faries, "Changes in the Motor Vehicle Law At a Glance," *Touring Topics*, Vol. XV, No. 9 (September, 1923), p. 24.
118 *Touring Topics*, Vol. XV, No. 12 (December 1923), p. 13.
119 E. J. Hopkins, *Our Lawless Police: A Study of the Unlawful Enforcement of the Law* (New York: The Viking Press, 1931), p. 3.
121 Walter G. Beach, *Oriental Crime In California: A Study of Offenses Committed by Orientals in That State, 1900–1927* (Stanford University Press, 1932), p. 72.
122 *Touring Topics*, Vol. XIV, No. 9, (September, 1922), p. 16.
123 Bogardus, *op. cit.*, pp. 69–70.
124 George Baker Anderson, "What Price Traffic?" *Nation's Traffic*, Vol. II, No. 6, (August, 1928), p. 12.
125 *Times*, November 7, 1926, pt. VI, p. 5.
126 *Ibid.*, November 2, 1926, pt. II, p. 10.
127 *Ibid.*, November 3, 1926, pt. I, p. 11.
128 E. B. Lefferts, "San Diego Police Plan Is Reducing Accidents," *Nation's Traffic*, Vol. II, No. 3 (May, 1928), p. 18.
129 *San Francisco Examiner*, June 11, 1963.
130 *Touring Topics*, Vol. XVI, No. 8 (August, 1926), p. 26.
131 *Times*, editorial "Green Drivers," July 29, 1926.
132 Millard, *op. cit.*, p. 33.
133 Frederick Russell, "There's No Place Like the Automobile," *Touring Topics*, Vol. XIX, No. 6 (June, 1927), p. 35.
134 Dan Jacobson, *No Further West* (London: Werdenfield and Nicholson, 1957), p. 37.
135 J. W. Livingstone, "And the Salesman Assured Me 'It's An Absolute Cinch': An Encounter With My First Automobile," *Touring Topics*, Vol. XIV, No. I (January, 1922), p. 16.
136 *Ibid.*
137 Edward Bellamy Partridge, "Flivver Complaint," *Sunset*, Vol. XLV, No. 1 (July, 1920), p. 37 ff.
138 Livingstone, *op. cit.*, p. 16.
139 Partridge, "Flivver-Complaint," *op. cit.*
140 Frank Prescott, "His First False Step," *Touring Topics*, Vol. XV, No. 2 (February, 1923), p. 16.
141 *Times*, October 10, 1925.
142 Eugene Brown, "Dancing Drivers," *Los Angeles Times*, May 24, 1926, pt. II, p. 4.
143 Denison, *op. cit.*, p. 216.
144 Freeman, *op. cit.*, p. 137.
145 Olive Gray, *Los Angeles Times*, October 20, 1926, pt. II, p. 1.
146 Rider, *op. cit.*, pp. lii–liii.
147 Olive Gray in *Times*, October 20, 1926, pt. II, p. 1.
148 Ullman, *op. cit.*
149 *Touring Topics*, Vol. XIV, No. 6 (June, 1922), p. 48.

150 Complete lyrics of this song are given in Floyd Clymer, *Treasury of Early American Automobiles: 1877–1925* (1950), p. 196.

151 Scott, *op. cit.*, pp. 35–36.

152 Quoted in R. W. Durrenberger, *The Geography of California in Essays and Readings* (Northridge, California: Roberts Publishing Co.), p. 184, from Margaret S. Gordon, *Employment Expansion and Population Growth* (1954), pp. 49–70.

153 Thomas D. Murphy, *On Sunset Highways: A Book of Motor Rambles in California* (Boston: the Page Co., 1921), p. 13.

154 *Times*, July 11, 1926, pt. III, p. 30.

155 Murphy, *op. cit.*, p. 13.

156 *Nation's Traffic*, Vol. II, No. 4 (June, 1928), p. 29.

157 Ernest McGaffey, "Living In the Age of Motorization," p. 35.

158 Leuchtenberg, *op. cit.*, p. 245.

John K. Galbraith, *The Great Crash, 1929* (Boston: Houghton Mifflin Co., 1954), pp. 179–181.

159 *Touring Topics*, Vol. XI, No. 1 (February 1919), p. 9.

160 *Times*, March 2–March 6, 1929.

161 R. T. Nicholson, *The Original Book of the Ford* (7th edition revised; London: Temple Press, 1924), p. 247.

162 *Touring Topics*, March and April, 1924.

163 Long, *Motor Camping, op. cit.*, p. 78.

164 *Touring Topics*, Vol. XIV, No. 4 (April 1922), p. 15.

165 *Ibid.*, Vol. XV, No. 9 (September, 1923), p. 23.

166 *Times*, January 5, 1919.

167 Joe Mears in *Touring Topics*, Vol. XXI, No. 2 (February, 1929), p. 46.

168 "Harold Lloyd's World of Comedy."

169 E. F. MacDonough to Nels Edwards, May 4, 1926, California State Archives, Division of Highways, Dept. of Public Works, Correspondence D127, 28, F1389.

170 Automobile Blue Book Publishing Co., *Automobile Blue Book 1920*, New York: 1920), pp. 466–469.

171 *Ibid.*, p. 48.

172 Hanna, *op. cit.*, pp. 41–56.

173 Frank L. Meline, Inc., *Los Angeles: The Metropolis of the West* (Los Angeles: by the author, 1929), p. 4.

174 *Touring Topics*, "The Auto Club Goes 'On the Air' " (January, 1923), p. 20.

175 Ernest McGaffey, "On Duty With the Highway Patrol," *Touring Topics*, Vol. XVI, No. 8 (August, 1924), p. 14 ff.

17fl

PART IV: LAND

1 McWilliams, *Southern California Country, op. cit.*, p. 12.

2 Carlson, *op. cit.*, p. 138.

3 Beatrice Larned Massey, *It Might Have Been Worse: A Motor Trip From Coast to Coast* (San Francisco: Harr Wagner, 1920), p. 129.

4 Murphy, *op. cit.*, p. 3.

5 Ben Blow, *op. cit.*, p. 166.

6 *Ibid.*, p. 51.

[7] Murphy, *op. cit.*, p. 15.

[8] Quoted from John S. Brown, "Suggestions to Travellers," in U.S. Geological Survey, Water-Supply Paper 490A, *Routes to Desert Watering Places in the Salton Sea Region, California* (Washington: 1920), by J. Smeaton Chase, *Our Araby: Palm Springs and the 'Garden by the Sun'* (New York: Little and Ives, 1923), p. 111.

[9] Ben Blow, *op. cit.*

[10] Caroline Rittenberg, *Motor West* (New York: Harold Vinal, 1926), pp. 49–50.

[11] California Highway Commission, *Biennial Report* (Sacramento: 1922), p. 9.

[12] Denison, *op. cit.*, p. 219.

[13] Hunt and Ament, *op. cit.*, p. 205.

[14] Frederick L. Paxson, "The Highway Movement 1916–1935," *American Historical Review*, Vol. LI, No. 2 (January, 1946), p. 263.

[15] *Service*, Vol. I, No. 1 (January, 1925), p. 8.

[16] Automobile Club of Southern California and the California State Automobile Association, *The State Highways of California—An Engineering Study* (Los Angeles: 1921), p. 9.

[17] *Ibid.*, p. 10.

[18] *Ibid.*, p. X.

[19] *Ibid.*, p. 10.

[20] Hanna, *op. cit.*, p. 48.

[21] Zettel, *op. cit.*, pp. 1–2.

[22] *Touring Topics*, Vol. XVIII, No. 6 (June, 1926), p. 21.

[23] Hanna, *op. cit.*, p. 49.

[24] California State Archives, Division of Highways, Department of Public Works, Correspondence, D 298, F2931-5.

[25] *California Highways*, Vol. II, No. 9 (September, 1925), p. 6 ff.

[26] California Highway Commission, *Biennial Report 1926*, p. 122.

[27] See, for example, Rachel Carson, *Silent Spring* (Boston: Houghton Mifflin, 1962), pp. 69–75.

[28] Frank J. Taylor, *California: Land of Homes* (Los Angeles: Powell Publishing Co., 1929), p. 29.

[29] Charles Francis Saunders, *Finding the Worth While in California* (New York: Robert M. McBride, 1930), p. 44.

[30] Earl Pomeroy, *In Search of the Golden West: The Tourist In Western America* (New York: Alfred A. Knopf, 1957), p. 218.

[31] *Ibid.*, p. 127.

[32] *Ibid.*, p. 223.

[33] e.g., Winifred Hawkridge Dixon, *Westward Hoboes* (New York: Charles Scribners' Sons, 1921), p. 79.

[34] Frederic F. Van De Water, *The Family Flivvers to Frisco* (New York: D. Appleton and Co., 1926), p. 13.

[35] Elon Jessup, *The Motor Camping Book* (New York: Putnam, 1921), p. 8.

[36] *Los Angeles Examiner, California: Its Opportunities and Delights*, p. 46.

[37] Rider, *op. cit.*, pp. lii–liii.

[38] *Touring Topics*, Vol. XVIII, No. 7 (July 1926), p. 43.

[39] Long, *Motor Camping*, pp. 202–203.

[40] *Touring Topics*, 1925–1926, *passim*.

[41] Pomeroy, *op. cit.*, p. 207.

[42] See "The Neals on Wheels," *Sunset*, Vol. XLIV, No. 6 (June, 1920), p. 66.

[43] Freeman, *op. cit.*, p. 162.
[44] Van de Water, *op. cit.*, p. 233.
[45] Long, *Motor Camping*, Appendix.
[46] Pomeroy, *op. cit.*, p. 148.
[47] J. B. Priestley, *Midnight On the Desert: A Chapter of Autobiography* (London: Heinemann, 1937), pp. 87–89.
[48] Quoted in The McWilliams *Southern California Country, op. cit.*, p. 135.
[49] Van de Water, *op. cit.*, p. 109.
[50] Miriam Van Waters in Southern California Conference on Modern Parenthood, p. 166.
[51] Van de Water, *op. cit.*, p. 13.
[52] Stephenson, *op. cit.*
[53] *Van de Water, op. cit.*, p. 123.
[54] Mary Carolyn Davies, "Motor Honeymoon," *Sunset*, Vol. LIV, No. 5 (May, 1925), p. 32.
[55] Long, *Motor Camping*, p. 97.
[56] John Keats, *The Insolent Chariots* (Philadelphia: J. B. Lippincott Co., 1958), pp. 186–187, 192.
[57] Chase, *op. cit.*, pp. 17–18.
[58] *Ibid.*, p. 5.
[59] *Ibid.*, p. 16.
[60] *Ibid.*, p. 61.
[61] *Times*, February 26, 1963, pt. I, p. 26.
[62] *Sunset*, Vol. LVI, No. 5 (May, 1926), p. 26.
[63] Hunt and Ament, *op. cit.*, p. 209.
[64] Howard J. Nelson, *op. cit.*, p. 81.
[65] E. V. Weller, California Motorlogues: Suggestions for One-Day and Week-End Motor Trips on the Highways and Byways of California (*San Francisco Examiner*, 1921), p. 40.
[66] Viertel, *op. cit.*, p. 75.
[67] California Highway Commission, *Biennial Report* (Sacramento: 1928), p. 81.
[68] *Los Angeles Evening Express*, May 31, 1919, pt. III, p. 1.
[69] C. E. M. Joad, *The Horrors of the Countryside* (London: the Hogarth Press, 1931), p. 24.
[70] *California Highways*, Vol. II, No. 12 (December, 1925), p. 14.
[71] Tunnard and Pushkarev, *op. cit.*, p. 179.
[72] Murphy, *op. cit.*, preface.
[73] Joad, *op. cit.*, p. 25.
[74] Joad, *op. cit.*, p. 24.
[75] Ogden Nash, "The Song of the Open Road," anthologized in J. M. Cohen (ed.) *The Penguin Book of Comic and Curious Verse* (London: Penguin Books, 1952).
[76] California Highway Commission, *Biennial Report* (Sacramento: 1922), p. 39.
[77] J. Horace Mc Farland, "The Billboard and the Public Highways," in *The Automobile: Its Province and Its Problems*, p. 95 ff.
[78] *California Highways*, Vol. IV, No. 12 (December, 1927), p. 22.
[79] *Ibid.*, Vol. V, Nos. 2–3 (February–March, 1928), p. 27.
[80] *California Highways*, Vol. I, No. 4 (April, 1924), p. 11. "Housing the Motor Car," *Touring Topics*, Vol. XVI No. 8 (Aug 1924) p. 21.
[81] *California Highways*, Vol. I, No. 4 (April, 1924), p. 11.

THE GREAT CAR CRAZE

[82] National Council for Protection of Roadside Beauty, *The Roadsides of California: A Survey* (New York: 1931), p. 30.
[83] California Highway Commission *Report of the Joint Assembly and Senate Committee on the Scenic Preservation of State Highways* (Sacramento: 1931), p. 3.
[84] *Ibid.*, p. 24.
[85] National Council for Protection of Roadside Beauty, p. 33.
[86] California Highway Commission, *Scenic Preservation Report*, p. 10.
[87] National Council for Protection of Roadside Beauty, p. 28.
[88] California Highway Commission, *Scenic Preservation Report*, p. 13.
[89] *Ibid.*, p. 14.
[90] California Highway Commission, *Scenic Preservation Report*, p. 10.
[91] *Ibid.*, p. 9.
[92] *Ibid.*, p. 8.
[93] National Council for Protection of Roadside Beauty, p. 37.
[94] *Ibid.*, p. 29.
[96] *Ibid.*, pp. 38–43.
[97] Application of George W. Dell of Lamanda Park, June 1, 1925, and recommendation by S. V. Cortelyou June 9, 1925, California State Archives, Division of Highways, Dept. of Public Works, Correspondence, D127, 28, F1388.
[98] Murphy, *op. cit.*, p. 56.
[99] National Council for Protection of Roadside Beauty, p. 32.
[100] Gordon, *op. cit.*, pp. 65–66.
[101] Leon Mirp in Los Angeles *Citizen*, May 30, 1924.
[102] *Times*, March 29, 1929.
[103] J. Allen Davies on "California Motor Vehicle Legislation," in West Publication Co., *West's Annotated California Codes: Vol. 66—Vehicle Code* (St. Paul, Minn.: 1956), p. 28.
[104] National Council for Protection of Roadside Beauty, p. 14.
[105] *Touring Topics*, Vol. XIV, No. 8 (August, 1922), p. 15.
[106] Chase, *op. cit.*, p. 58.
[107] Leslie T. White, *Me, Detective* (New York: Harcourt, Brace and Co., 1936), p. 8.
[108] Walter Woehlke, "Gasoline and Trout," *Sunset*, Vol. LVI, No. 4 (April, 1926).
[109] Harold Child Bryant, *Outdoor Heritage* (Los Angeles: Powell Publishing Co., 1929), p. 378.
[110] Los Angeles Board of City Planning Commissioners, *Conference on the Rapid Transit Question Called January 21st 1930* (Los Angeles: 1930), p. 16.
[111] Emily Barker Carter, *Hollywood: The Story of the Cahuengas* (Hollywood High School, 1926), p. 78.
[112] Automobile Club of Southern California, *The Los Angeles Traffic Problem* (Los Angeles, 1922), p. 17.
[113] Los Angeles Traffic Commission, *A Major Traffic Street Plan for Los Angeles* (Los Angeles: 1924), p. 12.
[114] George Baker Anderson, "What Price Traffic?" *Nation's Traffic*, Vol. II, No. 6 (August, 1928), p. 12.
[115] Hoffman, *op. cit.*, p. 246.
[116] City of Los Angeles, *Los Angeles Municipal Architecture* (Los Angeles: 1928).

[117] Automobile Club of Southern California, *The Work of the Los Angeles County Grade Crossing Committee* (Los Angeles: 1930), p. 22.

[118] *Ibid.*, p. 36.

[119] *Ibid.*, p. 17.

[120] Howard J. Nelson, *op. cit.*, p. 92.

[121] L. A. Board of City Planning Commissioners, *Rapid Transit Conference*, p. 6.

[122] Mel Scott, *Metropolitan Los Angeles*, p. 93.

[123] Marshall Breeden *The Romantic Southland of California* (Los Angeles: The Kenmore Publishing Co., 1928), p. 10.

[124] Inez Haynes Irwin, *The Californiacs* (San Francisco: A. M. Robertson, 1921), p. 38.

[125] Marshall Breeden, *Romantic Southland*, p. 22.

[126] *Ibid.*, p. 21.

[127] "The Garage A Part of the Home," *Sunset*, Vol. XLV, No. 5 (November 1920), p. 70.

[128] *Times*, September 26, 1926, pt. II, p. 17.

[129] John F. Harbeson, "The Automobile And the Home of the Future," in *The Automobile: Its Province and Its Problems*, pp. 58–60.

[130] Remi Nadeau, *Los Angeles: From Mission to Modern City* (New York: Longmans Green, 1960), p. 149.

[131] Mc Williams, *Great Exception*, p. 238.

[132] *Times*, June 1, 1925, pt. I, p. 4.

[133] *Nation's Traffic*, Vol. II, No. 4 (June, 1928), p. 29.

[134] Nadeau, *op. cit.*, p. 150.

[135] Ralph Hancock, *Fabulous Boulevard* (New York: Funk and Wagnalls, 1949), pp. 149–164.

[136] *Times*, September 26, 1926, pt. VI, p. 17.

[137] Battelle Publishing Company, *Building a Profitable Super-Service Station Business* (Los Angeles, 1927), p. 21.

[138] Douglas Honnold, *Southern California Architecture* (New York: Reinhold, 1956), p. 19.

[139] Battelle, *op. cit.*, p. 15.

[140] Matt Weinstock, *My L.A.* (New York: A. A. Wyn, 1947), p. 233.

[141] *Country Life* (April, 1927), p. 102.

[142] Battelle, *op. cit.*, p. 11.

[143] Upton Sinclair, *op. cit.*, p. 12.

[144] Ted Salmon, *From Southern California to Casco Bay* (San Bernardino: San Bernardino Publishing Co., 1930), p. 33.

[145] *Ibid.*

[146] Battelle, *op. cit.*, p. 32.

[147] *Ibid.*, p. 6.

[148] Gordon, *op. cit.*, p. 36.

AFTERMATH

[1] Weinstock, *op. cit.*, p. 236.

[2] Los Angeles Traffic Commission, *Annual Report* (Los Angeles: 1929), pp. 37–39.

[3] Robert H. Burrage and Edward G. Mogren, *Parking* (Saugatuck, Conn.: Eno

Foundation for Highway Traffic Control, 1957), p. 109.

[4] John Keats, *op. cit.*, p. 186.

[5] Victor W. Killick, *Can We Build Automobiles to Keep Drivers Out of Trouble?* (San Francisco: Reeves Publishing Co., 1940).

[6] Wilfred Owen, *Cities in the Motor Age* (New York: Viking Press, 1959), p. 7.

[7] Center For the Study of Democratic Institutions, *The City (One of A Series of Interviews on The American Character)* (Santa Barbara: 1962), pp. 30–31.

[8] Jane Jacobs, *op. cit.*, pp. 369, 370.

[9] Mumford, *op. cit.*, p. 510.

[10] San Francisco *Chronicle*, October 11, 1962, p. 23.

[11] Graves, *op. cit.*, p. 2.

[12] Nadeau, *op. cit.*, pp. 284 ff.

[13] Irving Bengelsdorf, "Sun, Cars, Still Air, Team to Give Southland—Smog," *Times*, May 26, 1963, pt. C, p. 1.

[14] See Wolfgang Langewiesche, "How Polluted Is the Air Around Us?" *Reader's Digest*, Vol. LXXXII, No. 497 (September, 1963), p. 117 ff.

[15] Anonymous, *Sunshine and Grief*, pp. vii, iii, 207.

[16] Gordon, *op. cit.*, p. 54.

BIBLIOGRAPHY

Unpublished Material

Braffet, James Harvey. "Vicarious Liability and The Family Purpose Doctrine," Unpublished Juris Doctor thesis, University of California, Berkeley, 1924.

California State Archives, Sacramento. Division of Highways, Department of Public Works, Correspondence, 1919–1929.

McEntire, Davis. "An Economic and Social Study of Population Movements in California, 1850–1944." Unpublished Ph.D. Dissertation in Economics, Harvard, 1947.

Nylander, Towne Joseph, "The Casual Laborer of California." Unpublished Master's thesis in Economics, University of California, 1922.

Reese, Paul Francis. "The California Highway Patrol: Its History, Organization, and Work." Unpublished Master's thesis in Political Science, University of California at Berkeley, 1940.

Letters to the author from:

> Automobile Club of Southern California.
> California Department of Motor Vehicles.
> California Highway Patrol.
> Los Angeles Air Pollution Control District.
> Los Angeles Police Department.
> National Safety Council.
> Standard Oil Company of California.

Veysey, Laurence Russ. "The Pacific Electric Railway Company since 1910." Unpublished thesis, Yale, 1953.

Public Documents

California Commission of Immigration and Housing. *Annual Reports.* Sacramento: 1919–1927.

———. *Bulletin of Information for Immigrants.* Sacramento: 1920.

California Crime Commission. *Report.* Sacramento: 1929.

California Crime Commission. *Report of the Joint Assembly and Senate Committee on the Scenic Preservation of State Highways.* Sacramento: 1931.

California State Division of Motor Vehicles. *First Biennial Report*. Sacramento: 1925.
City of Los Angeles. *Los Angeles Municipal Architecture*. Los Angeles: 1928.
Los Angeles Board of City Planning Commissioners. *Conference on the Rapid Transit Question, Called January 21, 1930*. Los Angeles: 1930.
————. *Annual Reports*. Los Angeles: 1928–1930.
Los Angeles County Regional Planning Commission. *A Comprehensive Report on the Regional Plan of Highways: Section 2E, San Gabriel Valley*. Los Angeles: 1929.
Los Angeles Police Department. *Annual Reports*. Los Angeles: 1919–1928.
Los Angeles Traffic Commission. *Annual Reports*. Los Angeles: 1924–1929.
————. *A Major Traffic Street Plan for Los Angeles*. Los Angeles: 1924.
U.S. Bureau of Public Roads and California Highway Commission. *A Report of Traffic on State Highways and County Roads in California*. Sacramento: 1922.
U.S. Bureau of the Census. *Statistical Abstract of the U.S.* Washington: 1919–1962.

Newspapers and Periodicals

Bulletin Of the Los Angeles City Teachers' Club. 1925.
California Digest. Sacramento: 1922.
California Highways. Sacramento: 1924–1929.
California Jewish Review. Los Angeles: 1925–1929.
California Real Estate. Los Angeles: 1925–1929.
California Southland. Pasadena: 1918–1929.
California Sports. Los Angeles: 1924.
Citizen's Advocate. Los Angeles: 1921.
Community. Riverside: 1927.
Country Life. April, 1927.
Hollywood Daily Citizen. 1922.
Look magazine, Sept. 25, 1962.
Los Angeles Citizen. 1919–1929.
Los Angeles Evening Express. 1919.
Los Angeles Illustrated Daily News. 1924.
Los Angeles Times. 1919–1929.
Nation's Traffic. St. Louis, Mo.: 1928–1930.
Pacific Golf and Motor. San Francisco and Los Angeles: 1915–1924.
Service. Los Angeles: 1925.
Sunset. San Francisco: 1919–1929.
Touring Topics. Los Angeles: 1916–1929. (*Westways*. Dec. 1950)
Transportation. Los Angeles: 1927–1929.
Van Nuys News. 1927.

Books and Articles

Albert, Allen D. "The Social Influence of the Automobile," *Scribner's Magazine*, Vol. LXXI, No. 6 (June, 1922), p. 685 ff.
Allen, Frederick Lewis. *Only Yesterday: An Informal History of the Nineteen-Twenties*. New York: Bantam, 1959.

Anderson, George Baker. "What Price Traffic?" *Nation's Traffic*, Vol. II, No. 6 (August, 1928), p. 12 ff.

Anonymous. *Sunshine and Grief in Southern California: Where Good Men Go Wrong and Wise People Lose Their Money: By an Old Promoter Forty Years in the Field of Real Estate*. Detroit: The St. Claire Publishing Co., 1931.

Anonymous. "Do You Give the Tramp A Ride?" *Sunset*, Vol. LIV, No. 5 (May, 1925), p. 15 ff.

Armand, Irma. "The Pedestrian," *Los Angeles Times*, January 3, 1919, pt. II, p. 2.

Automobile Blue Book Publishing Company. *Automobile Blue Book 1920, Volume 8: California, Nevada, Utah, and Arizona*. New York: 1920.

Automobile Club of Southern California. *The Los Angeles Traffic Problem*. Los Angeles: 1922.

————. *The Public Road System of California*. Los Angeles: 1928.

————. *The Work of the Los Angeles County Grade Crossing Committee*. Los Angeles: 1930.

————. and the California Automobile Association. *The State Highways of California: An Engineering Study*. Los Angeles: 1921.

Automobile Manufacturers' Association, Inc. *Automobile Facts and Figures*. Detroit: 1963.

Bacon, R. H. "Plans for Pedestrian Subways," *The Municipal Employee*, Vol. I, No. 10 (August, 1925), p. 27.

Battelle Publishing Company. *Building a Profitable Super-Service Station Business*. Los Angeles: 1927.

Beach, Walter G. *Oriental Crime in California: A Study of Offenses Committed by Orientals in that State 1900–1927*. Stanford University Press, 1932.

Bengelsdorf, Irving. "Sun, Cars, Still Air, Team to Give Southland—Smog," *Los Angeles Times*, May 26, 1963.

Beymer, William Gilmore, "Talion," *Los Angeles Times*, Sunday Magazine Section, February 13, 1927, p. 11 ff.

Blades, Paul H. "Amazing Tide of Travel," *Los Angeles Times*, July 17, 1921.

Blow, Ben. *California Highways: A Descriptive Record of Road Development by the State and by such Counties as Have Paved Highways*. San Francisco: by the author, 1920.

Bogardus, Emory S. *The City Boy and His Problems: A Survey of Boy Life in Los Angeles*. Los Angeles: Rotary Club of Los Angeles, 1926.

Breeden, Marshall. *California—All of It*. Los Angeles: Kenmore Publishing Company, 1925.

————. *The Romantic Southland of California*. Los Angeles: The Kenmore Publishing Company, 1928.

Broom, Leonard, and Phillip Selznick. *Sociology: A Text With Adapted Readings*. Evanston, Ill.: Row, Peterson & Co., 1956.

Brouillet, Ray U. *Objections and Answers*. San Francisco: by the author, 1925.

Brown, Eugene. "Dancing Drivers," *Los Angeles Times*, May 24, 1926, pt. II, p. 4.

Brownes, Leepson. "Motorizing the Olympic Games," *Touring Topics*, Vol. XVI, No. 9 (September, 1926), p. 17 ff.

Brunner, Edmund De S., and Mary V. *Irrigation and Religion: A Study of Religious and Social Conditions in Two California Counties*. New York: Doran, 1922.

Bryant, Harold Child. *Outdoor Heritage*. Los Angeles: Powell Publishing Company, 1929.

Burnham, John Chynoweth. "The Gasoline Tax and the Automobile Revolution," *Mississippi Valley Historical Review*, Vol. XLVIII, No. 3 (December, 1961), p. 435 ff.

Burrage, Robert H., and Edward G. Mogren. *Parking*. Saugatuck, Connecticut: Eno Foundation for Highway Traffic Control, 1957.

Canfield, Dorothy. *The Homemaker*. New York: Harcourt Brace and Co., 1924.

Carlson, Oliver. *A Mirror for Californians*. New York: Bobbs-Merrill, 1941.

Carson, Rachel. *Silent Spring*. Boston: Houghton Mifflin, 1962.

Carter, Emily Barker. *Hollywood: The Story of the Cahuengas*. Hollywood High School, 1926.

Caughey, John Walton. *California*. Englewood Cliffs, New Jersey: Prentice-Hall, 1953.

Center for Safety Education, New York University. *Man and The Motor Car*. Englewood Cliffs, New Jersey: Prentice-Hall, 1954.

Center for the Study of Democratic Institutions. *The City: (One of a Series of Interviews on the American Character)*. Santa Barbara: 1962.

Chase, J. Smeaton. *Our Araby: Palm Springs and the Garden of the Sun*. New York: Little & Ives, 1923.

Chessman, Caryl. *Cell 2455 Death Row*. New York: Prentice-Hall, 1954.

The Christian Century, "Our Motorized Society," Vol. XLI, No. 41 (October 9, 1924), p. 1298.

Cleland, Robert Glass. *California in Our Time (1900–1940)*. New York: Alfred A. Knopf, 1947.

Clymer, Floyd. *Cars of the Stars and Movie Memories*. Los Angeles: by the author, 1954.

———. *Henry's Wonderful Model T: 1908–1927*. New York: McGraw-Hill, 1955.

———. *Treasury of Early American Automobiles: 1877–1927*. New York: McGraw-Hill, 1950.

Coale, James J. "Influence of the Automobile on the City Church," in American Academy of Political and Social Science, *The Automobile: Its Province and Its Problems*. (Annals, Vol. CXVI, November, 1924), Philadelphia, 1924, pp. 80–82.

Cohen, J. M. (ed.). *The Penguin Book of Comic and Curious Verse*. London: Penguin Books, 1952.

Cohn, David L. *Combustion On Wheels: An Informal History of the Automobile Age*. Boston: Houghton Mifflin, 1944.

Connor, Tom. "His Majesty the Pedestrian," *Touring Topics*, Vol. XIV, No. 5 (May, 1922), p. 16 ff.

Corle, Edwin. *The Royal Highway (El Camino Real)*. New York: Bobbs-Merrill, 1949.

Crawford, H. L. *Selling Used Cars: The Used Car Advertising and Merchandising Encyclopedia*. South Bend, Indiana: Associates Investment Co., 1955.

Cronbach, Abraham. "Motors and Morality," *The Survey*, Vol. LV, No. 2 (October 15, 1925), p. 102.

Crowningshield, Daniel Smith. *The Jolly Eight: Coast to Coast and Back*. Boston: Richard G. Badger, 1929.

Davis, J. Allen. "Shall Everyone Be Allowed To Drive?" *Touring Topics*, Vol. XVI, No. 12 (December, 1924), p. 22 ff.

————. "New Rules for the Motorist," *Touring Topics*, Vol. XVII, No. 7 (July, 1925), p. 29.

Dench, Ernest A. *Making the Movies*. New York: The Macmillan Co., 1919.

Denison, Merrill. *The Power to Go: The Story of the Automotive Industry*. New York: Doubleday and Doran, 1956.

Dixon, Winifred Hawkridge. *Westward Hoboes*. New York: Charles Scribners Sons, 1921.

Durant, John. "The Movies Take to the Pastures," *Saturday Evening Post*, October 14, 1950, p. 24 ff.

Durrenberger, R. W. *The Georgraphy of California in Essays and Readings*. Northridge, Calif.: Roberts Publishing Co.

Erickson, Ursula Spier, and Robert Pearsall, (eds.). *The Californians: Writings of Their Past and Present*. San Francisco: Hesperian House, 1961.

Fairbanks, Harold W. *Southern California, The Land and Its People: A Reader for Beginners in Geography*. San Francisco: Wagner, 1929.

Faries, David R. "Crimes Involving the Automobile," *Touring Topics*, Vol. X, No. 12 (January, 1919), p. 17.

————. "Changes In The Motor Vehicle Law at A Glance," *Touring Topics*, Vol. XV, No. 9 (September, 1923), p. 24.

Fitzgerald, Harold J. "Auto Bloodhounds," *Sunset*, Vol. XLVI, No. 1 (January, 1921), p. 33 ff.

Flagg, James Montgomery. *Boulevards All the Way—Maybe*. New York: George H. Doran, 1925.

Ford Motor Company. *Ford at Fifty*. New York: Simon and Schuster, 1953.

Freeman, Larry. *The Merry Old Mobiles*. New York: Century House, 1949.

Furnas, J. C., and Ernest N. Smith. *Sudden Death and How to Avoid It*. New York: Simon and Schuster, 1935.

Galbraith, John K. *The Great Crash 1929*. Boston: Houghton Mifflin Co., 1954.

Gassaway, Gordon. "Scooting Stars," *Touring Topics*, Vol. XIII, No. 14 (April, 1921), pp. 18–20.

Geddes, Norman Bel. *Magic Motorways*. New York: Random House, 1940.

Gordon, Jan and Cora. *Star-Dust in Hollywood*. London: George G. Harrap, 1930.

Graves, Jackson A. *California Memories: 1857–1930*. Los Angeles: Times-Mirror Press, 1930.

Hager, Anna Marie and Everett G. *Cumulative Index—Westways, Touring Topics 1909–1959*. Los Angeles: Automobile Club of Southern California, 1961.

Hampton, Benjamin B. *A History of the Movies*. New York: Covici, Friede, 1931.

Hancock, Ralph. *Fabulous Boulevard*. New York: Funk and Wagnalls, 1949.

Hanna, Phil Townsend. "The Wheel and The Bell: The Story of the First Fifty Years of the Automobile Club of Southern California," *Westways*, Vol. XLII, No. 12 (December, 1950), pp. 41–56

Harbeson, John F. "The Automobile and the Home of the Future," in American Academy of Political and Social Science, *The Automobile: Its Province and Its Problems* (Annals, Vol. CXVI, November, 1924), pp. 58–60.

Harris, Joseph P. *California Politics*. Stanford University Press, 1961.

Hart, Joseph K. "The Automobile in the Middle Ages," *The Survey,* Vol. LIV, No. 9 (August 1, 1920), p. 493.

Heitner, Joseph. *Automotive Mechanics: Principles and Practices.* Princeton: Van Nostrand, 1953.

Hoffmann, Paul G. "The Traffic Commission of Los Angeles—Its Work on the Traffic Problem," in American Academy of Political and Social Science, *The Automobile: Its Province and Its Problems,* (Annals, Vol. CXVI, November, 1924), Philadelphia, 1924, pp. 246–250.

Honnold, Douglas. *Southern California Architecture.* New York: Reinhold, 1956.

Holt, Mrs. Helen Lucille. "California Women on the Firing Line for Safety," *Nation's Traffic,* Vol. II, No. 3 (May, 1928), pp. 36–37.

Hopkins, E. J. *Our Lawless Police: A Study of the Unlawful Enforcement of the Law.* New York: The Viking Press, 1931.

Hungerford, Edward. "California Takes to the Road," *Saturday Evening Post,* September 22, 1923, p. 27 ff.

Hunt, Rockwell, and William S. Ament. *Oxcart to Airplane.* Los Angeles: Powell Publishing Co., 1929.

Hunt, Rockwell D. *Fifteen Decisive Events of California History.* Los Angeles: Historical Society of Southern California, 1959.

Hurt, Elsey. *California State Government—An Outline of Its Administrative Organization from 1850 to 1936.* Sacramento: 1936.

Huxley, Aldous. *After Many a Summer Dies the Swan.* New York: Harper, 1939.

Irwin, Inez Haynes. *The Californiacs.* San Francisco: A. M. Robertson, 1921.

Jacobs, Jane. *The Death and Life of Great American Cities.* New York: Random House, 1961.

Jacobson, Dan. *No Further West.* London: Weidenfield and Nicholson, 1957.

Jessup, Elon. *The Motor Camping Book.* New York: Putnam, 1921.

Joad, C. E. M. *The Horrors of the Countryside.* London: The Hogarth Press, 1931.

Johnson, E. L. "Our Traffic Problem as an Officer Sees It," *Touring Topics,* Vol. XV, No. 9 (September, 1923), p. 25.

Keats, John. *The Insolent Chariots.* Philadelphia: J. B. Lippincott Co., 1958.

———. "Ask The Man Who Doesn't Own One," *Atlantic,* December, 1962, pp. 61–64.

Kelker, De Leuw & Co., *Report and Recommendations on a Comprehensive Rapid Transit Plan for the City and County of Los Angeles.* Los Angeles: 1925.

Killick, Victor W. *Can We Build Automobiles to Keep Drivers Out of Trouble?* San Francisco: Reeves Publishing Co., 1940.

Kloes, D. R. *California, Land of Contrast,* San Francisco: Fearon, 1959.

Knight, Arthur. *The Liveliest Art: A Panoramic History of The Movies.* New York: MacMillan, 1957.

Knoles, George Harmon. *The Jazz Age Revisited: British Criticism of American Civilization During the 1920's.* Stanford University Press, 1955.

Langewiesche, Wolfgang. "How Polluted Is the Air Around Us?", *Readers Digest,* Vol. LXXXII, No. 497 (September, 1963), p. 117 ff.

Lefferts, E. B. "San Diego Police Plan is Reducing Accidents," *Nation's Traffic,* Vol. II, No. 3 (May, 1928), p. 18.

Leuchtenburg, William E. *The Perils of Prosperity 1914–1932*. Chicago: University of Chicago Press, 1958.

Lindsay, Cynthia. *The Natives Are Restless*. Philadelphia: L. B. Lippincott, 1960.

Lindsey, Ben B. *The Companionate Marriage*. New York: Boni and Liveright, 1927.

Literary Digest. "Los Angeles And Its Motor Jam," Vol. LXXXI, No. 4 (April 26, 1924), p. 68.

Livingstone, J. W. "And the Salesman Assured Me 'It's An Absolute Cinch': An Encounter With My First Automobile," *Touring Topics*, Vol. XIV, No. 1 (January, 1922), p. 16 ff.

Long, John C. "The Mother's Part in Public Health," in American Academy of Political and Social Science, *The Automobile: Its Province and Its Problems* (Annals, Vol. CXVI, November, 1924), Philadelphia, 1924, p. 18 ff.

Long, John D., and John C. Long. *Motor Camping*. New York: Dodd Mead & Co., 1926.

Los Angeles Examiner. California, Its Opportunities and Delights. Los Angeles: 1920.

Low, A. M. *It's Bound to Happen*. London: Burke, 1950.

Luther, Mark Lee. *The Boosters*. Indianapolis: Bobbs-Merrill, 1923.

Lynd, Robert S. and Helen M. *Middletown: A Study in Contemporary Culture*. New York: Harcourt Brace and Co., 1929.

McClenahan, Bessie Averne. *The Changing Urban Neighborhood: From Neighbor to Nigh-Dweller*. Los Angeles: University of Southern California, 1929.

McComas, J. Francis (Ed.) *The Graveside Companion: An Anthology of California Murders*. New York: Ivan Obolensky, 1962.

McCrae, Lee. "Traffic Control in Los Angeles," *Nation's Traffic*, Vol. II, No. 6 (August, 1928), p. 13 ff.

McDowell, Syl. "Highway Hikers vs. Asphalt Turtles," *Touring Topics*, Vol. XV, No. 2 (February, 1923), p. 21 ff.

McFarland, J. Horace. "The Billboard and the Public Highways," in American Academy of Political and Social Science, *The Automobile: Its Province and Its Problems*, (Annals, Vol. CXVI, November, 1924), Philadelphia, 1924, pp. 95–101.

McGaffey, Ernest. "The Automobile Transforms Business," *Southern California Business*, Vol. II, No. 7 (August, 1923), p. 17 ff.

———. "Living in the Age of Motorization," *Southern California Business*, Vol. VII, No. 2 (March, 1928), pp. 30 ff.

———. "On Duty With the Highway Patrol," *Touring Topics*, Vol. XVI, No. 8 (August, 1924), p. 14 ff.

McGaughey, William H. *American Automobile Album*. New York: E. P. Dutton & Co., 1954

McGill, Vernon, *Diary of A Motor Journey From Chicago to Los Angeles*. Los Angeles: Grafton Publishing Corp., 1922.

McWilliams, Carey. *California: The Great Exception*. New York: A. A. Wyn, 1949.

———. *Southern California Country: An Island On the Land*. New York: Duell, Sloan, and Pearce, 1946.

Massey, Beatrice Larned. *It Might Have Been Worse: A Motor Trip From Coast to Coast*. San Francisco: Harr Wagner, 1920.

Mathews, Mitford M. (ed.) *A Dictionary of Americanisms.* University of Chicago Press, 1951.

Mavity, Nancy Barr. "The Woman at the Wheel," *Sunset,* Vol. LVIII, No. 4 (April, 1927), p. 31 ff.

Meline, Frank L., Inc. *Los Angeles: The Metropolis of the West.* Los Angeles: by the author, 1929.

Millard, Bailey. "Traffic Perils and the Law," *Sunset,* Vol. XLVI, No. 4 (April, 1921), p. 33 ff.

Mumford, Lewis. *The City in History: Its Origins, Its Transformations, and Its Prospects.* New York: Harcourt Brace and World, 1961.

Murphy, Thomas D. *On Sunset Highways: A Book of Motor Rambles in California.* Boston: the Page Company, 1921.

Musselman, M. M. *Get a Horse! The Story of the Automobile in America.* Philadelphia: J. B. Lippincott, 1950.

Nadeau, Remi. *Los Angeles: From Mission to Modern City.* New York: Longmans Green, 1960.

National Council For Protection of Roadside Beauty. *The Roadsides of California: A Survey.* New York: 1931.

Nelson, Howard J. "The Spread of An Artificial Landscape Over Southern California," in *Annals of the Association of American Geographers,* Supplement, Vol. XLIX, No. 3, part 2, September 1959.

Nelson, Warren H. "What the Automobile Has Done To and For the Country Church," American Academy of Political and Social Sciences, *The Automobile, Its Province and Its Problems* (Annals, Vol. CXVI, November, 1924), Philadelphia, 1924, p. 83-6.

Nevins, Allan. *Ford: The Times, The Man, The Company.* New York: Scribners, 1954.

Nicholson, R. T. *The Original Book of the Ford.* (9th edition, revised). London: Temple Press, 1924.

Nicholson, T. R. *Adventurer's Road: The Story of Pekin-Paris 1907 and New York-Paris, 1908.* New York: Rinehart & Co., 1958.

Norris, Frank. *The Octopus.* New York: Doubleday, 1901.

O'Connor, Robert. "Don't Try to Use Your Car As a Brewery Wagon," *Touring Topics,* Vol. XII, No. 8 (August, 1920), p. 19.

O'Hara, John. *Appointment in Samarra.* New York: Grosset and Dunlap, 1935.

Owen, Wilfred. *Automotive Transportation: Trends and Problems.* Washington, D. C.: The Brookings Institute, 1949.

———. *Cities in the Motor Age.* New York: Viking Press, 1959.

Pampel, George. "Motoring's Infant Days," *Touring Topics,* Vol. XVIII, No. 9 (September, 1926), p. 18 ff.

Parker, Samuel F. "There They Go—Several Hundred Strong," *Nation's Traffic,* Vol. II, No. 2 (April, 1928), pp. 27-28.

Partridge, Bellamy. *Fill 'Er Up: The Story of Fifty Years of Motoring.* New York: McGraw-Hill, 1952.

———. "Flivver-Complaint," *Sunset,* July, 1920, p. 37 ff.

Paxson, Frederick L. "The Highway Movement, 1916–1935," *American Historical Review,* Vol. LI, No. 2 (January, 1946), p. 263.

Pomeroy, Earl. *In Search of the Golden West: The Tourist in Western America.* New York: Alfred A. Knopf, 1957.

Post, Emily. *Etiquette*. New York: Funk & Wagnalls, 1923.

Pound, Joseph H. "Civilization and the Motor Car," *Rice Institute Pamphlet*, Vol. XI, No. 1, January, 1924, pp. 48–73. Houston, Texas.

Prescott, Frank. "His First False Step," *Touring Topics*, Vol. XV, No. 2 (February, 1923), p. 16.

Price, Edward T. "The Future of California's Southland," *Annals of the Association of American Geographers*, Supplement, Vol. XLIX, No. 3, part 2, September, 1959.

Priestley, J. B. *Midnight on the Desert: A Chapter of Autobiography*. London: Heinemann, 1937.

Read, R. W. "From the Front Platform," *Touring Topics*, Vol. XIV, No. 4 (April, 1922), p. 16.

Reade, Charles. "Pull Up By the Side of the Road," *Sunset*, Vol. LVII, No. 6 (December, 1926), p. 15 ff.

Rice, Craig, (ed.) *Los Angeles Murders*. New York: Duell, Sloan, and Pearce, 1947.

Rider, Fremont, (ed.) *Rider's California: A Guide-Book For Travellers*. New York: Macmillan, 1925.

Risenberg, Felix, Jr. *The Golden Road: The Story of the California Mission Trail*. New York: McGraw-Hill, 1962.

Riesman, David, and Eric Larrabee. "Autos in America: History Catches Up With Ford," *Encounter*, May, 1957, pp. 26–36.

Rittenberg, Caroline. *Motor West*. New York: Harold Vinal, 1926.

Robinson, W. W. *Panorama: A Picture History of Southern California*. Los Angeles: Title Insurance and Trust Company, 1953.

Robson, William A. "American Glimpses, VIII—Automobiles," *English Review*, June 1925, p. 814.

Ross, H. B. "Cupid In The Fog," *Touring Topics*, Vol. XVI, No. 10, (October, 1924), pp. 24 ff.

Russell, Frederick, "There's No Place Like the Automobile," *Touring Topics*, Vol. XIX, No. 5 (June, 1927), pp. 35–36.

Ryan, Don. *Angel's Flight*. New York: Boni & Liveright, 1927.

Salisbury, Ethel Imogene. *Boys' and Girls' California*. Boston: Houghton Mifflin, 1925.

Salmon, Ted. *From Southern California to Casco Bay*. San Bernardino: San Bernardino Publishing Co., 1930.

San Francisco Chronicle. "Gophers Killed by Essex Exhaust Gas," January 28, 1923, p. 71, col. 2.

————. "An Auto Man's Case for Heavy Traffic," October 11, 1962, p. 23.

Sann, Paul. *The Lawless Decade*. New York: Crown Publishers, 1957.

Saunders, Charles Francis. *Finding the Worth While in California*. New York: Robert M. McBride, 1930.

Scott, Mel. *Metropolitan Los Angeles: One Community*. Los Angeles: The Haynes Foundation, 1949.

————. *The San Francisco Bay Area: A Metropolis in Perspective*. Berkeley: University of California Press, 1959.

Searight, Frank Thompson. *The Doomed City*. Chicago: Laird and Lee, 1906.

Security Trust and Savings Bank. *'Since You Were Here Before': A Story of the Changes that Have Come to Los Angeles Since it was Host to the American Bankers Association in 1910 and 1921*. Los Angeles: 1926.

————. *Industrial Summary of Los Angeles for Year 1924*. Los Angeles: 1925.

Seldes, Gilbert. *The Movies Come From America*. New York: Scribner, 1937.

Sibley, Hy. "The Motor Dodo," *Touring Topics*, Vol. XVII, No. 10, (October, 1925), p. 17.

Sinclair, Andrew. *Prohibition: The Era of Excess*. Boston: Little, Brown and Co., 1962.

Sinclair, Upton. *Oil!* Long Beach: by the author, 1926.

Sloane, Julia M. *The Smiling Hill-Top and Other California Sketches*. New York: Scribner, 1919.

Smith, Kirkpatrick, Jr. "The One-Way Street," *Overland Monthly*, Vol. LXXXV, No. 2 (February, 1927), p. 42 ff.

Southern California Conference on Modern Parenthood. *Proceedings of the Southern California Conference Held in Los Angeles California December 15th, 16th, 17th, and 18th, 1926*. Los Angeles: 1927.

States Publishing Company Ltd. *Southern California at a Glance*. 1930.

Steffens, Lincoln. *The Autobiography of Lincoln Steffens*. New York: Harcourt Brace & Co., 1931.

Stephenson, D. D. "Tourists' Motor Camp," *Touring Topics*, Vol. XIX, No. 1 (January, 1927), p. 11.

Stewart, George R. *U.S. 40*. Boston: Houghton Mifflin, 1953.

Sullivan, Mark. *Our Times*. New York: C. Scribners Sons, 1923–35.

Taylor, Frank J. *California: Land of Homes*. Los Angeles: Powell Publishing Co., 1929.

Thrasher, Frederic (ed.) *Okay For Sound: How the Screen Found Its Voice*. New York: Duell, Sloan and Pearce, 1946.

Thorpe, Willard G. "Teaching Safety With Radio, Song, and Movies," *Nation's Traffic*, Vol. II, No. 1 (March, 1928), p. 15.

Tooke, Alfred I. "Festina Lente—or The Wisdom of Making Haste Slowly," *Touring Topics*, Vol. XVIII, No. 6 (June, 1926), p. 21.

Tully, Jim. *Jarnegan*. New York: Albert and Charles Boni, 1926.

Tunnard, Christopher and Boris Pushkarev. *Man-Made America: Chaos or Control—An Inquiry into Selected Problems of Design in the Urbanized Landscape*. New Haven: Yale University Press, 1963.

Ullman, Marie Russell. "Women Make a Difference," *Touring Topics*, Vol. XVI, No. 10 (October, 1924), p. 29 ff.

Van De Water, Frederic F. *The Family Flivvers to Frisco*. New York: Appleton and Co., 1926.

Van Loon, Hendrik Willem. *Man The Miracle Maker*. New York: H. Liveright, 1928.

Van Vechten, Carl. *Spider Boy*. New York: Alfred A. Knopf, 1928.

Vernon, Paul E. *From Coast to Coast by Motor*. London: A. C. Black and Co., 1930.

Viertel, Peter. *The Canyon*. New York: Harcourt, Brace & Co., 1940.

Wagner, Rob. *Rob Wagner's California Almanac, 1924*. Los Angeles: Times-Mirror Press, 1924.

Walker, Franklin. *A Literary History of Southern California*. Berkeley: University of California Press, 1950.

Ward, Leo C. "A Plea For Light Harness," *The Catholic World*, Vol. CXXVII, No. 761 (August, 1928), p. 562 ff.

Weinstock, Matt. *My L.A.* New York: A. A. Wyn, 1947.

Weller, E. V. *California Motorlogues: Suggestions For One-Day and Week-End Motor Trips on the Highways and Byways of California.* San Francisco: *San Francisco Examiner,* 1921.

West Publishing Company. *West's Annotated California Codes: Vol. 66—Vehicle Code.* St. Paul, Minn., 1956.

White, Leslie T. *Me, Detective.* New York: Harcourt Brace & Co., 1936.

Williamson, Alice M. *Alice in Movieland.* New York: Appleton, 1928.

Wilson, Harry Leon. *Merton of the Movies.* New York: Doubleday, Page, & Co., 1922.

Woehlke, Walter, "Gasoline and Trout," *Sunset,* Vol. LVI, No. 4 (April, 1926).

———. "Traffic Jams," *Sunset,* Vol. LVI, No. 3 (March, 1926), p. 40 ff.

Writers' Program (WPA), California. *Berkeley: The First 75 Years.*

Young, William P. *A Ford Dealer's Twenty Year Ride.* Hempstead, N. Y.: by the author, 1932.

Zettel, Richard M. *An Analysis of Taxation for Highway Purposes in California, 1895–1946.* Sacramento: 1946.

Films

"The Golden Age of Comedy," Hollywood, 1957.
"Harold Lloyd's World of Comedy," Hollywood, 1962.
"The Golden Twenties," (McGraw-Hill).
"America's Traffic Problem," (March of Time).
"Motor Mania" (Walt Disney).

APPENDICES

APPENDIX A

Private Automobile Registration

	Los Angeles County[1]	California[1]	U.S.[2]	Entire World[3]
1919	140,967	477,450	6,679,133	
1920	161,846	532,934	8,131,522	
1921	211,679	645,522	9,212,158	
1922	288,495	822,394	10,704,076	12,848,783
1923	411,451	1,056,756	13,253,019	15,847,824
1924	465,882	1,125,201	15,436,102	18,432,891
1925	505,865	1,224,831	17,439,701	24,589,249
1926	559,684	1,383,097	19,220,885	27,650,267
1927	601,637	1,479,411	20,142,120	29,687,300
1928	650,207	1,582,477	21,308,159	
1929	776,677	1,885,308	23,060,421	
1930	806,264			

[1] California Dept. of Motor Vehicles
[2] Automobile Manufacturer's Association, *Automobile Facts and Figures* (Detroit: 1963), p. 18.
[3] *U.S. Statistical Abstract.*

APPENDIX B

Population Growth

	L.A.[1] City	L.A.[1] County	Southern[2] California	California[3]
1900	102,479	170,298	304,211	1,485,053
1910	319,198	504,131	751,310	2,377,549
1920	576,673	936,455	1,347,050	3,426,861
1930	1,238,048	2,208,492	2,932,795	5,677,251

[1] Scott, *Metropolitan Los Angeles*, pp. 33–34.
[2] McWilliams, *Southern California Country*, p. 14.
[3] D. R. Kloes, *California: Land of Contrast*, Appendix.

APPENDIX C

Motor Vehicle Fatalities[1]

	L. A. City		California		U.S.	
	No. of deaths	Rate per 100,000 Population	No. of deaths	Rate per 100,000 Population	No. of deaths	Rate per 100,000 Population
1919	119	21.1	647	19.2	7,968	9.4
1920	142	24.1	734	21.1	9,103	10.4
1921	165	27.1	876	24.4	10,168	11.4
1922	187	29.5	960	26.0	11,666	12.4
1923	224	?	1,239	32.6	14,411	14.7
1924	267	?	1,254	32.0	15,528	15.5
1925	258	28.0	1,327	28.6	17,571	17.1
1926	286	28.4	1,464	30.2	18,871	18.0
1927	353	32.9	1,628	32.1	21,160	19.6
1928	337	29.7	1,755	33.2	23,765	20.8
1929	430	36.0	2,100	38.1	27,066	23.3

[1] U.S. *Statistical Abstract*, (Figures do not include motorcycle accidents, or collisions with trains and streetcars).

INDEX